A ROGUES' GALLERY

A 'Rogues' Gallery

Off the Record Encounters with
Figures of Fame, Folly and Fun 1950–2000

Peter Lewis

QUARTET

First published in 2013 by Quartet Books Limited
A member of the Namara Group
27 Goodge Street, London W1T 2LD
Copyright © Peter Lewis 2013
The right of Peter Lewis to be identified
as the author of this work has been asserted
by him in accordance with the
Copyright, Designs and Patents Act, 1988
All rights reserved.
No part of this book may be reproduced in
any form or by any means without prior
written permission from the publisher
A catalogue record for this book
is available from the British Library
ISBN 978 0 7043 7317 4
Typeset by Josh Bryson
Printed and bound in Great Britain by
T J International Ltd, Padstow, Cornwall

Every effort has been made to credit the illustrations used in this
book and the publishers apologise for any errors of omission.

CONTENTS

CONTENTS

PROLOGUE

It takes an ever shorter time for the past to become a foreign country. Now the new century is no longer new, even the latter half of the twentieth century feels foreign. They did things differently then. There was no such thing as celebrity. There was fame. If you did something sufficiently strange, if you climbed Everest or ran a four-minute mile, if you painted like Francis Bacon, or wrote like Amis or Osborne, or made surreal jokes like Spike Milligan, you could become famous, but not a 'celebrity'. Such people could walk down the street without being mobbed. That was reserved for visiting exotica like Marilyn Monroe, who for a few summer months of 1956 was Queen of England.

Social and political histories of this recent period have already proliferated. What follows is nothing of that kind. It is a snapshot album. The snaps I had the chance to secure as a reporter. Reporting is a spectator sport but often its most piquant moments are the ones that don't get used in your copy. These off-beat, off-camera glimpses of the famous I took down and hoarded for their own sake out of curiosity. Not all of the people I snapped were famous for long. Some were destined to become failures. Some were fakes who were seen through in due course. Most, however respectable, had a roguish streak. This did not make them any the less appealing. They were all fodder for the curiosity that drives most journalists to put up with their tiring and not often rewarding job and with the newspapers they have to serve. Dorothy Parker put our situation best. The cure for boredom, she said, is curiosity – adding: 'There is no cure for curiosity.'

THE FIFTIES

ARTHUR MILLER

The woman Britain would have liked to adopt as its own arrived at London airport in the summer of 1956 to an unprecedented brouhaha of cameramen fighting for her picture. Marilyn Monroe had come to make a movie with our own near-royal thespian, Sir Laurence Olivier. She had just got married to America's leading dramatist, the intellectuals' hero, Arthur Miller. And here they were, only two weeks into their honeymoon. The next morning a more orderly press reception was held at the Savoy, presided over by Sir Laurence himself. Not yet aware that keeping everyone waiting was a tactic Monroe had raised into an art, he decided to 'warm up' the waiting newsmen. Ten minutes passed, then twenty. A glaze of desperation began to form over his face at her non-arrival. Olivier ad-libbed on and on but when she finally appeared all this was forgotten in the excitement of hearing her speak. Instead of the super-gentility of Royal Windsor porcelain here was the breathy, sexy, almost baby voice of Hollywood. She was looking forward, she breathed, to getting to know the lovely English countryside…on a bicycle! Offers of bicycles came pouring in. And in a day or two photographs appeared of Marilyn riding in Windsor Great Park near her rented home with her cute, caressable bum on the saddle of an English bike. Beside her pedalled the gaunt, unsmiling Miller. By then joy at her presence was unconfined. For a summer England went Marilyn mad. She could have been Queen for the asking. No, I didn't get any nearer her than press conference range. Hardly anybody not in the film studios did. They closed Marks & Spencer so that she could look around, fearing otherwise she might be crushed in a stampede.

But by the time the filming was over and she was ready to depart it was rumoured that the honeymoon was over also. Olivier had learned the truth of the observation made by her Hollywood director, William Wyler, that directing Monroe was 'like working with Hitler'. Her lateness for work, her innumerable retakes and her insistence on being directed by her acting coach from the New York Actors' Studio, the insufferable Paula Strasberg, had not only driven Olivier to fury but opened the first cracks in her marriage to Miller. In trying to keep the peace between her and Olivier, Miller had turned her paranoid suspicions on himself as well. They had believed they were the magic that could transform each other's lives. It had failed. 'England had humbled both of us,' Miller concluded in his autobiography *Timebends*.

To me he was the more interesting member of the partnership – author of the most impressive American plays of the decade and a target of the UnAmerican Activities Committee, where he refused to name names, unlike most of its victims, to the Communist-hunting-and-hating members of the House of Representatives.

A few years later, when I was writing a book on the fifties, I caught up with him in New York and heard the story from the horse's mouth. By then he had been given a thirty-day suspended prison sentence for contempt of Congress (later quashed by the Supreme Court). I was staying at the Chelsea Hotel on Manhattan's run-down 23rd Street, a notorious hang-out favoured by bohemians and deviants of many kinds. Its cheapness compensated for the battered décor and faint perfume of marijuana that permeated the corridors. But I was surprised to learn that Arthur Miller was a long-term resident, two floors above me. It seemed an unlikely spot for a world-famous playwright to pitch his cell. 'I come here to write,' he explained when he invited me up. 'But watch out when you take the elevator. A girl was shot on my corridor last week.'

Miller was a big man, smoking a big pipe over his typewriter. The Marilyn years were over. He was alone. I asked him what 'UnAmerican' meant and how could it be applied to someone with his distinguished record. 'Broadly it means pro-Communist. Really it's a catch-all for holding any kind of opinion which is minority or unorthodox – like being anti-capitalist or anti-big business or atheist or pro-abortion.' *Death of a Salesman* could have qualified as anti-capitalist and *The Crucible* had exposed the anti-Communist McCarthyite paranoia for the witch hunt it was. The first had been received with stunned silence and audible sobbing in 1948. In 1952 the first night of *The Crucible* was more sinister. 'A sheet of ice formed over the audience as it sensed the relevance of the theme to what was currently happening. I was standing in the theatre lobby afterwards and people who had greeted me on the way in passed me on the way out as if I wasn't there at all.'

I could not understand why were Americans so conformist – why did they so readily turn paranoid? He took a moment to consider this. 'I think the thing Americans fear above everything is being a failure. The worst thing that could happen is losing your status as a success. Being no longer welcome at certain houses or parties or even restaurants. After *The Crucible* I was expelled from the ranks of the accepted. It was the only work of serious protest against McCarthy and the terror that I know of. The most disheartening thing was the way intellectuals and creative people chickened out of the fight. They behaved as if nothing terrible was happening. One got to understand how the Germans made peace with Hitler. They weren't shooting writers in America, only disgracing them, and look how few stood up in defence of their freedom. It was our Holocaust.'

What was it like appearing before the House Committee? 'The humbug and cynicism of the whole persecution burned right through me to my backbone. The night before I was due to attend I got a message through my lawyer from the Committee chairman, Representative Francis E. Walter. It offered to cancel my appearance on one condition: that Representative Walter would be photographed with my wife, Marilyn.' How do you react to a thing like that? 'You laugh,' he said grimly. And how did she feel? 'She was real mad.' At that stage his autobiography was still years into the future and I was the first to publish this pathetic stab at bribing a man who was then America's conscience.

'Let's go get some lunch.' This was to be the first lunch of a long if intermittent acquaintance and it provided an insight into his rugged, unegotistic character.

We walked up Broadway to Times Square. Not to a stars' restaurant like Sardi's where Miller would be recognised and fussed over but to a sandwich bar so modest that it seemed little wider than a hole in the wall. He ordered salt beef sandwiches and a bottle of celery pop. Towering above every other customer, he looked round with affection at the scuffed décor, the bottles of sauce on the wooden tables. 'This place hasn't changed,' he said appreciatively, wrapping his massive hands round a hot sandwich. 'I used to eat here when I was a kid of eighteen, driving a truck. I delivered auto parts for a living.' Looking at his heavy windcheater, open-neck shirt and bristle-brush hair I thought how easily he could pass for a truck driver. Maybe at heart he still was. 'Yes,' he said. 'It's a handy little place, this, very convenient for Broadway. And I like their celery pop.'

John Osborne

In the fifties American theatre seemed much superior to our own diet of West End light comedy or the pretentious verse drama of T. S. Eliot and Christopher Fry. But on his visit to England with Marilyn the play Miller had wanted to see was *Look Back in Anger*, to which Olivier unenthusiastically escorted him. To Olivier's surprise he enthused over it. The play achieved amazing notoriety during its short run. The ranting of its anti-hero, Jimmy Porter, against the dull complacency of the time – the English Sunday with its pompous Sunday papers as the only available entertainment, and the powerlessness of a proletarian outsider like himself to do anything to change it – was a striking departure from the good manners and underplayed emotion of typical West End acting. It caused much offence to audiences and to many critics at the Royal Court Theatre but its many revivals brought in the customers, which saved the theatre's policy of putting on new playwrights. It also made the author, John Osborne, a name everyone knew, which was why I found myself looking for him at an unobtrusive address in Chelsea – Woodfall Street – which was tucked away behind the then highly fashionable King's Road.

I had for the first time taken with me a cumbersome piece of new technology, a tape recorder, which came in a substantial metal case containing two revolving spools as big as dinner plates, and a heavy motor to drive them. By the time I found his front door I was panting with the burden of carrying it. I was expecting rather apprehensively to be confronted by an 'Angry Young Man' – as the theatre's publicity had provocatively described him. He opened the door of the small, mews-type house and looked at my case with surprise. He had never seen one either. He courteously helped me get it going on the floor between us. We played back a test run to see if it was working. How long and slender his hands were, I noted, how smooth the elongated oval of his face, how quiet his voice and polite his manner. He wore a bow tie and a cashmere sweater. Only a quizzical curl to his long lips suggested ready wit, possibly ready contempt. The Angry Young Man label was clearly a libel. The long narrow sitting room was bookish, a writer's room. I did not know then that the house actually belonged to Mary Ure, the fiery Glasgow blonde who originally played the dumb wife at the ironing board who infuriates Jimmy Porter by refusing to rise to his taunts. He had moved in with her from his houseboat on the Thames.

From time to time one or other of us glanced down at the machine to see if its spools were revolving. 'Do you think it's still listening?' I knew of his years touring provincial reps which reminded me of my own spent touring provincial newspapers. While I was playing Northampton, Leeds or Manchester he was playing Leicester, Kidderminster or Derby. 'But I heard you were a journalist before that?' 'I started on the *Gas World.*' 'And I started on *The Bicycle!*' It was a bit of a bond. At the time he was writing unperformed plays I was trying to write unpublished books. How long did it take you to write this one? 'About three weeks – with interruptions.' And to get it on? 'It was rejected by every management I could find in the *Writers' and Artists' Yearbook*. About twenty-five of them. Until George saw it. No one but he would have put it on.'

George Devine at the Royal Court was the only manager in the theatre known by his first name apart from his exquisite opposite, 'Binkie' Beaumont, the all-powerful boss of H. M. Tennent's in the West End. The theatre was divided between Binkie's theatre of comfort for the middle classes and George's theatre of disturbance for the non-conformist young audience. The former took care to make money. The latter paid no heed to losing it on plays he believed in. Osborne was his first hit playwright. How did that feel? 'Well, I haven't made a fortune, if that's what you're wondering. But it's nice to be able to buy the books you want without have to get them from the library.' But what made him, a success, want to denounce England? 'The people in charge,' he said. All the same the prevailing impression he made was of traditional Englishness. Not just the pipe, the appearance, the clothes but the attitudes. For instance his love of the Music Hall – we discovered that we both went to Collins, a hall which was still in business – and his love for Max Miller (who was part inspiration for *The Entertainer*, his next play). Then there was his admiration for the language of the Book of Common Prayer for which he was to take up the cudgels against modernisation. 'Actually I couldn't live anywhere but England. I think the English people on the whole are gentler and kinder than other people.' Look back in anger? He looked back with a sense of loss to an England, as he put it, 'where the pound was worth a pound'.

I remembered these sentiments the next time he was provoking public outrage. His mild manner deserted him as soon as he picked up a pen. Within weeks he was describing the royal family as 'the gold filling in a mouthful of decay'. His ferocious jibe was not so much at the royals as at the surrounding decay. Next came his letter to his compatriots, 'Damn You, England'. It was sent to the left-wing magazine *Tribune* from a holiday address in the South of France and addressed to: 'My countrymen – I mean those men with manic fingers leading the betrayed body of my country to its death. My favourite fantasy is four minutes of non-commercial viewing as you fry in your hot seats in Westminster.' (He later regretted posting the letter and called it 'a slovenly, melodramatic misuse of my so-called gift for rhetoric'.) It fell to me to write a response in the form of a *Daily Mail* leader column. I began: 'John Osborne's letter of hate reads more like the howl of a betrayed lover who feels powerless to affect the world he lives in…' To the paper's surprise a large majority of the letters that poured in were in his support. It was a time of dangerous confrontation with the Soviet Union, which was attempting to cut off Berlin. Nuclear threats were being bandied about. People were genuinely scared and said so. They probably agreed with Jimmy Porter that, if the Big Bang did come, 'it wouldn't be in aid of any good, brave cause but for a Brave New Nothing Very Much, thank you'.

Over the following years I had to review his many subsequent plays. Some were very powerful – *Inadmissible Evidence* for example – in others he seemed to lose his theatrical touch. One of them, *West of*

Suez, a reflection on the now defunct British Empire, ended with a burst of machine gun fire to finish both the characters and the argument. This seemed lazy to me and I condemned it. Three weeks later I saw it again on transfer to a West End theatre and I realised that up to that point it had been a very interesting play. It was not often I changed my mind on a second viewing but this one had to be acknowledged. 'I am about to eat humble pie,' I wrote, going on to explain why. Next day came a postcard: 'We think it very stylish of you to change your mind – J. O.' Success came and went for him, as unhappily as his wives. Our relations fluctuated, sometimes on the telephone, sometimes face to face, whenever he was causing trouble. 'Why should I talk to you?' 'I thought we knew each other.' He reviewed a book of mine about the National Theatre vituperatively and at length, not because of the book but because of the theatre, which he hated for giving some of his plays unworthy productions.

His last years were mostly silent except for some sizzling polemical journalism – at which he could have made a Swiftian career. Here he is in full thunder against the substitution of the Alternative Service Book for the 1662 Book of Common Prayer:

> The vile infelicities, the customs-and-excise speak, the liturgical insensitivities of the new versions, their failure of imagination, poetry and beauty show the aim is now overt: to change utterly the form and faith of the Church of England, to cause the wholesale destruction of those who once sheltered and thrived within its national mysteries.

Whatever his shortcomings, the ability to use the English language like a newly-whetted blade was not one of them. I last saw him shortly before his death, staying as usual at the Cadogan Hotel. We drank our champagne to the memory of its former guest, Oscar Wilde. Unlike some theatre colleagues not half as talented as he was, I mourned him.

THE REBEL COURT

Osborne's Jimmy Porter opened the door for a host of malcontents: Alan Sillitoe's Arthur Seaton of *Saturday Night and Sunday Morning*, John Braine's Joe Lampton of *Room at the Top*, Keith Waterhouse's *Billy Liar*, all of them more successful as films than as novels. But these were Northern misfits kicking against the barrier that constrained the working class. Their heroes were monosyllabic compared with the abrasive, excoriating eloquence of Osborne's anti-heroes. They were part of the dissent that marked the supposedly conformist fifties, at least in its second half. The revolutionary headquarters for non-conformist writers was a theatre – the Royal Court, Sloane Square – however posh its neighbourhood and however nineteenth-century its façade. George Devine's benign but uncompromising leadership and willingness to back the unpopular attracted working-class talent, playwrights like Arnold Wesker and actors like Albert Finney, Tom Courtenay and Nicol Williamson, who no longer had to suppress their aggressively provincial or lower-class accents. At the Court they were precisely what was wanted. No accent was more unabashed than the Yorkshire vowels of Tony Richardson, Devine's right-hand man who directed all Osborne's early plays. Tall, lean, ruthless, energetic, he was a fiery counter-balance to the more judicious Devine – he provided the acceleration while George did the steering.

Tony had come up to my college at Oxford, Wadham, as if blown by hurricane from his native Shipley, and occupied an adjoining staircase. Once you got used to his breakneck hurry he was extremely stimulating. The moribund college dramatic society was soon reeling under his assault, presenting bizarre choices of play such as *Perkin Warbeck* by the Jacobean John Ford. The production hardly drew the crowds and lost the society £800, an alarming sum in the late 1940s. Tony showed not the least contrition at the inquest into the accounts held afterwards in the Junior Common Room. 'But Tony,' said a plaintive voice, 'Why choose this play?' Tony unwound to his full height: 'It hadn't been donn for three oondred and twenty years and ah wanted to know why!' He glared at us daring anyone to question this obvious need. There was a pause. 'Well,' said a more resigned voice, 'we know now.' (I have never heard of another production of *Perkin Warbeck*.) I was soon involved in other of Tony's adventures, including an ambitious production of *Romeo and Juliet* at Oxford Playhouse prior to a tour. Audition had failed to produce agreement on a suitable Juliet. Time was getting short when Tony burst into a meeting triumphantly: 'Ah've found her! Ah found her on top of a booss!' She was an undoubtedly beautiful girl called Julia but a stranger to the stage. By the end of rehearsals she had still not discovered much about its requirements of voice and projection for all Tony's efforts. But decorative she was and he designed the production to show her off physically while distracting attention from her acting with great swirling crowd movements – 'A producer's holiday' was I think *The Times'* verdict.

At the Royal Court, where he and Devine worked in harness for eight years, no one could mistake a Tony Richardson production. By the time George resigned, worn out and ill (he was to die within a year), Tony and John Osborne had founded Woodfall Films and were making a fortune from Osborne's *The Entertainer*, starring Laurence Olivier as the seedy music hall comedian down on his luck, and were about to make another from *Tom Jones*, adapted by Osborne from the Henry Fielding novel and starring Finney. With that under his belt Tony took off for a more exotic life in California and work in Hollywood. Passing him one day in an airport lounge I asked why did he not return to England sometimes and work in the theatre again. He gave me a dazzling smile: 'But you see ah just adore *movies*!'

LINDSAY ANDERSON

Lindsay Anderson, the other film director who found a comforting home for a while at the Court, was also a Wadham man, as Devine had also been, a remarkable record for one college in such a short period. I came to know him because of a postcard he sent after I had reviewed his production there of *The Fire Raisers*, a parable by Max Frisch. In the middle of the Cold War, with both sides stacking up nuclear weapons on a theory of safety called Mutually Assured Destruction, its symbolism needed little guessing. A blindly naïve Herr Biedermann welcomes perfect strangers into his house who wish to stack drums of petrol in his basement. By all means, he assures them. More and more fuel is steadily added. But he is confident they have no sinister intentions. Even when they ask him if he can supply them with a match he is eager to oblige. Biedermann, played by Alfred Marks, was made up to have an uncanny resemblance to our own prime minister, Mr Macmillan, as I pointed out. The postcard said simply: 'I know one is not supposed to write to critics – but thank you. Lindsay Anderson.' So our friendship began.

He hated everything middlebrow or complacent, such as West End theatre or popular English cinema (*Four Weddings and a Funeral* later aroused his particular spleen as 'everything that is wrong with British filmmaking'). He resolutely refused to compromise with commercial values. 'Surely,' he used to say, 'we should aim at perfection?' Not many directors did so. His impatience, though he tried to conceal it, was of the officer class. He had been born in India, son of a future general, product of a public school (Cheltenham, which he was to use as the setting for *If...*, later the winner of Best Film at Cannes).

When we first met he was directing Richard Harris, the star of his gritty rugby-playing film, *This Sporting Life*, an extrovert so belligerent that he made Lindsay's technique of quiet, deadly dominance almost invisible. They were engaged in a foolhardy two-man enterprise, Gogol's *Diary of a Madman*, adapted as a soliloquy for the Royal Court stage. At first I thought Lindsay was being uncharacteristically passive, perhaps as a technique for wearing out Harris's ego by letting him talk endlessly about the ways he was going to hold an audience for nearly two hours with the ramblings of a madman. It never wore out. As he was in need of frequent alcoholic stimulation his boasting grew wilder as the day wore on. What I did not realise until Lindsay's diaries were published years after his death was that, for perhaps the only time in his life, Lindsay was suffering a crush, a masochistic infatuation for Harris (who was rampantly heterosexual). In private he would endure his insults and commands. He even allowed Harris to point at the ground and snarl, 'Heel, Lindsay! Heel!' The resulting show was not a peak in either of their careers.

Harris went on to become rich, famous and ever more bombastic after *Camelot*. Almost every memory I have of him is of late or all-night drinking sessions at which he would attempt to seduce whichever woman I was with. It was an instinctive reaction like a seal ensuring he dominated any female on his territory. He would explode with a 'God! Look at that bum!' – indicating a female perched on a Savoy bar stool who had caught his ever-alert fancy. Sadly, but perhaps not surprisingly, he ended his days living alone at the Savoy. He was so bored that he would slip out into a nearby alleyway to a pub called The Coal Hole where he hoped to buttonhole someone into listening to his repetitive tales of self-admiration. He wasn't, unfortunately, quite as great an actor as he thought and never exceeded the performance Lindsay got out of him in *This Sporting Life*.

Lindsay worked on at the Court with a memorable series of plays by the writer from whose novel that film was made, David Storey. One, *The Changing Room*, exposed the backstage tensions of rugby league players like his former self. Most were ruthlessly realistic studies of Yorkshire family life, where terse conversation carries overtones of emotion which no one can openly express. Storey, a much underrated writer, reached the apogee of this technique in a play called *Home*. A combination of his extraordinary script and the opportunity to work with Anderson brought to the Royal Court the unlikely West End duo of Sir John Gielgud and Sir Ralph Richardson. Set outdoors in the grounds of the 'home' the play was almost devoid of action. Its characters sometimes sat down on garden chairs, sometimes stood up, beginning to converse but drifting away into silence because none of them could finish a sentence. It was only gradually that audiences realised it was a home for people with dementia. The silent sympathy that Gielgud and Richardson created between them was palpable – sometimes touching, sometimes amusing, sometimes tragic. Audiences sat in rapt silence listening or waiting. On the second night, I was informed by a fellow reviewer who was present, the silence was so deep that a mouse wandered on stage, looked around and departed without attracting any attention. 'I suspect it had been rehearsed by Lindsay,' he said.

When he died in 1994 Lindsay had not made a major film for years. His insistence on total control as a director and his search for perfection gave him a reputation for being 'difficult'. It made it near-impossible to raise the backing for the films he still wanted to create. His fame rests on no more than five films, each extraordinary and original. He was hurt when they went unappreciated by the many. He was a demanding friend, always on the verge of scorn for some aspect of English smugness or triviality in tastes. His mockery often included by implication your own. Lunching with him somewhat resembled being lashed with birch twigs after a sauna – a bracing and really quite agreeable test of endurance. Of course, he admitted he was 'difficult'. 'It is the duty of an artist to be difficult – to bite the hand that feeds him.' He never neglected that duty.

SAMUEL BECKETT

The playwright whose work was most often produced at the Court was not Osborne but Samuel Beckett. George Devine, a friend of his, directed the first English productions of *Happy Days*, *End Game* and *Krapp's Last Tape*. By then *Waiting for Godot*, greeted with total incomprehension in 1955, had been acknowledged a modern classic. But Beckett himself remained an enigma who dwelt in Paris and never gave interviews. So when word came that he was attending rehearsals of one of his plays at the Court there was great anticipation. At the theatre he was 'Sam' to everybody, almost a fellow thespian. I am not sure why but there was a party, possibly connected with his birthday, in the upstairs bar at which I found myself sitting next to his long, lean frame on the floor – there were never enough chairs at the Court. To be so close to the famous bird-of-prey profile was a little awesome. But he was genially relaxed over his beer and had been watching cricket at Lords (he was a member of MCC and had earlier played for Trinity College, Dublin).

There was an unspoken understanding that he never talked about or explained his work. I noticed that when someone looked like venturing on personal territory he rose from the floor saying, with a gracious smile, 'Sorry, I just have to go to the lav.' It so happened that earlier that day I had been asked to tape a TV piece to camera connected with the forthcoming play. With an excusatory laugh, I said, 'I've just been given three minutes to camera to describe your work for a television programme.' He leant forward with interest. 'Oh? What did you say?' 'Well, I said that lately your plays have been getting shorter and shorter. An hour. Half an hour. Fifteen minutes. Five…I wondered, will you be able to go on?' The eagle head considered this. 'I hope so,' he said at last. 'But I doubt it.'

THE SUEZ SPLIT

The first days of November 1956 had the gathering tension that precedes a full-blown hurricane or earthquake. It felt afterwards that, although nothing had actually lost its roof or fallen down, everything had been shaken and cracked and might collapse very soon, especially Great Britain. At 2am on the Sunday Russian tanks began rolling into Budapest to crush the self-governing style of government their Hungarian fellow Communists had set up. Meanwhile a British invasion force was steaming with maddening slowness and deliberation from Malta towards the Suez Canal, which had been nationalised by a defiant Colonel Nasser. Only half a dozen years earlier I had been 'defending' it as part of the British occupying army. It was a bare desolate stretch of canal which I was assigned to defend with few troops. One consolation was that on emerging from my tent I would sometimes find a stately, shapely liner of dazzling white a few hundred yards away, apparently ploughing graciously through the sand in the early morning sunshine. Sometimes for relief from the heat I would drop into the canal after such a liner had passed to be borne along effortlessly on its following wave. The sensation was exhilarating. You could have surfed for miles at walking pace, only it would have been tedious to have to walk back again. A less welcome realisation was how deeply the Egyptians hated our being there, a dislike warmly returned by the average squaddy. No wonder Nasser was a popular hero.

Earlier that year the last of our garrison, once eighty thousand strong, was withdrawn under an agreement negotiated by Anthony Eden. Three months later he was trying to take it back again. The barefaced cheek of nationalisation caused furious resentment and horror in Britain among people who, like him, had been brought up to believe that the Canal was the vital link that connected our widespread empire. Eden had waited too long to succeed Churchill and when he did reach Number 10 seemed a weak, ineffectual leader. He was determined to prove otherwise by toppling Nasser – with help from the French and a secret agreement with the Israelis. But not from the Americans, who were being kept in the dark. This was extraordinarily bad judgement from a supposedly ace diplomat.

The country was deeply divided about his gamble – party against party, newspaper against newspaper, even family members against one another. *The Daily Express*, which I was helping to put to bed every night, was one of the most belligerent, stopping little short of calling Nasser a 'Wog'. The tedium of normal fifties politics became a whirlpool, in which the plight of the brave Hungarian rebels was all but forgotten.

On the eve of our invasion a protest meeting in Trafalgar Square turned ugly. Mounted police struggled vainly to stop a mob rushing down Whitehall towards Downing Street. A worried meeting of the Cabinet, which was beginning to realise that Britain could not afford to go to war without American approval and financial backing, must have heard from outside the chants of 'Eden Must Go!' I passed through the square on the way to Fleet Street in time to see the hero of the Left, Aneurin Bevan, hoisted on a plinth where he declared: 'If Eden is sincere in thinking his plan will work…' – dramatic pause – 'then he is too *stupid* to be prime minister!' To the delight of the crowd. But a very different emotion was boiling at the *Express* offices. The paper was demanding that Nasser be taught a lesson. I and one other night sub-editor expressed dissent, saying Eden was mad. We were surrounded by a growing crowd of night staff and backed more and more tightly against a wall. Their mood was ugly. 'Our boys are going in!' they chorused menacingly. 'Our boys are going in!' No actual violence was done to us but I was shaken, mainly by the transformation into warmongers of these normally quiet, sedentary men who spent their break times discussing cricket or the best way to combat greenfly.

Thanks to the displeasure of Eisenhower, interrupted in his bid to be re-elected president, and the duplicity of his secretary of state, John Foster Dulles, the invasion was ignominiously called off almost as soon as it began. I doubt if our troops reached as far as my old Canal stamping ground before they were turned back again. But this botched venture made the loss of Britain's ability to act alone as a great power plain to the world. No more was heard from the 'teach Nasser a lesson' school who had been in the majority until the attempt failed. Had Eden kept his nerve, had Nasser fallen as a result, he would have been wildly popular and acclaimed, at least for a time. But it was Nasser who survived to triumph and Suez which lived on as a one-word symbol for acts of political folly. The Empire that the Canal was supposed to pin together very soon fell apart.

The Daily Express

Despite the fervour of the *Express* nothing could save Eden, who was shuffled into oblivion as quickly as possible. At that time the *Express* sold four million copies and set the pace for popular newspapers which were largely broadsheets like itself. The aim of many thrusting young journalists was to work in its art deco palace of black glass, known to its inmates as 'the Lubianka'. Indeed to work in Fleet Street but never to have been on the *Express* was rather like serving as a soldier but never having been under fire. When its courteous deputy editor, Edward Pickering, offered me a vacancy as a sub-editor I accepted eagerly, though it was not what I wanted to be and despite his warning that, like a subaltern on the Western Front, a sub's expectation of survival was about three weeks. But the paper was made by its sub-editors. It was their responsibility to rewrite and dress up stories in *Express* style, steaming and rattling through the day's news with excited toots of scorn and whistles of amazement. Life at night in the huge 'ballroom', where every department was within shouting distance, was lived on your nerves. The subs were nervous of the chief sub, a caustic martinet, who in turn was nervous of the night editor, an aggressive Yorkshireman who, rather than waste time removing the cigarette from his mouth, blew the ash off it noisily, sometimes in your face. He, in turn deferred to the 'back bench' of assistant and associate editors who came and went with rapidity. They were arranged in a hierarchy culminating in the chair of the editor, Arthur Christiansen, more often occupied in my time by Pickering, his deputy.

Christiansen, a Fleet Street legend who had taken over the editorship at the age of twenty-nine, seldom appeared on the floor but controlled the paper by writing a daily Bulletin which was pinned up in a glass case on the wall, every evening at 6pm. His aim was to make the columns exciting to his favourite imaginary reader – 'the man in the back streets of Derby'. His Bulletins, which analysed what he thought good or bad about that morning's paper, were a powerful influence. He seemed to know exactly who was responsible for the high points and the lows. 'Have you seen the Bulletin?' we always asked each other as we began work on the next day's paper. People who looked pleased with themselves had been singled out for approval. Others slunk cowed to their work, hoping nobody knew it was their piece that had been found wanting. A typical Chris comment would run: 'Let me quote this morning's Page One Centre Column for the sheer virtuosity of its intro. "The honeymoon was definitely over when the bridegroom threw the bride out of the railway carriage window..."' It wasn't until later that the reader discovered that the train was on fire. On a signboard hanging from the ceiling above our desks was the word IMPACT in enormous letters, like a battle cry.

The atmosphere grew tenser as the clock on the wall approached first edition time at 10pm. You would hold up copy that was ready for the printer above your head and shout, 'Boy!' Middle-aged messengers older than most of us would collect it and drop it down a wooden chute to land on the head printer's desk on the floor below. These 'boys', cockneys to a man, knew the foibles of everyone in authority and who had got it in for whom. George and Laurie, one thin and nervy, the other plump and relaxed, worked as a team and were our chief source of office gossip. "Ear about that new ponce of an assistant editor? 'Ad a right up-and-downer wiv 'is nibs, din't he? 'E won't last long, mark my words.' Besides knowing the psychological state of play they also knew of suppliers of certain luxury goods at curiously low prices – television sets, refrigerators, champagne or cigars. 'Fancy one of them new big tellys? Could get one for you Tuesday.' One didn't ask how. One night the front page lead story went missing. It had been sent down but the head printer swore he had never received it. Consternation at ten to ten. Desks were searched savagely. Then Laurie sauntered over to the chute, whose opening was covered by a glass lid. He lifted it and peered in. 'There's your lead. Stuck 'alfway down.' The bundle of paper was out of reach. Laurie came up with a heavy weight attached to a metal cable and lowered it down the chute just in time. Such was the state of technology at the mightiest newspaper in the land.

Heat, din and smell were then essential ingredients in newspaper production. The heat rose, along with the smell of printers' ink and hot metal, from the composing room below the editorial floor. Linotype machines clattered under the hands of compositors who earned far more than most journalists. Their unions had a stranglehold on the management – if they stopped work there would be no paper the next day. For example, every galley of type came up plentifully scattered with mistakes or 'literals' and had to be sent back for correction. Of course the operators could have made fewer mistakes. But corrections were paid for at a higher rate and setting them was reserved as a bonus for compositors who were nearing retirement.

By twenty or twenty-five past ten the rotary presses in the basement began to turn, reaching the floor above with a muffled roar and deep vibrations. The whole building stirred like ship putting to sea. It was a satisfying sensation. Nearby within a few hundred yards presses were turning also at the *Daily Mail*, *Daily Telegraph*, *The Times*, *Daily Mirror* and *News Chronicle*. Fleet Street's fleet was leaving harbour. Recalling it now is like conjuring up the days of the stage coach before the coming of the railways. The presses are now sited miles from the offices, the linotype machine is extinct along with its quirky operators, and editorial floors no longer resound to the clatter of a hundred typewriters or shouts of 'Boy!' Computer screens are silent. Their mice don't even squeak. When it all came to an end a powerful sense of camaraderie was lost. The staffs of rival papers knew each other because they took their breaks for refreshment in the same somewhat squalid watering holes. Enough valedictory pieces have been written about the Street's intake of alcohol, but this habit had a virtue. Everyone knew what the others were doing and thinking. In half an hour's stroll from hostelry to hostelry you would know what stories were hot as well as who had quarrelled, resigned or been fired.

Summary dismissal was a hazard even at the highest level, even for Christiansen whose position was assumed to be unassailable. For years he had retained the capricious favour of the *Express* proprietor, Lord Beaverbrook, by leaving the politics of the paper entirely to him. After suffering a heart attack he was invited by Beaverbrook to convalesce at his holiday home in the West Indies. After three weeks with the Lord in the sun he sailed home and arrived one evening looking pink and fit, greeted his staff, wrote his Bulletin and then was asked by his embarrassed deputy, Ted Pickering, to go upstairs to see Beaverbrook's son, Max Aitken. He learnt that during his voyage Beaverbrook had dismissed him and appointed Pickering in his stead. No one knew why. His health did not look suspect. Could it have been that his frequent television appearances were making him better known than the Beaver himself? Or was Beaverbrook emulating Henry VIII once more, by ordering summary execution of former favourites? No one saw Chris on the editorial floor of the *Express* again. Except for myself. One evening a few days later I saw him leaning on a filing cabinet at one end of the ballroom, his pink, pug-like face resting on his fist with a faint, bemused smile. It was the evening break and there were few people about. For a few moments he contemplated the empty battlefield that he had dominated for so long. When I looked up again he had vanished like a ghost – which I suppose by then he was.

Pick, as he was universally known, was the editor I admired most out of the many I have written for. He showed no sign of emotion in any crisis beyond raising one eyebrow and thoughtfully stroking the ridge of his prominent nose before pronouncing a decision. The paper's Prodnose, a former naval commander of stern aspect, who searched the galley proofs for grammatical errors or solecisms of style, came dancing up to him one night waving a piece of copy which I recognised as my own. 'You can't print this!' he cried in near apoplexy. 'This tomfoolery! This…whimsical nonsense!' Pick took the galley proof, which was to accompany a picture page of film stars sunning themselves on Riviera beaches while we all shivered in a bad English February – a desperate expedient to fill a gap for lack of anything better. He read it gravely. 'Of course you are right,' he said, 'but it is just the sort of whimsical nonsense we need in tomorrow's *Express*.'

Caption writing of more than an identifying line was a new departure at that time. The easing of post-war restrictions on newsprint made it possible to make photographs big. The *Express* picture page was created by a gifted lay-out supremo, Harold Keeble, who left his mark on most of the popular papers in the Street. He was a short, plump, husky-voiced visionary who stood at a long lectern along one side of his office wielding tracing lay-out paper and chinagraph pencils with which to crop photographs. The best news pictures in the world would be submitted every night in the hope of catching his eye. Every picture agency from Magnum downwards competed to make 'Photonews'. Sometimes they were the latest portraits by Karsh of Ottawa or Richard Avedon of New York. The decks were also cleared for photographic essays from Anthony Armstrong Jones, later Lord Snowdon. Keeble was always hoping that something better than he already had would come through the door at the last minute. The floor was littered with discarded layouts and prints while the clock ticked towards the deadline and often past it. My role was to provide a half-column which told the story in such a way that the reader would think: what marvellous pictures! But he gave me less and less time in which to do it. People would drift into the office just to watch him scheme pages on enormous sheets of tracing paper with the fat pencil grasped in his left hand. He liked to give the impression that this was only an interruption in his rich social life. One evening he announced that he would be leaving early because of an important dinner he was hosting. He picked up a white telephone, one of his status symbols, to give instructions to a butler or valet at his flat. 'Baines? I'm a little behind schedule, so would you decant the Bechavelle now? Oh and Baines…use the William IV decanters.'

One night we were confronted with a surprising photograph of T. S. Eliot out dancing with his recently married second wife, Valerie, who for years had been his secretary and as his widow was to forbid all would-be biographers. The austere Eliot dancing? And smiling? Keeble was intrigued. 'See what you can find out.' Already his left hand was itching above the lectern with some such headline as 'Nobel Laureate Cuts A Rug'. Nervously I rang up the poet. I had first heard his voice on a recording of him reading his work. It amazed us at school. Was this old maidish voice, bereft of any expression except a weary resignation, really the right way to read *The Waste Land*? Now I heard it again, cautiously answering the telephone. 'Dancing? Yes, I have been stepping out a little since my marriage. In fact I am thinking of having dancing lessons as I have not danced for some years.' I hoped the conversation would develop but, 'I never give interviews to the press. But I would like a copy of your photograph. If you send it I may perhaps have something to say to accompany it.' I was to ring again the next evening. He began by confessing that he often could not remember his own poems. 'When my wife quoted a line the other day I did not recognise it as mine.' He usually wrote from ten until one – 'though I would much rather be doing something else'. I asked if he had enjoyed working in a bank when he was younger. 'They were valuable years, far from dull. I never thought about poetry in the day. At night I could write with a fresh mind. I recommend such a job to young writers.' He was currently working on a play which had taken two years. 'A long time to entertain the same characters. Like making a long train journey with travellers whose conversation you have exhausted. That is all I have to say. Goodbye.' I was left clutching my shorthand. I still wonder if he ever took the dancing lessons.

The *Express* of those days was produced regardless of expense. It had a very large staff of reporters at home and abroad and paid handsomely for serial rights to such things as the early James Bond novels or exclusive Paris fashion pictures. It liked to chronicle the doings of rich or sophisticated café society, though there was a 'black list' of individuals of whom Beaverbrook desired no mention to be made – unless it was to their discredit. Lord Louis Mountbatten was a prime example. It was an *Express* principle to translate for the man in the back streets of Derby any foreign phrase. Frowning at a piece of agency copy the foreign editor came across the ballroom floor to consult the night editor. 'Stockholm says the Nobel prize for literature will not be awarded this year because of an...' – he paused – '*embarras de richesses*. We can't print that!' There was a lengthy pause for deliberation. 'Better make it "for lack of funds".' Beaverbrook controlled the executives by telephone from his apartment near the Ritz at Arlington House. He often wanted to know why a certain story was not in the *Express*, especially about Sotheby's auctions in which as an art collector he was interested. One night in Pick's absence the night editor took the Beaver's regular evening call and emerged looking shaken and angry. 'What's up Ray? Didn't the old man like today's paper?' Ray blew the ash off his cigarette with extra venom. 'Gorgin! We missed a story on Gorgin!' There was a long silence among the subs. 'Who's Gorgin?' someone asked at last. 'Gorgin! The fuckin' painter!'

Lord Beaverbrook

The *Express* reached a circulation of 4.3 million copies under Pickering and it was typical of Beaverbrook to choose this moment to deliver the unexpected stab in the back, on Christmas Eve, of all days. To add ridicule to injury Pick was not straightforwardly fired but demoted to the editorship of the *Farming Express*, a minor weekly publication in the group. Fleet Street was dumbfounded but Pick remained as unperturbed as usual. He soon crossed over to the Mirror Group. From that point on the *Express* began its long slide from the top. Beaverbrook changed editor three times in as many years before Time relieved him of his irresponsibilities. His eighty-fifth birthday was celebrated by a lavish dinner for six hundred thrown by Roy Thomson, a fellow Canadian given to buying up any newspaper in sight. He owned two hundred including *The Times*. With an escort of Canadian Mounties and Indian Chiefs Beaverbrook was wheeled to an exclusive top table for two – himself and Thomson, who was not a byword for conversational brilliance other than the sentence, 'A commercial television licence is a licence to print money.'

By this time I had left the *Express* and was reporting the occasion for the rival *Daily Mail*. Photography by flash then required a large heavy box of equipment connected to the camera by a cable. I offered to carry the *Mail* photographer's box for him so that I could follow him up to the top table. I wanted to hear what the 'little nut-brown man' was saying. Precisely nothing, was the answer. The two press lords sat in deep Canadian silence. We did not know then that Beaverbrook was about to die. It did not stop him from making a good speech about his apprenticeship in newspapers, adding that it was time for him to become an apprentice once more – 'somewhere, sometime, soon'.

A Rogues' Gallery

When he died a week or two later the obituaries called him a 'master journalist'. He was more of a master *provocateur*. His gift was to spot outstanding journalists and drive them, out of anxiety to please him, to perform better than they knew they could. When he had had the best out of them he would discard them without a moment's remorse.

At least Beaverbrook cared first and foremost what his papers said. 'I run my newspapers for political and propaganda purposes,' he told a Press Commission. Profit was a very secondary motive with him – unlike some proprietors to come. He was called wicked but we had not then heard of Robert Maxwell or Rupert Murdoch.

ROCK & ROLL UNITED

1956 was also the year when young people in Britain began to rock:

> One, two, three o'clock, four o'clock rock!
> Five, six, seven o'clock, eight o'clock rock!
> Nine, ten, eleven o'clock, twelve o'clock rock!
> We're gonna rock around the clock!

This oddly stirring chorus was first heard that year accompanying the title of a film, *Blackboard Jungle*. Its pistol-cracking beat unlocked some kind of floodgates of repressed vitality in the young. It was crude, it was energetic and it vibrated through teenage minds like no previous spell had done. They rose from their cinema seats dancing wildly in the aisles, ripping out seats that got in the way of the jiving, bouncing and bopping. In fact it was not as young a sound as they thought. It was played by a band called Bill Haley and his Comets, who were the wrong side of thirty. They arrived the next year to tour Britain, having sold twenty-two million records. 'Man,' ran their publicity man's greeting in the *Daily Mirror*. 'We really are hoping to meet you British cats.' But the British cats were a shade discomforted to see that Mr Haley was a plumpish man with a kiss curl and a tartan jacket, concealing braces. Hardly suitable for a teen icon. The words rock and roll occurred frequently in the limited vocabulary of Haley's lyrics. Soon rock 'n' roll was forever united in mutual bondage.

Until then popular music in the fifties had been a heyday for ballad singers, mostly hoping to emulate Frank Sinatra. It was a world of sentimental conformity they presented where Mr Wonderfuls promised some enchanted evening with a stranger in paradise.

A Rogues' Gallery

England produced its own balladeers from factory bench or building lot – Dickie Valentine, Frankie Vaughan, David Whitfield joined by restrained songstresses such as Petula Clark, Alma Cogan and Ruby Murray, who at one time was selling one of every four records purchased in Britain, mainly of a hit called 'Softly, Softly'. They were of a different species from Elvis Presley, who was the first singer not to moon about 'April Love', 'Love and Marriage' or promise 'Friendly Persuasion'. His lyrics were nakedly aphrodisiac, like his hips, leaving no room for doubt what was meant by 'Good Rockin' Tonight'. Britain could not equal this but it tried. Pop stars were discovered, groomed, renamed and presented by managers such as John Kennedy and his partner Larry Parnes, who maintained a stable full of hopefuls in a spacious apartment. They included Cliff Richard (formerly Harry Webb), Marty Wilde (Reg Smith to his parents), and others renamed Vince Eager, Billy Fury and the like.

It was to witness the magic of this transformation process, the minting of pop stardom, that I went along to a basement somewhere off the Bayswater Road where a single was being cut by the recently launched Marty Wilde, who was bidding to become Cliff Richard's rival. Rock 'n' roll discs emerged from dark, airless chambers lined like padded cells with acoustic material. The floor, covered in cables and cigarette butts, was overlooked by a sinister square window cut in one wall. The Control Room. The recording manager was called Ivor, who looked unhappy. 'Let me hear your A,' he said to one of the Wild Cats sprawling on a bench. A boy called Liquorice smote his A. The Wild Cats gave out little nervous jangles of notes. One of them lit a cigarette and placed it between the strings at the top of his guitar's fretboard, where it stuck out horizontally emitting blue wisps. They, like us, were waiting for Marty Wilde. I was told he earned an unimaginable £1,000 a week.

'OK, Group, let's have a run-through,' said Ivor to four much older men. They stood round a microphone facing each other in a hollow square. The parts on their music stands were marked 'Boy 1', 'Boy 2' and so on. They were the backing, or the 'Wah Group'. 'OK boys, take it from your first Wah…bah-di-dah-di…waah!…Bah!…Aah!…Bup!'

They leaned into the mike passing a cigarette packet round as they

32

waahed in harmony.

'Where's Marty?' boomed a voice from the Control Room, not for the first time. Attention stiffened as a portly American entered the studio. 'That's Mort – he wrote the song,' whispered my neighbour. 'Mort Shuman. You know, Shuman and Pomus. They wrote *Teenager in Love*. That was Marty's first hit.' Their present offering was called *It's Been Nice*. It was a boy's complaint to a girl whom he had expensively entertained but who was saying goodnight, it's been nice, but she had to get up early in the morning....

Marty arrived late because he had been announcing his engagement at a special press conference. He rushed in with his manager, the sleek Larry Parnes. He was tall and had a pleasant, open, South Londoner's face. No tuning was necessary for him. He held his guitar back to front. He was going to slap it, not play it. 'Take one,' boomed the Control Room. His face creased as if in pain, Ivor raised both hands and beat them in the time-honoured manner: 'Er, one. Two. Three...' The Wild Cats twanged, the Boys waahed and Marty sang:

> I don' wanna hear you say
> It's been nice
> But Goo'night
> Godda geddup really early in the mor-nin'

'I just feel it needs a piano in there to bump it out,' said Mort unhappily.

'But we never use a piano. Did we ever use a piano?'

'I just feel it. I could so easily fill in...'

'You don't understand our laws, Mort,' said Mr Parnes swiftly. 'You are an American. The minute you touch that piano the union could withdraw every player.'

'But I don't even want to be paid!'

'Listen, Mort, it'll be a great record. If I didn't think it would do a quarter of a million I wouldn't make it!'

During the next take Mort, a heavy man, rode an imaginary horse full tilt at the drummer.

Mr Parnes explained to me how Reginald Smith, a bus driver's son from Greenwich, had become Marty Wilde. 'He's a big tall boy, he must be a friendly boy, but with character. Marty – that's a friendly name. But Wilde, that's the spirit!' Marty, when he came over, seemed unassuming to a fault. He drank a glass of milk. He said he didn't think much of his voice, as such. 'It'll last about two years. Then I'll be big as somethin' else.'

The afternoon wore on, take after take. A wilting feeling set in. 'Marty!' said Control sharply. 'That last take was sensational. But LEAVE OUT THE TAPPING.'

Marty looked affronted.

'But me tappin's important!'

'Leave it out.'

'*Please*! Can't Marty keep his tappin' in?'

'Marty, you want a great record? A really great record?'

Ivor rallied the weary troops. 'Just one more take. For kicks. Keep it groovy!'

It was take twenty-six when I slipped away. I was exhausted. The record did not make the charts.

QUEER TIMES

Philip Larkin's dictum that sexual intercourse began in 1963 would have rung truer if he had added the words 'to be freely admitted'. In the fifties it was discreet and not talked about. If of the same sex variety it was often a source of private shame and fear of prosecution, yet it was in the fifties that the first steps to legalise such behaviour in private were taken by the appointment of a Home Office committee to examine the law. It was headed by Sir John Wolfenden, formerly headmaster of a public school and therefore presumably conversant with what he was inquiring about. Strangely he claimed in his memoirs that in 1954, when his committee began its work, 'most ordinary people had never heard of it'.

If so they must have sedulously ignored press reports of the trials of prominent homosexuals who were the targets of a campaign of police persecution in the early 1950s. Alan Turing, the genius of Bletchley Park, was prosecuted in 1951 and though not imprisoned killed himself as a result. Sir John Gielgud was caught 'cottaging' by one of the plain-clothes police provocateurs who preyed on public urinals. Though he was only fined, his career suffered a ten-year setback in which he was reduced to doing one-man Shakespearean recitals. In 1954 the law fell on the young Lord Montagu of Beaulieu who together with two friends was imprisoned for gross indecency on the evidence of two RAF men. They had been promised their own immunity from prosecution for giving it. The case was notable for the declaration in court of one of the co-defendants, journalist Peter Wildeblood, that he was a homosexual. 'I am no more proud of my condition than if I had a hare-lip but I am no more ashamed of it than I would be of being colour-blind.' People just did not make public admissions like that in 1954. A few famous queers, as they were then called – no one would have dreamed of applying the word 'gay' to them – scarcely troubled to conceal the fact. Noel Coward was an unabashed example. But Terence Rattigan saw very clearly that homosexual characters had to be disguised in his plays as heterosexual. Newspapers knew who the queers were but avoided even giving their readers heavy hints. Interviewers like myself knew better than to broach the subject of sexuality to a queer subject, even if the interviewee was being quite explicit.

As I was to learn early on when I went to interview Frankie Howerd, then at the peak of his career as a comedian on stage and radio. When I got off the train from Leeds I was astonished and flattered to find that a chauffeur-driven limo had been sent to meet me at the station and deliver me to his residence. My escort was a delicately dressed, pretty young man who introduced himself as Terence. As the Rolls purred westward he gave me a warm smile. 'Frank is so looking forward to meeting you,' he said. I couldn't think why. I was nobody, an unknown provincial journalist from a Yorkshire evening paper.

I was shown into a spacious drawing room where another smartly dressed young man brought me tea on a tray. Clearly it was an all-male household. After some time Mr Howerd – Frank, as I was invited to call him – erupted into the room looking breathless and dishevelled, as was his style on stage. He was a torrential talker, expressions of amazement and horror chasing across his moon-like countenance. His eyebrows and eyes frequently searched the ceiling as if for something he had lost. With arms flying he paced the carpet restlessly. It was like being at close quarters with a highly strung horse. It was not done for effect. He was making no attempt to be funny or putting on the stage persona. He was recalling with passionate resentment his long struggle to get started as a comedian, even at the bottom of variety bills. 'It took me thirteen years to get a break. Not to have a success. Just to *get in*. So I've always been frightened of failure.' In that way, I suggested, he reminded me of Sid Field, the great unrecognised comedian from the Midlands, who waited years for recognition and lived in the daily expectation that it would be abruptly taken away again. Like Howerd, he established a deep complicity with his audience. 'He was my idol,' interrupted Howerd. 'When I saw him for the first time I went home and wept – wept! – cried my eyes out. I knew I would never be as good.' But it was Sid Field's old dressing room at the Prince of Wales that he was now occupying. 'You see, basically what I do is, I confide my *suspicions* to the audience. "Oo… What? They're a funny lot, this lot. See what they're up to now?" I'm saying one thing and underneath I'm thinking another.'

Which was what, I began to realise, he was doing there and then. He had stopped shooting about and was perched on the other end of the sofa. 'There's something I've been wanting to ask you…but no, no. I couldn't possibly. It wouldn't be right.' Why not? 'No, it's my problem.' As he spoke he was rubbing his tummy. 'I have this trouble, a hernia, you see, gives me a lot of discomfort.' Innocently I mentioned that I had had trouble with a hernia myself. He was on me in a flash. 'Let me see, it may be we've got the same problem…' Before I could object he had me lying prone on the sofa with his hand inside my shirt, massaging my abdomen. 'You don't mind, do you? Me doing this?' I remained as politely non-committal as I could. Was he genuinely interested in my navel or was there something else? Nothing happened. I was not responding on the lines he hoped. He patted my stomach off-handedly and got up. 'I should see a good physio if I were you. He could put you right.' As I tucked in my shirt I caught sight of him exiting through an inner door. Soon Terence sidled in. 'Frank wants to know if there's anywhere you'd like to be taken in the car?'

I said I could manage fine, thanks, and walked away down Holland Park. It was exactly like having failed an audition. But then I didn't want the part. Later I learned how frequently he made these attempts and how depressed he often was by his own behaviour. We used to chat years later at after-theatre drinks parties. Neither of us ever referred to our first encounter.

TONY HANCOCK

It may well be that all great comedians are haunted men off stage. It was certainly true of the two who dominated the fifties – Tony Hancock and Spike Milligan. I never met the Hancock whom I, like most of the nation, adored on radio and then television. He did not exist. Anthony Aloysius Hancock, unemployed actor and layabout of Railway Cuttings East Cheam, was the loving invention of two South London scriptwriters, Ray Galton and Alan Simpson. But it was Tony Hancock himself who gave him his crumpled belligerence, resigned self-pity, suppressed resentment and the air of a man who cannot believe what is happening to him. In him the public saw something of themselves. He grumbled and protested for England. Sadly he did not realise it was his character, not himself, that turned people on. He sacked his scriptwriters in order to prove that he could do better on his own. It was my misfortune to have to tell him that he was wrong.

His new stage show – Hancock's Unduly Prolonged Half-Hour, it might have been called – was to be tried out at Southsea and then on tour. I was told to review it. I protested that it was unfair to judge a new venture on its first try-out but the paper was adamant: Hancock was a national institution held in such affection that anything he did was news. So on a bleak Monday evening in a thinnish house I sat waiting and hoping for the best. I could not believe what I saw. A portly middle-aged Hancock was attempting to carry off the act he had used at the post-war Windmill Theatre, originally inspired by ENSA and the Gang Shows. No doubt it went down all right in those undemanding days when would-be stand-ups, who had made their fellow-servicemen laugh, jostled for position on the variety stage. Hancock still had energy but his sight gags and imitations of officers were no longer relevant nor even comprehensible to a new generation that did not remember the war. He even used the old 'Up periscope!' routine when the officer bending over it is struck in the eye. There was sporadic laughter from the bald heads in the orchestra pit but the house felt chilly with disappointment. I rang my office afterwards to say the show did not yet merit review. 'Sorry, they're waiting for it. The editor expects…' I tried to convey Hancock's massive mistake as kindly as I could.

Next morning my hotel bedroom telephone rang. 'Mr Hancock would like to see you.' He was staying at the same hotel. 'Try to cheer him up,' said his publicity lady, who fetched me. Hancock looked angry – worse, wronged and hurt. 'Go and sit over there.' He gestured to a stool which had been placed against a bare wall, like a seat in the dock. 'Why shouldn't you face the music for a change?' For the next twenty minutes I tried to explain tactfully why I thought the show wasn't working, without saying plainly that he had lost his touch. What his act needed, of course, was a Galton and Simpson script but their names were taboo. Suddenly he gave up on me and turned away – he no longer wanted to discuss it. He seemed to be no longer tuned into the rest of the world. From then onwards things went from bad to worse for him until they ended in another hotel room in Australia. By that time the nation had adopted other idols.

SPIKE MILLIGAN

Spike, the comic genius, had passed the war as Gunner Terence Milligan, meeting and joking with a fellow Gunner Harry Secombe along the way. Born in Poona where his father was an Indian army captain, he had begun life cosseted by servants. Then came a traumatic return to unemployment in South East London, until call-up. After the war he scratched a living writing radio comedy scripts for unfunny comedians like Derek Roy. A reunion with Secombe and introduction to Peter Sellers led to a show at first called Crazy People being broadcast very doubtfully by the BBC, whose high-ups could not see anything to laugh at. But in 1951 several million ex-service listeners recognised its surreal send-up of pompous authority with joy. *The Goon Show* changed comedy in ways that are hard to define but needed no explanation to its fans. The demands of writing over a hundred scripts gave Spike nervous breakdowns.

Verbal anarchy remained his weapon against a world he distrusted. I could never make out whether he was in fact mad or, like Hamlet, pretending to be. His mercurial mood-changes were a byword. Sweetness and light could suddenly turn dark, melancholic and even savage to those close to him. His famous put-down of Prince Charles – 'the grovelling little bastard' – was not, however, one of those moments. He interjected it at an award ceremony when someone was reading out a fulsome, overlong tribute to Spike from his royal fan. Anything to break it off. Spike never apologised for anything. He simply sent HRH a postcard saying, 'I suppose that's the end of the knighthood.' In fact, it wasn't. He got an honorary one as an Irish citizen which, thankfully, was never used. It was hard to imagine calling him 'Sir Spike'.

Few people, I think, found him comfortable to be with. He needed to dominate any company. An American network TV show being made at Elstree studios hired and fired writers with great rapidity. At one point both of us were on the payroll and, Hollywood studio fashion, writers were assigned to a 'writers' table' at lunch in the canteen. Every day I watched bumptious pairs of American comedy writers monopolise the conversation with their smart gags. Then Spike would arrive, sit down and within minutes interrupt them with a long, much funnier story of his own, silencing them for the rest of the meal.

He could also become extremely serious about the planet's future. He was campaigning to save the rainforests before anyone. I remember being lectured by him, all alone in his room, on the threat of over-population. He went on working himself into ever more heated indignation for what felt like at least an hour until I began to feel an overmastering urge to interrupt and point out that, as the father of five children, he had made more than his fair contribution to the problem. But it was not wise to contradict Spike. He loved Irish jokes and attributed his surreal humour to his own Irish father, who had woke him up in India at three o'clock in the morning to say urgently: 'Son, I never shot a tiger.' 'Why do you have to tell me that now?' 'Well, I've got to tell *somebody*.' His anarchic tendencies could be breathtaking. Once at a reception in a publisher's plush offices, someone in our group remarked on a fancy Impressionistic painting hanging on the wall alongside us. 'I wonder who that's by? It's not signed.' Spike took a pen and wrote 'Spike Milligan' in large letters right across the bottom. 'It is now.'

His mind worked sideways like flashes of lightning. At an *Oldie* lunch the editor, Richard Ingrams, sitting beside him, explained that we were having bread-and-butter pudding because it was Lent. Without missing a beat Spike asked, 'Oh. When do we have to give it back?' One of his oldest buddies was Harry Secombe – 'the finest straight man in comedy'. One day he told him: 'I hope you die first. I don't want you singing at my funeral.' There spoke the troubled and troubling Spike.

DIANA DORS

Britons may have been publicly secretive about their sexual habits but it was understood that they were permitted to enjoy public titillation. The breasts were the erogenous zone available for inspection in the fifties. Mammary development was universally admired and respectably desired, although the Page Three girl had not yet made her appearance. In a curious way women's bodies responded to public demand, as they have through history. Boobs burgeoned like prize melons (often with a little artificial help) for about ten years. Then just as mysteriously, they shrank. By the mid sixties they had been flattened almost out of sight. But in the fifties whole careers could be built on their amplitude – at its most extreme in the Hollywood of Jayne Mansfield and Jane Russell. Britain put its best bust forward on the well-upholstered Diana Dors (37 - 24 - 35, as the newspapers kept reminding us). When she was nineteen in 1951 she began appearing in forgettable films with titles like *Lady Godiva Rides Again*. But she was best known for magazine pictures posing amid a bath of bubbles. She made a notorious appearance at the Venice Film Festival of 1955. She entered reclining in a gondola in a mink bikini supported by straps of giant jewels. Anything less like current British film stars – Celia Johnson, Deborah Kerr or Vivien Leigh – it was not possible to imagine.

She may not have been in their class as an actress but for a time she was the highest paid female in British films, which was not bad going for a cheery working-class girl born in Swindon and named Diana Fluck. She did prove to be a capable character actress after she shed the glamour. In later years when she was living a genteel life in the Sunningdale belt of the Home Counties, and was by no stretch of the imagination 37 - 24 - 35, she talked about the fifties with amusement.

'I was the first home-grown sex symbol of austerity Britain, a sort of living seaside postcard. Men have always been hung up on breasts and in those days it was the only part of the female body which could be shown off. The Americans, who started it, were the biggest hypocrites. On American television they insisted on putting a gauze across my bosom. If I was filmed wearing a bikini, the bottom half had to cover my navel. Then we would shoot it again in a different bikini for British audiences. It was all a gigantic con. You see, we never really showed anything. Under those archly arranged bath bubbles there was a flesh-coloured body stocking.'

The stories of her wild life of sexy hoopla were also, she suggested, a bit exaggerated.

'I resented being marketed as a female Errol Flynn. The real me would rather stay home than go to orgies – but who would want to hear that? I always wanted to be a star with a cream telephone but it couldn't be done with the films I was offered. I had to become a sex symbol on tiger skin rugs in mink bikinis.'

LADY DOCKER

Besides the occasional sex symbol like Miss Dors, Austerity Britain varied its escapist diet of royal princesses, debs and film stars with another fantasy – that of extreme wealth. As a forerunner of celebrities to come, one of the most photographed women of absolutely no importance was Lady Docker. Everyone knew of Norah Docker for the simple reason that she had a gold car. It was a gold-plated Daimler with a gold radiator grille, gold bumpers, gold headlamps and mountings and of course a gold Daimler symbol on the bonnet. The joint image, woman and car, was constantly in the newspapers, sometimes accompanied by a shadowy figure in the background. This was her husband, Sir Bernard, who, like the tar-baby, never said nuffin'. To a public whose wildest dream of fortune was to win £75,000 on the pools, Norah's car was the Golden Calf, an object of veneration. She lived up to it in her invariable costume of mink coat and cap. She had decreed that the Daimler should be upholstered in zebra skin. 'Mink,' she explained quotably, 'is too hot to sit on.' If anyone knew that, it would be her.

I spent one Sunday escorting the Dockers round a Yorkshire pit village and coal mine, at the invitation of the miners themselves. It was a regal visit. Pitmen pink with pleasure ushered her with many a 'this way, my lady' into the cage and down below to glimpse the underground mysteries. Norah was a sport. She risked her high heels. At the pithead the car underwent constant gaping inspection, for she never walked anywhere. She even took lunch with them on the platform of the miners' social club. In return she invited forty miners to visit her on her ocean-going yacht moored at Monte Carlo. They went – and she danced a hornpipe with them. She was a natural mixer, with a somewhat cloudy past. She had begun her career as a café dancer (at the Café de Paris, a café of class). She had a Gaiety Girl's facility for marrying rich husbands. Sir Bernard was her third.

Norah ably fulfilled her only function, which was to be motored hither and thither to parties sitting on her burnished throne like Cleopatra – and, like Cleopatra, to exhibit occasional tantrums of temper. A glass of champagne was thrown either at or by her at the fashionable Caprice restaurant. More headlines. Then she was banned from Monte Carlo by Prince Rainier himself for having stamped on the Monaco flag – a paper version serving as table decoration – in a fit of pique. Then her life turned pure Cinderella, as midnight struck with a ring of doom. Gone suddenly was her golden coach. Gone the yacht. Gone the retinue of photographers. Sir Bernard, who accompanied her everywhere like a big dog, had run out of brandy. He was ousted as chairman of the Birmingham Small Arms company, which inconsiderately revealed that it had been funding the car (actually five of them), her wardrobe and their gilded lifestyle as a business expense, which was now inappropriate. The glamour had all been for publicity's sake. Norah stoutly claimed that it had been worth far more to the company than any money of theirs that she had spent. But the game was over. Having been famous for so long for being rich – or supposedly so – this odd couple vanished overnight, not to the kitchen cinders but into some tax haven, never to be heard or thought of again.

CAMPAIGNERS

Imagine the contrast between Norah and another good time girl who earned her notoriety by becoming a burden on the public conscience. Ruth Ellis is still remembered because of her death on the end of a hangman's rope on 13th July 1955. Britain still largely tolerated the death penalty for murder or treason as a necessary evil. But when it came to hanging a good-looking nightclub hostess of twenty-nine, who had shot her faithless lover outside a Hampstead pub in a classic example of *crime passionnel*, doubts began to gnaw. Her motives have remained controversial, the subject of more than one drama, but it was more and more felt inhuman that she should hang for it. The Home Secretary refused her a reprieve, to general dismay. The day of execution, then the hour, approached. Few people's minds were on anything else as the clock's hands reached nine. It felt almost as if a friend was about to die. The barbarity of the act of judicial murder at last sank in when people saw it visited on a woman – the last woman to suffer it in Britain.

According to her letters Ruth Ellis acknowledged that she ought to die but in too many other cases miscarriages of justice had been identified, too late to help any of the victims. The result was the forming of a national campaign for the Abolition of Capital Punishment, led by an MP, Sidney Silverman, the broadcaster Ludovic Kennedy and many writers, notably Arthur Koestler, who had spent weeks under death sentence in the Spanish Civil War. He had described in a memorable book his sensations on hearing men taken from the neighbouring cells each night and then listening for the shots.

But formidable numbers remained in favour of the death penalty – they still are. I did not need convincing. Like many reporters of Assize

Courts in those days I had more than once witnessed the donning of the black cap when the judge pronounced the words, 'And be hanged by the neck until you are dead…and may the Lord have mercy on your soul.' The figure slumped in the dock would then be smartly manhandled out and down the steps to his doom. I had passed chilly early mornings waiting outside desolate county jails while the hanging took place on the other side of the wall. There was always somebody among the little crowd assembled to make an ill-received attempt at ghoulish humour as we waited for the notice of execution to be pinned to the prison doors. I once asked a prison governor at a social gathering what he felt when he had to attend a hanging. He practically dropped his drink. In parched, offended tones he replied: 'All I can tell you is that it is over very, very quickly.' Not always, if some of the tales of bungled drops I heard were to be believed.

I had another memory which made this subject uncomfortable to contemplate. Dr Johnson famously said that the knowledge that one is to be hanged in a fortnight concentrates the mind wonderfully. But he did not speculate on what it does to the mind of the man who sentences him. I used to wonder that about the minds of the Assize judges, snug in their lodgings on the evening of passing such a sentence. Sometimes you could hear the strains of a violin being played within. I myself had had this experience to live with, if only on a minor scale, when I was too young to cope with it. When Cyprus was still a British colony it recruited a regiment of mixed Greek and Turkish ethnicity to serve in the British army. A detachment of the Cyprus Regiment arrived one evening to mount a night guard at my camp beside the Canal in the desert. I showed them their posts and quarters and went off to bed. All too soon I was urgently awakened. One of the guards, a Greek, lay dead of a stab wound. Everybody appeared to know who had stabbed him. Indeed the Turkish culprit smiled pleasantly and demonstrated the knife stroke employed. He looked as if he had done a good deed.

After I had given my evidence at the subsequent court martial I was asked to join the bench of officers to make up its number. 'It'll be useful experience for you,' said the brigadier who was presiding. The accused Turk again demonstrated his knife thrust. When it was time for the verdict each of us was asked in turn to give ours, without further discussion. What could it be but guilty? Then the brigadier proceeded to pronounce sentence. As he did so I became uncomfortably aware that I'd just helped sentence a man to death. 'Don't get upset about it,' said the brigadier cheeringly as we adjourned for a drink in the mess afterwards. 'These things are all reviewed in London by the Judge Advocate General's department. They may never carry it out.' We never heard. I hope that the Lord, or Allah, or Whoever, had mercy on his soul. It was more than we did.

SITTING DOWN FOR CND

So the fifties, when we were told there were 'no good, brave causes left', produced a healthy crop of civilising campaigns. The campaign to abolish hanging was joined by a campaign to reform the law on homosexuality. When Wolfenden's committee reported in 1957 that the law should be changed to decriminalise consenting homosexuals in private, its conclusions were rejected by a Conservative government and nothing whatever was done about them. Again a selection of the great and the good rallied in support behind the MP, Leo Abse, Lord Attlee and the philosopher A. J. Ayer (an active heterosexual) among them. That was joined by an abortion law reform campaign, featuring David Steel. All these causes had to wait for the sixties for fulfillment but changes in underlying public opinion take time. It was the fifties that began the process.

But by far the biggest and most disturbing campaign was the Campaign for Nuclear Disarmament. It is difficult more than fifty years later to see CND as anything more than a futile sideshow which failed to convert the nation. But futile was not how it felt at the time. The world was only on the brink of adopting nuclear weapons as standard. It was an urgent priority to stop them if possible. The atom bombs which ended the war against Japan had been received with a mixture of awe and relief. People of my generation, who fully expected to be called up in time to fight a war of attrition against the fanatical Japanese and their death wish, could only be glad to have the prospect lifted. And was not the Bomb an Anglo-American monopoly? This assurance lasted only until March 1950 when the Russians announced they had one too, developed in a staggeringly short time. The American reaction, that they should try to make an immensely more powerful hydrogen bomb, was debated by atomic scientists with doubt and anguish. Would it work? And how could it be ethically justified? The advisory committee on atomic energy, headed by J. Robert Oppenheimer, father of the Los Alamos atom bomb, unanimously advised the president not to proceed with it – 'providing by example some limit to the totality of war'. Some members added they thought it wrong on ethical principle.

For a few hopeful months it looked as if morality had triumphed. Then a German physicist, a pre-war refugee from Nazism who had proved brilliant at Los Alamos, revealed at his trial that he had been passing on nuclear secrets to the Russians for the past six years. Klaus Fuchs settled the matter. President Truman ordered the scientists to get to work immediately on the H-bomb. By 1952 the US had a tower mounted device which vapourised Eniwetok Atoll, sending a radioactive cloud twenty-five miles high. A tit-for-tat game followed: 1953 – the first Russian H-bomb test; 1954 – America's first aerial bomb; 1957 – the Russian Sputnik demonstrated they were capable of launching not only a satellite but a nuclear missile through space. And in 1957 the British caught up with their own H-bomb, assuring us, we were told, of 'a place at the top table'.

The military may have enjoyed capping each others' threats but it was no comfort to the public who had no say at the top table or any other. It was hardly reassuring to be told that in the event of nuclear attack Britons would get four minutes warning – just time to whitewash the windows against radiation. A government White Paper admitted that there was 'no means of providing adequate protection against nuclear attack'. And with that the subject was apparently closed. No wonder any thinking person felt scared about the future. In 1957 the decade became the Fearful Fifties. It was that state of mind that led to the forming of CND – an attempt by ordinary people to protect themselves by changing the minds of the politicians who ultimately controlled the Bomb. The alarm was first sounded by intellectuals. At an inaugural meeting the veteran philosopher Bertrand Russell suggested the human race was worth preserving, the novelist J. B. Priestley urged them to 'reject the evil thing forever' and the historian A. J. P. Taylor, after listing in horrific detail the effects of the H-bomb, asked the packed audience at the Central Hall, Westminster: 'Does anybody here want to do this to another human being?' – silence – 'Then why are we making the damn thing?'

The Campaign began with a three-day march over Easter 1958, from Trafalgar Square to Aldermaston, the heavily protected nuclear research establishment. It was not spectacular – no more than five-thousand strong – and was derided by the newspapers that covered it. But the following year, marching in the reverse direction, the march attracted twenty thousand people to Trafalgar Square and grew steadily year by year. Most of the marchers were young – they had the most life to lose – and the scene was enlivened with trad jazz bands, folk singers, students in rave costume as well as ordinary couples in ordinary clothes, some of them with pushchairs. But they had the endorsement of leading members of the intellectual and artistic worlds – such as Michael Foot, Benjamin Britten, Henry Moore, E. M. Forster, Peggy Ashcroft, Doris Lessing, Iris Murdoch, John Osborne, Michael Tippett and many more. Above all it had a universally recognised banner and badge – the symbol of a cross with its arms sunken to the semaphore sign for N and D.

Aldermaston was soon an institution, an alternative Easter parade. But it was not affecting political policy. Although a Gallup poll announced that thirty per cent of the public now supported disarmament, peaceful marching seemed unlikely to change anything. Bertrand Russell withdrew from the presidency and founded a more militant body, the Committee of 100, to direct displays of civil disobedience or direct action. It made its first assault in December 1958, at an RAF base at Swaffham in Norfolk, which hosted nuclear rockets. We were not an impressive body, perhaps seventy-strong, marching through the damp, dank Norfolk lanes wrapped in anoraks, knitted hats and brandishing a few banners and Thermos flasks. But we meant business. Some distance short of the base we were met by the assistant chief constable of Norfolk. He was courtesy itself. 'I have to warn you that the airfield you are approaching is government property. Any attempt to enter it will render you liable to prosecution.' Such, our leaders told him, was our intention, indeed our purpose in coming all this way. These were the opening moves in a chess game which lasted all afternoon. As fast as marchers scrambled in to sit down beside the hangars they were carried away, limp and unresisting, out of the gates. Meanwhile others scurried past to take their place. The chief constable finally called up vans and announced that any further trespassers would be arrested and taken to police cells to await trial. This was Saturday and the courts did not sit until Monday. 'It is our purpose to be arrested and tried,' explained our spokesman.

We mustered for the last time outside the gates ready for the assault when a voice called out: 'Quiet time, Quakers!' When I looked back the wet grass verges were occupied by meditating Quakers, their eyes fixed on some goal far from Norfolk. Then came the charge against the police cordon. Many got through. A few escaped arrest and got out again, among them myself. I urgently needed to telephone a report to the waiting *Observer*. It made the front page. The local magistrates obligingly helped the story to run by remanding about forty campaigners in custody over Christmas. Some of these protesters were elderly clergymen. A wave of public sympathy swept the newspapers. It made our little direct action, now a minor national outrage, seem worth while.

BERTRAND RUSSELL

The ultimate demonstration of direct action came two years later when a rally and march down Whitehall was announced, to be led by Bertrand Russell himself (at the age of eighty-eight). It was being prophesied that police counter-action would lead to widespread imprisonment including that of him, its leader. Which was how I came to be taking tea with the philosopher and watching his quivering hand lift a heavy Georgian silver teapot to pour me a cup in the parlour of his small house in Chelsea. This was a meeting I had never dreamed of experiencing. As a philosophy student I had venerated Russell. In fact my interest in the subject was owed almost entirely to his lucid little book, *The Problems of Philosophy* (published first in 1912), which I had read as a boy. It shocked me into realising how unreliable our assumptions about the world are. The thought of discussing such topics with him personally was like having the ultimate tutorial.

In the flesh, looking like a snowy-crested ostrich, all beak and deeply furrowed cheeks, his eyes glittered, not necessarily with bonhomie. I soon discovered that there was not going to be any philosophical chit-chat. 'I am no longer inter-ested in philosophy,' he informed me, 'I am only inter-ested in the survival of hu-man-ity.' His gravelly voice articulated each syllable precisely, like a Victorian speaker – which he was. We discussed the forthcoming march to promote British disarmament. If he was advocating multilateral nuclear disarmament, I ventured, he would have every thinking person's heartfelt support. But the British were not enthused by disarming all on their own. After all we had only recently had to fight and win a major war. He looked at me sadly. 'What you young people do not re-a-lise is that Britain is no longer an important force in the world. What you do not com-prehend is the very con-sider-able dimi-nution in our power and prestige.' Of course he was right. Our diminution had been demonstrated only recently at Suez but Britons were still loath to admit it. 'So our only useful role is to set the world a moral example.' And was he prepared, as a moral example, to go to prison that Friday? 'I do not look forward to it but if it will help the cause, I con-sider it my duty.' He smiled at my reaction. 'I have already spent time in prison. In fact I wrote one of my books there. They allow you to write, you know. They also gave me the Bible to read. There is some inter-esting reading in the Bible.'

Friday 18th February 1961 was cold and bleak but Trafalgar Square was bursting with thousands of excited demonstrators. After the speeches a column set off very slowly down Whitehall. At their head, flanked by police horses, walked our foremost philosopher. In front of him, walking backwards in order observe what happened, was myself. He did not speak to the supporters surrounding him. His eyes seemed to be focused somewhere above Big Ben. The objective was the Ministry of Defence, then housed not in Whitehall but around the corner from Parliament Square in Great George Street. When the head of the march reached the Ministry its tail was still waiting to get out of Trafalgar Square. As instructed by leaflet, we sat down on the pavements as a vigil. These were cold pavements for bottoms, many of them attached to well-known faces. Someone thoughtfully brought a blanket to wrap round the frail leader. People continually came up to stare at him or photograph him. A tweedy woman in a feathered hat was carrying a bag from which she produced a Flit gun for dispersing insects. She carefully flitted Russell with disinfectant. 'I've made my protest,' she said loudly as she was hurried away.

When all the protesters were at last seated, blocking the pavements of Whitehall from end to end, a notice was produced which Russell was to affix to the doors of the Ministry. Helped to his feet he proceeded up the steps accompanied by a supporter with a hammer and tacks. A very senior police officer in a braided cap intercepted him. It was his duty to inform Lord Russell that nailing his notice to the door would constitute the offence of defacing government property, which carried serious penalties. Russell looked thoughtful for some moments. This was not the offence for which he had intended to be martyred. During the silent stand-off a voice, like a stage prompter, said quietly, 'There's some sticky tape here, sir.' Russell pondered longer, stock-still like Socrates in the snow. Then he pronounced: 'I do not consider the use of sticky tape is a matter of prin-ciple.'

The protest was stickily taped to the doors and we all went home. I saw nothing ridiculous in this. Our disobedience had remained civil throughout – too civil for the police to make any arrests. It made one proud of British *sangfroid*. Russell did go to prison briefly later that year after another rally. The charge was incitement to civil disobedience. As the magistrate pronounced sentence there were cries of, 'Shame! An old man of 88!' The magistrate observed that he was therefore old enough to know better. Russell served only a week, spent in a hospital bed, but it caused a stir around the world.

In his last years under the influence of a young American, Ralph Schoenman, Russell allowed his name to be used for foolish causes – until he realised what was happening and dismissed Schoenman. For a time this devalued his influence. But where now is a British philosopher of equal prestige ready to risk a prison sentence for the future of mankind? The last one who was not too old, not too busy, not too keen on his own comfort to do so was Bertrand Russell. It was an honour to sit on a pavement with him.

THE SIXTIES

SATIRE – OR SAUCINESS?

In 1960 the Edinburgh Festival was regarded rather like a restful break for London newspaper critics. Nothing urgent was likely to happen. Deadlines were not pressing. So I, a mere novice reviewer, was not obeying the accepted form by writing about a late night show in addition to the main bill at the Lyceum Theatre, while my colleagues were enjoying their whisky and soda. A poster stuck out in the foyer had simply announced: '10.45pm BEYOND THE FRINGE' and nothing more. As it was listed in the official programme I reasoned it was my job to be there. The large auditorium was not at all full and no other critics were visible. I was considering an unobtrusive departure when four young men in grey pullovers wandered on to the open stage. I thought they were students about to set the scenery when one of them sat down at an upright piano and played the national anthem. We rose – it was still the customary practice to play it at theatre performances. Just as we were resuming our seats he began it again. People hovered uncomfortably between sitting and standing. 'Who is that fellow who keeps playing God Save the Queen?' asked one of the others. 'Must be some foreigner – can't be English.'

'You can tell that,' said the tall lanky one. 'By the way he plays it sitting down.'

This was a different way of starting a show. We were used to revues that began with song-and-dance and girls in fishnet tights followed by sketches full of double entendre. Ten minutes later it was evident that a new species of revue was being unveiled before our eyes. The respected institutions of British life were being held up one by one to ridicule. This was still a country where people Knew Their Place. It was not the place of the young to imitate the prime minister and make him sound a clueless old buffer.

It was not done to joke about the Four-Minute Warning we had been promised of a nuclear attack. 'I'll have you know that some people in this great country of ours can run a mile in four minutes!' Nobody dreamed of sending up the heroics of British war films or solemn lieder recitals or cripples who wanted to play Tarzan with one leg. It was very rude to parody Sir Laurence Olivier in Shakespeare history plays and films: 'O saucy Worcester! Dost thou lie so low?' As for the church – how familiar was this all-purpose Anglican sermon in elongated Oxford vowels comparing life to a tin of sardines. 'And y' know, there's always a little bit in the corner that you can never get out.'

After ad-libbing a breathless notice to the effect that revue was now slaughtering sacred cows wholesale and would never be the same again, I staggered back to join the whisky drinkers in the old Roxburghe Hotel's big leather armchairs while wee Scottish mice ran in and out of the long curtains. When my hasty paragraphs appeared in print not a few of them were asked by their papers why they had not reported this interesting event. They were there the next night, by which time the week's run was sold out. It was exciting to see previously impermissible liberties being taken and laughed at so loudly. The Four Parodists, two from Oxford, two from Cambridge, hardly knew one another. They knew they were good, but how good? And how far would it take them? Peter Cook was already scriptwriter of a successful London revue. Jonathan Miller had qualified as a neurologist at a London teaching hospital. He was performing as a holiday before intending to begin a more serious career in neuro-science. The donnish Alan Bennett was having a break from lecturing on medieval history while researching a thesis on the Retinue of Richard II. Dudley Moore, organ scholar turned jazz pianist, spoke in a blend of Dagenham and Oxford accents. At five-foot-two he felt overshadowed by the loftiness of the others. Tensions were beginning to appear in the large flat they were sharing, looked after by Miller's doctor wife, Rachel. Theatre managements were hastening up to Edinburgh to see them. The air fizzed with giddying possibilities. But Dudley Moore was desperate. 'They won't do it, you know,' he confided to me. 'They're intellectuals.

One's goin' to be a bloody doctor and the other a bloody don. Not interested in show business.'

They soon were, though. Supposing they could spare time to do it, was this the moment for overturning revue as we knew it? From gut instinct I assured them it was. They were speaking for a new decade and a new wave of grammar-school educated meritocrats.

The conformist fifties were over. The saucy sixties were beginning. I felt a twinge of envy that they, not much younger than my wartime generation, had arrived at the launching pad for new comedy at the ideal moment for take-off. Not without some dark moments of doubt. The next time I caught up with them was in Brighton on their pre-West End try-out. No one was in at the Theatre Royal. I found Alan Bennett in a café in a wet raincoat looking exceedingly lugubrious, even for him. How was it going?

'Dreadfully. They walk out every night. The seats go up like pistol shots.' But, I suggested consolingly, Brighton was notorious for discouraging receptions. 'They go to the theatre purely for the pleasure of walking out. It was all a great mistake,' he said mournfully. 'We should never have gone on with it.' Their producer, Donald Albery, did not show much confidence by paying them only £75 a week – though that was more than junior doctors or lecturers earned. 'Sensation – The Theatre Came of Age Last Night' was London's response at the intimate Fortune Theatre. Not everyone was bowled over.

'They're too young to know the meaning of good taste,' I overheard one patron say to another on leaving. By now the show was being described as 'satire' by commentators. In truth it had no political or social agenda beyond mockery of the elders who ran the country – youth's eternal urge to cheek the masters. But it had not been done before so publicly and accurately. Satire had become a buzzword.

THAT WAS THE SHOW

After Beyond the Fringe had conquered New York and *Private Eye* had won a small but discerning readership the time seemed right to certain high-ups at the BBC to cash in on the so-called Satire Boom with a Saturday night show to be called *That Was The Week That Was*, soon abbreviated by those involved to TW3. Journalists were sought as scriptwriters because they knew the stories behind the news and could write to tight deadlines. I and a colleague and friend on the *Daily Mail*, Peter Dobereiner, a genial master of the deflating one-liner, were already seeking relief from long newspaper nights by writing sketches for London cabaret shows.

We sent in a one-minute sketch and were summoned to meet Ned Sherrin, the show's producer, and its anchorman, one David Frost. We were invited to watch a pilot which rambled on less as a comedy but a topical TV magazine like *Tonight*, where Sherrin had cut his teeth. A lot of editing was needed. During the crises which frequently arose shortly before the show was due on-air in the coming weeks, Sherrin displayed his Noel Cowardish cool. '*Lovely* to talk to you,' he always began before telling you that a substitute line, joke or entire sketch was needed that very afternoon. '*Suaviter in modo, fortiter in re* – remember that, Lewis,' my old Latin master had advised. Ned was a living demonstration of it. Frost's manner on the other hand was intensely warm to the *n*th – even, *p*th – degree. He began with the drawn-out gushing, 'Hell-l-lo!' To which he was soon to add, 'Good evening and welcome!' He gave out an assumed air of stardom although at that time few people outside Cambridge had heard of him. He embodied a new breed – the professional media presenter with a blank face like pastry waiting to be shaped beneath a forward-pointing roll of hair, like a wavelet curling over the sand. To call his accent classless was not to do it justice. It echoed all levels from assumed top drawer to guttersnipe whine, which he curdled into an insinuating sneer on the punchline – followed by: 'Seriously, though, he's doing a grand job.' In the goldfish bowl of television hosting he was perfectly at home.

The number of complaints about TW3 was announced weekly by the BBC like a cricket score. By the end of the first month they had reached five hundred and the show was an established hit. Among those insulted were the prime minister, Members of Parliament, the churches and the Roman Catholic hierarchy of cardinals. Odd though it now seems the most notoriously rude sketch had been about a wrathful Roy Kinnear being deflated by Millicent Martin when she told him his fly buttons were undone. Fly buttons! Where are they now? This illustrates how impossible it was to recapture in later years the impact of a topical show which got people home early from the pubs in order to watch. Repeats of clips look embarrassingly dated, the jokes incomprehensible or lame. Ephemeral it had to be. The lines were so topical they dropped dead after use.

People hardly believed that the respected BBC could be so recklessly, riskily impudent. The sense that the audience was agog for the next installment was stimulating to a writer. So was the immediacy of performance, sometimes on the day the sketch had been written. As we lived on opposite sides of London, collaboration between Dobereiner and I often consisted of long, silences on the telephone, in a metaphorical postal district: London, TW3. At our back I could always hear Time's winged chariot hovering near – a BBC taxi, engine panting, outside my front door, waiting for a script. It must have cost a fortune in taxi fares but when I suggested posting less urgent ones, Ned almost raised his voice: 'Never! We wouldn't get them for a fortnight!' That apparently was the length of time it took for a letter to travel from the BBC post room to the department concerned. So the meters ticked on and the scripts were carried by hand, like precious papyri.

You never knew till afterwards what would be a hit or a miss. Sometimes sketches were 'improved' by an over-confident David Frost, who harboured illusions of being gifted as a comic performer. He also had, we discovered, a habit of borrowing the scripts for frequent cabaret performances, without payment. Nobody was making serious money out of the show's success but he had firmly set his course for lucre, lots of it. Rarely was a script vetoed on orders from on high. One of ours, about the Vietnam horrors, was banned on orders of the usually tolerant director-general, Hugh Carleton-Greene. It was written in the easy-going meter of *Hiawatha* and featured chiefs like the Mighty Lyndon Johnson and his sycophant, the Little Harold Wilson. Our anti-war sentiments were not at fault; we had overlooked the fact that the Little Harold Wilson would soon be deciding whether or not to renew the BBC Charter.

The traditionalists won in the end. After two series the BBC announced it would be 'inappropriate' for the show to continue into 1964 when a general election was to be held – the very time, you might have thought, when it could give useful service. Again protests rolled in, this time about the show's axing on such a transparent pretence. We went on writing for the show's sequels but none had the edge of the initial burst of subversion when the public first recognised that its elders were often not its betters.

WINSTON CHURCHILL

The last day of January 1965 was one of the bleakest of an exceptionally cold winter. Not the day to choose to spend clinging to unprotected scaffolding up a half-erected City tower block of exceptional unloveliness. That was the vantage point opposite the portico and columns of St Paul's assigned to reporters of Sir Winston Churchill's funeral. As the procession wound its way slowly up the streets to Ludgate Hill, no one was in a position to take notes. Fingers, too frozen to write, were jammed deeply into pockets. The crowds hedging the pavements below at least could shelter each other from the cutting north-easter. Their faces were frozen masks, keeping their emotions well concealed in a British manner. But their tribute was their silence – two miles of utter silence. A pall of memories hung over the flag-draped coffin containing the best-remembered Briton of the past half-century.

To the great majority the memory was of a voice; a voice that had done unquantifiable service in uniting a beleaguered nation in the early disasters of the war and its few victories. How fortunate that in such adversity we could listen to a master of language, producing one memorable phrase after another. The harsh, rumbling delivery turned the word 'Nazi' into a rasp that schoolboys loved to imitate and the syllables 'Herr Hitler' into a pinprick of contempt. He knew the value of his props – the cigar and the siren suit, the naval cap or the unique Homburg whose crown seemed several inches taller than other people's. Unlike the dictators he led us in formal and rather old-fashioned dark suits complete with gold watch-chain. The jut of the chin and the V-sign did more than any uniform could to inspire British confidence.

A Rogues' Gallery

Yet my first sight of him in the actual flesh was a never-forgotten disillusion. In May 1945, he toured the country to solicit our votes. As the election cortège wound through true-blue Buckingham, the market square was crowded with curious schoolboys from nearby Stowe, some of whom sported boaters in his honour as an old Harrovian. At last his vehicle arrived with him displayed on the back of it and the cheers died in my throat and in the throats of many others. Before us was the wreck of the man we had followed. Everything about him sagged, his jowls sinking into his collar as if he would be asleep like a dog any minute. He hardly made the attempt to raise the walking stick between his knees to acknowledge the crowd. After he had rolled on my friends looked at one another with dismay and doubt. This man was simply too exhausted to go on running the country. It looked as if, had he won, he would be dead at his post in a year.

Instead he went on holiday and made sure that his version of the Second World War and his place in its history would get into print first. One of the historians arduously assembling the material was Bill Deakin, a don at Wadham, my college. So at regular intervals the lodge would be filled with huge hampers from the South of France addressed to him from 'W. S. Churchill, Hotel de Paris, Monte Carlo', to provide fuel for the task. After his second tenure at Number 10 and his reluctant handover to Eden, of whom he had well-founded doubts, he had little else to do but take holidays down there and paint. There an enterprising American director of Pathé News, Jack Le Vien, persuaded him to let him make a biographical film based on the vast news film footage available. I became involved in this enterprise as writer of the book to accompany the film, *The Finest Hours*. Churchill, then in his eighties, was not available but all his photograph albums were, for use as illustrations. I was invited to inspect an unoccupied Chartwell and the still secret underground war rooms in Whitehall, unaltered since the day the war ended in 1945, and left to collect dust.

The film commentary was already recorded from Churchill's own words by the actor Patrick Wymark and we assembled in a private theatre in Wardour Street to see the final cut. Orson Welles had been engaged to read Churchill's speeches over it when required. Welles arrived, mountainous in a fur-lapelled overcoat. He settled in the stalls and took out a slim cigar. In the midst of his florid face his babyish mouth made an O-shaped opening into which the cigar fitted perfectly. After the lights went up an anxious Le Vien looked at him. 'Well, Orson?' Then followed a masterly display of the imperceptible takeover.

'I'm beginning to hate Churchill, England and everything. This guy is hitting every line like he was John of Gaunt. But you're using him as a messenger, a spear-carrier. There's method in Churchill's oratory. When it gets too rich he has a method of throwing it away and this produces a frisson. This man is filling every line as if it was a Shakespeare History – one of the duller ones. Of course I'm not knocking him, he's one of the best actors in England, but that style is driving us out of the theatre – we can't endure it. He's never that funny little urchin peeping out between the pillars, which Churchill is.'

'You're right, Orson, you're right,' said Jack Le Vien again and again. By the time we left the theatre it was eagerly agreed that the right man to do the commentary, as well as the speeches, was Orson Welles. What Churchill thought of it we never discovered. When he was shown it in his private cinema he simply grunted 'Fine' and ordered champagne. Like it or not, it would earn him a substantial percentage. And nine months later he was dead.

My last glimpse of him, like the first, did not do justice to his heroic stature. Till his last years he had kept up the habit of attending the House of Commons, which had been his club since 1900. Not in order to speak. He probably had nowhere else to go. I was never a member of the Westminster press corps but occasional assignments took me there to sample its gossipy, villagey atmosphere. I often enjoyed a drink with an old friend, Norman Shrapnel, the *Guardian* sketch writer known for his unique style of sophisticated amusement at the proceedings. For all his high complexion and snowy moustache, which gave him an Indian Army air, he was shy in company. He detested the rowdier bars which some MPs frequented in order to mix with journalists they hoped to impress. Norman refused to know any Member personally. He explained that he wanted to preserve 'the purity of my hatred'. I remember gazing down from the gallery one afternoon when Churchill was occupying his seat below the gangway. He was curled up like a small black ball, listening to (or dozing through) the debates he used to dominate. But his entrances and exits from the chamber still did dominate whatever was going on. Shrapnel described the scene so tellingly that I cannot do better than quote from his book on Parliament, *The Performers*.

'We watched with agonised fascination – failing to hear a word from whoever was speaking – as the pallid, ancient hulk moved in pitiable slow motion, like a giant refusing to accept that it was extinct. This sole survivor from Queen Victoria's Parliament would lurch inch by precarious inch to his place, impatiently rejecting helping hands that sought to steer him. He would sit for an hour or two, hunched like a premature statue of himself, occasionally exchanging greetings with some old colleague. And the whole nerve-wracking performance would be repeated in reverse when he made his exit. It seemed an eternity before he reached the bar of the House, turned and made his bow, then stumped out to his waiting wheelchair. Excruciating as it was to the nerves it provided a theatrical experience nobody who saw it would willingly have missed. Did he know every eye was on him? Of course he did.'

And now every eye was on him again as the draped coffin was shouldered very slowly and carefully up St Paul's steps and in due course down again. It was the silence with which it took place which was so eloquent. Seldom have so many people kept silent for so long. In it there was a unity of spirit that we had not felt for twenty years. When the gun carriage disappeared there was a feeling of lack, of emptiness, of how we were going to miss him. For many of us he was 'our time', a time of danger and defiance not experienced since. It meant something to have been alive in Churchill's time. There, vanishing, was the end of it.

ESMOND ROTHERMERE

Kenya was one of the first British colonies to feel Mr Macmillan's prophetic 'wind of change blowing through Africa' at the end of 1963. Despite memories of the atrocities committed by the Mau Mau, its leader Jomo Kenyatta had emerged from prison as the main political force, its first black prime minister, waiting to become president on its independence as a republic. I saw some of the country's late colonial days as a beautiful but supposedly decadent 'place in the sun for shady people'. I wanted to know how they were adapting to the prospect of black rule. I did not meet any Evelyn Waugh characters. Some long-established planters were optimistic that their rights to their land would be respected (though many sold out) and hoped that their labourers and their families, if well treated, would remain loyal. One very old Harrovian who had been farming deep in the Bush since the 1920s was ready for trouble from the surrounding Kikuyu tribesmen. He carried a big stick, which was hollowed out to contain a sharpened bicycle spoke, and dyed his beard and moustache with Stephens black ink. 'It doesn't do to let them see you're getting old.' He admired Kenyatta. 'I wouldn't take on his job. They talk of the hospitals and schools they're going to build but they'll never keep up with African fecundity. They're so bloody fecund! That's what will do for them in the end.'

The country was ravishing but the street slum dwellings that already surrounded the perimeter of Nairobi were squalid, crime-ridden and desperate. The educated Kikuyu ladies who were expecting shortly to be ministers' wives were seeking advice from white ladies on dinner party-giving, etiquette, *placements* etc. There seemed to be confidence in Kenyatta, known affectionately as 'the Mzee' (the old man), then in his seventies. Sadly I was not introduced to him until his death fifteen years later. Awaiting a state funeral he was lying on a slab with a name ticket tied round his huge big toe and his trademark flywhisk in his grasp – immobile just when he needed it. I loved Kenya and especially the Masai who greeted the tiny two-seater plane that landed me on the upper slopes of Mount Kilimanjaro. With their spears and their cattle they guarded the plane while I made my call. On the way back the pilot said, 'Have you got something to give them? Money's no good.' My bag held nothing but 35mm film cans of silvery metal. 'Just the thing,' said the pilot. They eagerly put them to use as adornments to their earrings.

An unexpected result of my journey was a summons when I returned to the office by the *Daily Mail*'s proprietor, the second Lord Rothermere. Nobody saw him, usually. He remained aloof on the top floor of a separate building overlooking the Thames. The only sign of him on the editorial floor of Northcliffe House was a graffito on the lavatory wall which observed: 'Lord Rothermere is a cunt.' Beneath, in tiny capitals, was a response: 'NO I AM NOT.' The flair of his uncle, Lord Northcliffe, and his father, the Fascist-supporting first Lord Rothermere, seemed to have passed him by. Having been brought up purposely in ignorance of the source of the family's wealth he had little idea what to do with the newspaper stable he inherited. Sometimes he would betray this.

A veteran *Mail* writer told me that he once used the phrase 'Home Page' to Rothermere's evident bafflement. 'The Home Page is for Home stories.' 'Thank you very much, I've been waiting a long time for someone to tell me that.' At his club he was heard to say he'd just changed the editor of the *Daily Mail*. 'I've tried a short fat one. Now I'm tryin' a long thin one.' The fat one, William Hardcastle, went on to be the founder editor of Radio Four's *News At One*. The thin one, Michael Randall, achieved the distinction of being made 'Editor of the Year' at the same time as the *Mail* was awarded the title of 'Newspaper of the Year'. That was the year Rothermere sacked him. I called on him warily, wondering why he'd sent for me. When I was shown into his office he was clearly wondering the same thing.

'You're Lewis?' he asked, glancing at his blotter where my name was written. I confirmed it. There was a considerable silence. 'Been abroad?' he ventured. 'Yes, sir…Africa, sir,' I said , trying to be helpful. 'I know, I know,' he drawled in his upper-class manner. 'What part of Africa?' Surely he read the paper? He must have noticed my articles. 'Kenya, sir.' 'I know, I know.' A pause. 'What's goin' on down there?' He hadn't read them. 'Independence, sir.' 'I know.' His appetite to be told what he already knew seemed boundless, 'How's that goin' to go orff?' As this had been the subject of my articles the question seemed otiose. I summarised in simple terms, remembering from the back of my mind that this very press lord had once commissioned Evelyn Waugh to write an article for a huge fee. Was it possible that I was looking at the actual model for Lord Copper in *Scoop*?

Esmond Rothermere had one undoubted gift: for making the wrong decision. He had recently purchased the *News Chronicle* and merged it into the *Daily Mail*, to see the great majority of its affronted readers desert within weeks. No wonder – the two newspapers were chalk and cheese. He had bought into commercial television creating Associated Rediffusion, which lost a great deal of money. He sold out again just when it was turning the corner and about to become, in his fellow press lord Roy Thomson's phrase, 'a licence to print money'. He was tall and toweringly handsome and was said to play a very good game of tennis. He lived an eighteenth-century grandee's life at Warwick House in the precincts of St James's Palace, filled with spacious salons, gilded mirrors and painted ceilings. When attending one of his receptions you were greeted by liveried footmen in white gloves offering quails' eggs on silver salvers. The hollow at the heart of this splendour was the absence of a Lady Rothermere. His second wife Ann had left him publicly and humiliatingly for Ian Fleming, creator of James Bond. He eventually remarried and retired to his villa on the Côte d'Azur to general relief, relinquishing control of the papers to his son, Vere.

MR CAP AND BIG BILL

Early in 1965 the North Sea was causing a great deal of excitement. There were rumours of an imminent oil strike that might transform Britain's economy. For three months the first oil rig to venture as far as one hundred and fifty miles offshore had been drilling into the seabed in lonely mystery. It was called 'Mr Cap'. A helicopter known as Whisky November and I were paying it a visit. It was the longest over-sea helicopter ride at that time in the world.

After two and a half hours in the co-pilot's seat in the narrow cockpit I was beginning to wish I had some reading matter. The rotor blades screamed above my head, the immersion suit sucked at my neck and we had seen nothing but three small fishing boats in all that expanse of frothing grey unfriendly sea. Then the pilot's voice spoke in my earphones. Although we were sitting side by side, radio was our only means of hearing what each other said: 'Just passed the point of no return.' The what? 'Not enough fuel left to make the return trip. So we'll have to find the rig now.'

This lent a certain urgency to my scrutiny of the horizon. I assumed an oil rig would be a tall pylon-shaped object like a derrick protruding clearly from the sea. But our view was constantly being obscured by white curtains of rain. The voice in my ear spoke again: 'Like to have a go? Just take the stick between your knees and keep it steady. There's nothing to it.' I found that moving the stick even a little to either side had immediate effect so I desisted from experiments. We droned on. Then rounding another curtain of rain I saw an insect sitting on the surface. It was the shape of a grand piano. The rounded end bore a pale blue saucer perched on four Meccano fingers.

'There it is!' I turned excitedly to the pilot who was calculating something on a chart. In my eagerness to point it out I swung the stick round with me. I could not believe the result. The helicopter seemed to have fainted. It keeled over sideways and began to slide swiftly down towards the sea, the hungry sea, the sea that was just waiting for a fool like me to make such an error. The pilot sprang to life, grabbed his stick and struggled to right the craft. Minutes later he set it down on Mr Cap's flat cap as delicately as a teacup on a saucer. The rest of the party of visitors climbed out of the body of the helicopter looking a little pale. 'Bit bumpy that last part!' I smiled and said nothing. The wind tore at our faces as we descended to the deck. Forty feet beneath the sea snapped and slapped at the three piano legs viciously. It is nobody's friend.

On board were forty muddy men in helmets, known as roughnecks and roustabouts, who were taking home £100 a fortnight to Sunderland, where they spent it all, often on drink because slippery Mr Cap was kept wisely dry – indoors. A handful of leathery Texans directing them lounged in their cabins reading the *Wall Street Journal*, which was delivered regularly, often only two days old. The skipper, the man I had come to see, was a baby-faced giant, his chin as wide around as his helmet. He was Mr Kilgore, or 'Big Bill'. He was the personification of an oilman, having been one since he was sixteen.

'What'll you all have to eat?' was his greeting. Large sizzling steaks were served all round. Big Bill let on that he tipped the scale at two hundred and forty pounds. Most of it was steak.

'Do Not Confirm Or Deny Reports' said a prominent notice on the dining room wall.

When Big Bill invited me into his office he cleared every scrap of paper off his desk first. 'How deep have you got?' 'That's a good question.' There were two shaven-headed German geologists aboard waiting to analyse samples of the drilled core every ten feet down. When a drill hits a pocket of gas the result is a blow-out, sending a plume of muddy fluid into the air. Big Bill's jacket was plastered with mud that looked as though it had fallen from a great height. He would not confirm or deny this. My own drilling was getting nowhere. 'Listen,' he said, his usual beginning, 'if we did strike oil nobody on this rig need know but me and the geologists.' But ashore was buzzing with speculation that they had. 'Yes, I read it in the papers.' Why all the secrecy? 'Listen, people who have rented concessions out here would give a lot to know what we are finding.' How big was the gamble? 'Listen, the rent of each one hundred square miles of sea is £6,250 payable to the British government. A rig costs £6,000 a day to run. Get my meaning?' And what are the chances of striking oil first time? 'Hundreds to one. So, Mr Lewis, if we *did* find any gas or oil in commercial quantities, I don't think we would say very much about it, do you?' There was just time to get the re-fuelled helicopter back by daylight, and leave Big Bill, who had six children and homes in Sunderland, Houston and New Orleans, to his *Wall Street Journal*. We were all soon to learn what he knew then. I did not offer to pilot the chopper on the return trip.

Jacques Tati

It was a standard Paris apartment building round a central courtyard hidden off the Champs-Elysées and the name on the bell was Tatischeff. The voice on the entry phone said simply 'Montez!' Coming out of the ancient lift I was confronted by two closed doors. I chose the wrong one and found myself in the broom cupboard. Watching me was a tall figure in the other doorway. 'Par ici, Monsieur,' said Jacques Tati gravely as I extricated myself from the mops and buckets. It seemed an appropriate way to make Monsieur Hulot's acquaintance.

I had come partly to pay homage, partly to ask what he was up to. It had been twenty years since the speed-mad postman of *Jour de Fête*; nearly fifteen since *Les Vacances de Monsieur Hulot*; ten since his parody of a fashion-conscious lifestyle, *Mon Oncle*. Hulot, so beloved of English audiences, had vanished like a benign apparition. I said that we missed him. 'Ah, the English,' said Tati, 'they understand my films in England. Not so well in France.' Why had it taken so long to come up with another? 'I make only films that I like. Can you ask more? Why should I make a lot? Each man has only a certain amount to say.' The next film would be in colour and widescreen. 'If you make a mistake in seventy millimetre it is a big mistake.' Shooting would begin soon – perhaps I would like to attend? I would hear from him when the time was ripe.

I had almost forgotten about it when three years later the message came: 'Monsieur Tati is shooting *Playtime*. You would be welcome on location at Vincennes.' I was eager to watch him at work, creating a world sharply observant of ours but so bizarre and intriguing that the mere presence of Hulot with his angular walk and half-masted trousers, pipe and hat courteously raised, makes the behaviour of those around

75

him look absurd. I knew by his name, Tatischeff, that he descended from a Russian count serving at the Tsarist embassy in Paris. He was sent to England young, to learn the family business of picture framing. He enjoyed English hobbies, especially rugby football. He constructed a variety act by miming various kinds of sport. There was nothing particularly French about his work. Such dialogue as there is in his films is used as another sound effect. 'Say, how do they say Drug Store in French?' asks an American voice of a French sign which says 'Drug Store'. The chatter of high heels and the bird-like cries of guests at a party are used like colours from a palette. Who can forget the eloquent '*zoink*' of the swingdoor at M Hulot's holiday hotel?

On a desolate patch of waste ground on the edge of Paris, beyond the Vincennes Metro terminus, a cluster of white office blocks in miniature was growing like exotic fruit. Some of them moved as I watched. Cardboard thin, they were mounted on wheels and could be manoeuvred along rails. Some were quite large, some only giant cereal packets. Shot from below they would pass for the canyons of modern Paris. A maze of newly laid tarmac surrounded them with a road system of baffling signs and painted prohibitions.

The pavements looked busy with groups of passers-by who were recruited every day from the actual streets of Paris for fifty francs a session. Tati always hand-picked real people as extras. At a grandiose, unfinished hotel, the 'Royal Garden', a gang of workmen were moving immense sheets of plate glass into position – except that there was no glass, only the illusion created by the placing of their hands. Tati was to exploit this mime to hilarious effect when the main entrance's glass door shatters on the opening night. A quick-thinking commissionaire picks up the great gilded boss of the door handle and continues to usher in the guests with ceremonious sweeps of an imaginary door.

Directing complex street scenes was taking a long time – longer still because of the frequent interruptions by the telephone bell mounted on the wooden hut which served as production office. It was, he explained, 'the money' calling. As usual costs were overrunning, alarmingly so to 'the money'. And as usual Tati would not let that disturb his perfectionism. When the lunch-break came he put aside his look of harassment and sat in the canteen among his junior assistants, as among equals. Anyone familiar with the pretensions of film directors would have marked this easy informality. He was soon entertaining us with mime. A chef tasting a cauldron of soup with his nose alone was followed by President de Gaulle presenting medals and decorations. Unfortunately the cushion on which these lay was always on the opposite side from the one to which he turned. Tati, a man of six-foot-two, seemed to rise to an even more rarefied altitude.

He saw exciting possibilities in the scale of 70mm film. 'Nobody wanted me to film with colour and stereophonic sound – that was for cavalry charges – but I want to progress.' He demonstrated by drawing thumbnail sketches how much could be happening in the depth as well as the width of the frame. 'You can tell several stories at once'. The consequence was that you need to see *Playtime* at least twice to take in all that is going on. And the cost…he gestured wearily. 'Some of the conversations about money are not at all amusing. I am not here making money. I am making a film. After I won an Oscar for *Mon Oncle* I could have had whatever money I asked for – provided I made the same films over again. M. Hulot Goes Ski-ing. Hulot In New York, Hulot Goes West…' He grimaced. 'Hulot is not the hero of *Playtime*. Everybody is the hero and everybody is funny. Only they do not know it.' As we left to go back to the cameras a prop man was waiting for Tati beside the path holding the Hulot pipe by its little round bowl. 'Regardez!' he said and puffed three perfect smoke rings in quick succession. It had probably taken all morning to perfect. 'Bien, très bien,' said Tati passing on. Three aged and scarred vagrants of the Paris streets sauntered past. 'I can use the one in the middle,' said Tati to his assistant.

The next time we met was in a London editing suite. He was running the concluding frames. They showed the tourists' coach leaving for the airport trapped at a grid-locked roundabout. The overhead camera showed the traffic slowly revolving in a solid block. The sound track suddenly added a fairground waltz on a wheezy organ. Tati watched my reaction closely like a boy doing a conjuring trick. It worked beautifully. 'Vous voyez?' In order to pay for the film to be finished he had remortgaged his home and sacrificed the future rights in his work.

A Rogues' Gallery

When *Playtime* at last appeared there were few cinemas with the required wide screen and sound equipment which wished to risk exhibiting it. It never got an American distribution. Critics were respectful rather than rapturous. I doubt if it even covered its costs. A mistake in 70mm is a big mistake. But was it a mistake? I believe it will be seen eventually as his most daring film, perhaps his masterpiece. But he was never allowed to film on that scale again or given the freedom which he would not compromise. The film industry does not indulge an artist who wants total control. To have achieved that four times in his career was heroic. An even rarer achievement was to impose his view of modern life on his audience, a more humane and far funnier view than anybody else's. He died trying vainly to raise money for a film called, appropriately, *Confusion*.

THE MAHARISHI

In the sixties the Maharishi Mahesh Yogi arrived in Britain. He had come from the Himalayas to offer us Transcendental Meditation, which was not a religion since he did not mention or worship God, nor require one to love one's neighbour. What he offered was personal bliss. The purpose of meditation was to attain 'bliss consciousness' for its own sake. This was so different from the usual emphasis on sin, salvation and self-denial that I was intrigued, like thousands of others.

Conventional Christians did not take him seriously. The press reported his doings with the strong implication that he was a fake holy man. There was confrontation on BBC radio between him and Malcolm Muggeridge, the self-appointed spokesman for sanctity at that period, who rejoiced in being a reformed sinner. Self-restraint, he told the Maharishi, was absolutely necessary to those of a greedy, sensual nature. 'If I allowed my nature complete freedom I should be like a pig in a trough,' he declared. 'Restraint unnatural, mmm?' responded the Indian sage sweetly. 'Natural way is that man should be more sensible than pig.'

I went to visit the Nash house in Regent's Park where he based his Spiritual Regeneration Movement. He had picked a propitious moment to start one. All kinds of hippie-ish experiments were being pursued, with or without the aid of mind-expanding drugs. The house was humming with candidates for spiritual regeneration, some of them sitting in states of what looked like shock. It was explained that they were attempting to enter the trance-like state of bliss consciousness. The Maharishi's entourage, seemingly all American since he had just visited the United States, rushed about looking tense and purposeful as if bliss were the last thing they were capable of.

A Rogues' Gallery

But when I entered his presence the guru himself radiated geniality and *joie de vivre*. He was seated as usual on a goatskin ('to prevent chill'). Stroking the stems of a bunch of fragrant freesias, he assured me he was very often in states of bliss. He offered to initiate me next day. Would there be a fee? 'Bring no money but flowers and clean handkerchief.' I took both and also my wife Patricia, so that we could compare notes afterwards. He took our hankies and flowers over to a corner shrine where a portrait of his own Himalayan master was surrounded by little coloured lights. Then he confided to each of us separately the mantra we were to repeat over and over to induce the meditative state. One's mantra was personal and must not be revealed to another living soul. 'Mantra has no meaning. Just as well repeat "Tick-tock". But same mantra does not suit all personalities.' Mine was the name of a Hindu deity and I suspect that a few names taken from the Hindu god catalogue served many thousands of disciples. We were told to work on the technique regularly for a week before coming back for further instruction.

Late that night when all was silent we tried mantra meditation with many doubts that it would lead to anything. Nor did it to begin with. After twenty minutes I was thoroughly bored although peaceful – both my breathing and my pulse had slowed. Then something like a distant boom vibrated softly inside my skull. My mind seemed to lift and float away out of my control. All bodily sensation drained away. My legs were weightless, as if hollow. My clothes made no impression on the body inside them. As the floating continued I became sharply conscious of the ticking of the alarm clock which I had left in the next room, timed to go off after half an hour. I could hear human voices and footsteps from outside the window, although there was nothing there but our silent garden.

The trance-like state was weakening and I reinforced it by repeating the mantra. Almost at once I began to feel that I was travelling horizontally and effortlessly on my back, as if borne up in water. Even when the alarm clock sounded the floating sensation persisted. When Patricia retrieved the alarm and switched on the light I remained motionless, as if paralysed. 'Time to wake up!' I opened my eyes but could not speak for a while. We had agreed to write down our experiences before attempting to discuss them. Patricia had had similar sensations but a totally different reaction to them. She had been horrified by the mind-opening feelings. She wrote, 'It was as if one had been taken into limitless, infinite space. It was shocking. I no longer had a self – I felt like an atom. It was not a journey and a space I was ready to go back to again.' Whatever the interpretation of our sensations, it did not correspond to bliss. But my senses had certainly been heightened. I checked that the alarm clock could not normally be heard ticking from the next room. The voices and footsteps outside must have come from the nearest road, thirty or forty yards away across the length of two gardens. We agreed that we had entered a trance induced by suggestion implanted along with the mantras by the charismatic power of the Maharishi. But the major sensation, like that of a jaw opening inside the skull cavity, was not repeated the next morning when I tried again. The mantra had a soothing, quietening effect but it did not open any doors.

The only time I was to experience it afresh was on our return visit to the Maharishi a week later. Again he was in infectious high spirits. His whitening beard bobbed with animation as he explained what happened during successful meditation. He called it 'making contact' – but with what? 'Deeper and subtler phases of awareness. Pure consciousness of transcendental nature. Nothing remains of outer world. Nothing! Absolute divorce from everything.' This seemed a plausible description of my experience. The mantra had reduced all distractions of sense and thought, the orchestra of awareness, to nothing. One was conscious only of consciousness itself.

'Let us meditate together,' he said. I watched his eyes flicker rapidly, darting from side to side. He was not looking at me but suddenly, without any recourse to a mantra, I was in the trance preceded by the same jaw-opening sensation inside the head. I felt unable to stir any part of my body. I continued to watch his eyes as I seemed to float gently backwards. He did not move. I could not. Nothing moved. But somewhere in the tall room there was now a humming, a deep, voiceless hum beating slowly, as if some huge organ pipe were vibrating on a very low frequency. A tremolo filled the room.

The Maharishi snapped back to normality as though the conversation had never stopped. As we said our farewells I was searching the room for pipes that might have been the source of the sound. There were no pipes of any description. 'What was it?' we asked each other eagerly once we were outside, for we had both felt it. Whatever we had experienced Patricia found wonderful – this time she didn't want it to stop. He must have made the sound, we agreed – but how? Once again some unknown source of energy seemed to be involved. Can consciousness radiate an unknown and inexplicable force which one day may be recognised as a natural phenomenon? Had it accompanied the Maharishi into his state of bliss where we could not follow him? When the Beatles took up the Maharishi with enthusiasm, I wondered if they tuned in to the floating and the deep, deep sound. I never experienced either of them again. Their occurrence seemed to depend on the presence or active encouragement of the Maharishi himself.

DOM ROBERT

Holy men come in all kinds of forms. I don't know if the Maharishi qualified as one. He was certainly the most exotic guru I had the fortune to meet. The church also has its holy men – even the relaxed old Anglican Church, where excessive holiness is regarded with some suspicion. One of these made a great impression on me and changed my thinking. Dom Robert Petitpierre was a Benedictine monk. He looked the part – tall, beaky-nosed, with thick-lensed spectacles beneath his tonsure. You could go back five hundred or a thousand years and find monks in the same long black habit who looked just like him. He was a deeply-read, quick-minded scholar with a sonorous drawl interrupted by loud explosive laughter. He could well have been a public school headmaster. He was, among other things, an experienced exorcist and the first time I met him in London he had an appointment with some demons after our lunch. I knew better than to ask him to talk about them. He invited me to visit his monastery; 'I think you might find it intriguing, perhaps even helpful.' At that point religion meant little to me but because I liked him, I went.

Nashdom Abbey was buried in the lush woodland of south Buckinghamshire and the first thing you noticed about it was the smell. This was compounded of wood and polish, candle wax, incense, and some further unnamable ingredient – 'Sanctity?' suggested Dom Robert with a fleeting smile when I mentioned it. The sprawling white house covered with dark bottle-green window shutters did not look English. It had been designed by Edwin Lutyens for a Russian prince with an opulence typical of the early 1900s. Hence the name, Nash Dom, Russian for Our House. It was like a superb dacha, hemmed in by wonderful woodland, on an English scale.

A Rogues' Gallery

Opposite the garden front stood a giant oak tree on a hillock which the setting sun lighted like a cathedral. I never tired of contemplating its huge limbs and cavernous depths as I ate my silent suppers in the dining room. It dated back to the early eighteenth century. I counted two hundred and fifty rings in the stump of a fellow oak nearby that had been recently felled. Behind it grass paths led away through Spanish chestnuts, beeches, birches and more beeches, a mysterious treescape. Along the paths monks in black cowls could be glimpsed pushing barrows full of tools until the bell tolled them back into chapel.

Time counts as much in a monastery as on a ship, the bell chiming not the next watch but the next office: Prime and Terce, Sext and None, Lauds, Vespers and Compline, the last devotion before bed. At Compline the monks confessed they had sinned exceedingly 'by my fault, my own fault, my own most grievous fault'. After the Compline hymn, asking to be defended through the coming hours 'from nightly fears and fantasies', the Abbot prayed for all of them to be granted 'a quiet night and a perfect end'. He sprinkled the cowled monks with holy water as they passed before him, bowing from the waist like penknives, on the way to their cells and the Silence. The Silence used to last over twelve hours, until after mid-morning Mass (it has been much relaxed since then). The house sailed into the night like a white vessel on an ocean of silence.

Silence had virtues I had not expected. It banished triviality and polite chatter and enabled you to be alone among other people. When I remarked on the sense of peace it created, Dom Robert was caustic: 'When people talk about the peace of the monastery, we spit. It's hectically busy.' This was true for the monks, who were under pressure from the timetable every minute of the day. Absurd conflicts would arise over such matters as the amount of washing-up liquid someone else was using. The downside of monastic fellowship was that they could never get away from each other. Sometimes the stress boiled over. The prior, a keen, young martinet, disappeared one day without a word – to be discovered months later living a married life with a former nun. A revered abbot had been found dead one morning on the gravel path beneath the first floor library windows.

The peace of the monastery was more apparent to the visitor than to the inmates. One night the silence was broken for me by the current abbot, Dom Augustine, who invited me to his bed-sitting room for 'a talk'. It was also the office from which he ran the monastery. He made us a cup of tea on a gas ring and lit a large square pipe. 'I suppose,' he began, in order to dispel any notion of pomp, 'you'll be wondering what I wear under this habit.' With that he lifted it to reveal stout navy blue football shorts. He had joined the monastery when he was halfway through training to be a doctor. 'As a postulant, then a novice, you are weighed up by the other monks as to your suitability. Can you stand the strain of spending five hours a day in prayer? Can you put up with the required obedience, as well as the chastity and poverty? Are you really called to this life? They all say they are. Some believe it most sincerely – and are wrong.'

Do monks miss women? The inevitable question amused him. 'Of course they do!' So why give up sex along with so much else – your property, money, clothes, even the name you were born with? Most of all your freedom? 'In order to do the job. Our job is to love God. If you can do that, the love of your fellow men follows. We believe there should be places where these commandments are put into practice, through prayer.' What was professional prayer like? 'At its best it is like the eloquent silence between two lovers.' But, he admitted, the silence sometimes remained empty. 'You are left looking for God with no consciousness of his presence.' An outsider might conclude that was because there was no God there to contact. 'Yes, we all know that kind of state.' And how did you know if you had succeeded in making contact? 'It's the realisation that deep down inside you there is a point of peace and union with God.' Was that what he expected to find in death? 'I don't know what we shall find. But monks are more ready to face death than most people because they train for it – like an examination.'

Dom Robert was more than ready for his examination. 'Enough of this life,' he would say, 'I want to get on with the next. Death can't come soon enough for me.' Life was keeping him busy, however. He was exorcising a council flat in nearby Slough where 'dreadful things' had been done and were now causing havoc for the present inhabitants. During the war he had worked as a priest in Soho. There had been plenty to exorcise there, he said. He recalled a young woman whose leg suddenly assumed a rigid horizontal position above the ground as she proceeded to drag him and two other monks all round the chapel with an uncanny strength.

A young man in the next guest room, who had come to consult Dom Robert, kept me up most of the night. He was scared of what his demons would do to him if he went to sleep. What demons? 'Look,' he said, pulling up a trouser leg. His calves looked a bit discoloured. 'They pinch me,' he said. 'It's like having pins stuck into your eyes and legs and arms.' He indicated that the most intimate parts were not immune from attack. Why him? He did not explain except for a dark hint that 'I should never have got involved with them.' When I mentioned this encounter to Dom Robert, smoking his pipe under a Spanish chestnut, he seemed unbothered. 'I've already had a talk with him. The first thing is to show him that he's not as interesting as he thinks he is. Possession can become a way of life – an excuse not to do any real work. As for the demons, he's been exorcised before, more than once. So if there were any, they've gone.'

My regard for the monks did not for a moment make me want to be one of them. I could not have stood their driven routine for a week. But they made no demands on me. They discussed their beliefs, if asked, with outspoken candour. 'As a monk do I miss personal fulfillment?' pondered large, genial Dom David. 'I don't think I know what that means.' When I asked whether they felt what they were doing was important: 'Not always. Day after day goes by following the routine and you sometimes wonder, does any of it matter?' Dom Edward, a carpenter with a rich London accent, asked me if I knew Camberwell and the Walworth Road market. 'Do you suppose many of them stall keepers says their prayers? Well, we say 'em for 'em.' Every monk went through dark nights of self-doubt. The abbot said, 'You have to come to terms with what you are and make the best of that. If you can't be Shakespeare, try to be Marlowe. If you can't be Marlowe...' When I took my leave I thanked the guest master, Dom Cuthbert, who had welcomed me, to my surprise, saying: 'Come in. You'll find lots of people just like you in here.' Up to a point he was right.

I went back to Nashdom as a fairly regular guest to be refreshed by contact with the spiritual energy that somehow seemed to be generated there. But when monks died they were not replaced by many newcomers. The day came when the remnant of the community decided to sell the house for a large sum and move somewhere more modest. Nashdom remained ghostly, empty amid the woods except for one space which the monks retained. Their graveyard. One day long after they had gone I slipped into the locked grounds and along the overgrown paths. Ranged in rows in the clearing were plain wooden crosses inscribed merely with the monastic names of the brethren and a date. Dom Robert's was among them. His death had not come as soon as he would have liked but it had come. I hope that it was the new beginning that he expected.

DANILO DOLCI

In the days before *The Godfather* the Sicilian Mafia had little of the spurious glamour that it acquired from the blockbuster film series. Since the Allied recapture of Sicily, when the US Army thought it could best restore order by releasing all the Mafia prisoners from the jails, they had lost no time in re-infiltrating all aspects of Sicilian life and politics. Even the beggars on the steps of Palermo Cathedral were paying protection money to the Mafia for their pitches. All attempts to put the Mafiosi back behind bars seemed to come to nothing. The same seemed to be true of the Anti-Mafia Commission recently appointed with much public drumbeating by the Christian Democrat government in Rome. I was trying to find out why.

The answer in Palermo was simple: there was no need for a commission because there was no longer a Mafia. 'Non esiste piu, signore,' I was informed again and again. The chief of the flying squad, weighed down with medals, assured me, 'There used to be forty Mafia killings a year. Last year – ninguno. Not one.' A moment later he went to greet the judge of the high court where twenty-one Mafiosi drug-dealers were currently on trial. The two men grasped each other round the shoulders to exchange the warmest of brotherly kisses. Despite the non-existence of the Mafia the *Giornale della Sicilia* each morning recorded violent deaths in and around Palermo, all victims of anonymous gunmen. Palermo's murder rate was currently twice that of Rome. I even heard whispers that a killing could be arranged for two hundred thousand lire – not a large sum.

Palermo was an oppressive city, like a great rotting compost heap of crumbling *palazzi*; and overcrowded slum alleys where the washing lines met above the traffic and women milked cows into buckets on the pavement. Palermo's central prison, the ill-famed Ucciardone, was a blank-walled hulk whose inmates often failed to reappear at the end of their sentences, usually because they had 'slipped on the stairs'. I engaged one of the horse-drawn *fiacres* that stood outside the opera house and asked to be shown the night life of the old town. It was a memorable ride lasting into the small hours. The driver explored all avenues of nocturnal squalor at no extra cost. We plunged into the labyrinthine streets where people slept ten, even twenty, to a room, Giuseppe informed me. From time to time we pulled in at bars to refuel. The men at the bar regarded their drinks with looks of pessimism, even despondency, until Giuseppe provoked them into bursts of unintelligible Sicilian dialect. I tried incautiously to convey that I would be interested in meeting any members of the Honoured Society, as the Mafia was known. Deep silence followed. One did not speak openly of such matters. At the next bar I suggested I would like to get to know the attractions of the city. Ah, they exclaimed, 'The catacombs!' Death was a principal attraction in Palermo, which exhibited its desiccated corpses of yester-century upright and fully dressed. I remarked to Giuseppe after we left that there were never any women present in the bars. 'Women? You desire women? I will take you where you get women.' I didn't *want* women, I explained. 'You prefer boys? I will take you...' Late-night Palermo was not joyful. There were no bands of strollers, no strum of guitar music. A watchful brooding silence waited for something unpleasant to occur.

I learned that the one person who would talk openly about the Mafia was Danilo Dolci, the social reformer who had espoused the cause of the Sicilian poor and taught them to raise themselves by their own efforts. He was infamous for having got villagers to mend their own roads, for which service he was put in prison. He was also awarded the Lenin peace prize, though he was no Communist. Some called him 'the Gandhi of Sicily' but where could I find him? Go west, I was told, to Partinico, Montalepre, Castellamare. Anyone there could direct me. Not so. Dolci seemed to be as mysteriously taboo as the Mafia, which had always been most active running the markets in western Sicily.

In Castellamare del Golfo, a wretched little town on the Tyrrhenian Sea, a white banner protruded from a doorway in a fly-blown side street. In Italian it said HUNGER STRIKE. Fasting was one of Dolci's favourite methods of operation and sure enough the striker was he. He was lying on a bed sipping from a bowl of warm water. He looked like a powerful, well-built priest in solemn black with bulging brow and gold-rimmed spectacles. Around the walls stood a peasant audience of locals. On the walls posters asked 'Why Was Nardo Renda Killed? and 'What Happened In The Pink Warehouse?' Everyone knew the answers but none would break the Mafia law of silence. The few prosecutions of Mafiosi seldom obtained convictions because no one dared give evidence against them. Dolci's aim was to get people to speak of what they knew and some were doing so, nervously, around his bed. His hunger strike was also calling attention to the fact that West Sicily's political boss and Member of Parliament was in cahoots with the Mafia, who saw to it that he was always re-elected. Bernardo Mattarella had recently held a conference with the local Mafia leaders – that was what had happened in the Pink Warehouse. Dolci had denounced him at a press conference. The Commission had promised to investigate but done nothing. 'So he is still in power,' said Dolci. 'Progress is impossible until people speak out about what they know, dangerous though it is. In the week I am fasting they make years of progress.' The tape recordings of their testimony were being sent to the Anti-Mafia Commission.

Dolci's protest looked almost pointless. How could he hope to change anything by lying on a bed in a poor house on a dingy street in a rundown Sicilian town? Because of the network of admirers and supporters he had in many other countries the Mafia thought it wiser to leave him unmolested. But for how long? He was at heart an academic, not a crusader. But now, to his satisfaction, Mattarella rose to the bait and sued Dolci for defamation. In typically dilatory Italian legal fashion the case was being heard on one day a week at Rome's Palace of Justice. I arranged to catch the day when one of Dolci's prize witnesses was to give evidence. Dolci gave me a rendezvous at which to meet him in Rome. It was the palm court of an inconspicuous hotel – 'Behind the fifth palm on the right.' Sure enough he was waiting there, with his back to the wall. He introduced his witness. Salvatore Capria was a small, knobbly-faced peasant from Montalepre, home of the famous dead bandit, Giuliano. His brother had been killed by the Mafia. He had been told by the mayor that if he gave evidence he would never work again. He shrugged. 'I haven't worked for six months anyway.' Previous witnesses had been spat on and called spies when they went home. In the passageway outside the court Salvatore was walking up and down. 'Non ho paura. Niente paura,' he was muttering to himself. Paura – fear. The word that subjugated Sicily. He was telling himself he didn't have it.

'Capria!' shouted the usher. I walked into court behind him and saw what he saw. At the foot of the circular benches sat Dolci on one side, on the other Mattarella. He had a politician's face from which all compassion had vanished long ago. He had been a minister in every Christian Democrat-dominated government for twenty years. He was 'Signore Sicilia'. One of his henchmen had been found on a Sicilian road machine-gunned, with a stone in his mouth to indicate that he had talked. The behaviour in court was not like that at the Old Bailey. People pottered about, chatting and shaking hands, waving to friends. Somebody delivered the evening paper to one of the judges on the bench, who settled down to read it as the case proceeded. When a sudden row erupted between counsel, who leapt to their feet shouting, the presiding judge beat his desk with his bare hands. 'Basta!' he shouted, 'Basta!' Mattarella's counsel was bullying Salvatore, who sat tightly clutching the sides of the witness's chair. Cutting through the verbiage he decided to say loudly what he had come to say, regardless of the consequences. 'Mattarella met Giuliano in Montalepre. My wife's cousin, who was one of Giuliano's band, was present.' The noise ceased as he went on. He named names besides that of Giuliano, who was secretly suspected of complicity in a notorious massacre. He recalled being invited himself to join the bandits for a promised thousand lire a day. They told him they were under Mattarella's protection.

Mattarella was staring at this little peasant open-mouthed, then tossing his head in angry denial. But an electric current could be felt circuiting the court. Even the Romans knew this was damning evidence. Mattarella's career was over. He was dropped in the next government reshuffle. Salvatore set out on his three-day journey back home. Dolci went on campaigning, speaking out, helping the wretched and writing books. Western Sicily remained as derelict as ever. The Mafia, without Mattarella's help, was still a force to be feared. But one man had made a dent in it. Such examples were rare in Sicily.

MI5 AND KGB

'Sorry I missed you in Moscow last year. I could have invited you out to my dacha.' The speaker was Viktor Louis, the most mysterious journalist I met either in or out of the Soviet Union. Technically he was a correspondent for the *London Evening News*, a sister paper of the *Daily Mail*, and for some American magazines. This did not explain how he was able to live like a millionaire. In Moscow his cars were legendary – a Mercedes, a Land Rover, a Porsche – when all the normal Russian journalist could hope to drive was a Moskvich. He travelled the world with a freedom unknown to Party high-ups. And he regularly produced spectacular scoops. He broke the story of Khrushchev's fall from power two days before it was announced. He predicted the Russian invasion of Czechoslovakia. He knew the latest Russian space exploit before anyone else. How?

Although the Cold War was at its height and the Cuban Missile Crisis a recent memory, the Soviet government had recently opened its borders to British tourists and I had taken my family on what was almost a freebie in order to report what it was like to holiday there. Pretty grim, was one answer. No place to go for a laugh. But interesting. After Khrushchev's fall the country had returned under Brezhnev to its old Stalinist ways of suspicion, surveillance, inhibition and prohibition. In Leningrad you still saw the flash of steel teeth, witness to the siege when dental filling was not obtainable. The chief occupation of the tourist, like the citizenry, was waiting. Waiting for permits, for service in restaurants, for hot water in hotel rooms. Everywhere you were followed by KGB minders in black coats and every night I telephoned the paper in London the call was very audibly tapped and recorded. Men in grey phone boxes reported your movements to some unseen controller. In Moscow alleyways young men would furtively beg the jeans off your legs or even the shoes off your feet. Unsmiling matronly tour guides would light up at the offer of a Western fashion magazine to look at. Everywhere people were fascinated by the pushchair of our youngest. It might have been the only pushchair in the Soviet Union.

Against this drab, glum background the lifestyle of Viktor Louis stood out like an exotic jungle fowl. And here he was, suddenly, at London airport accompanying a 'dissident Russian novelist' whom he had just escorted from Moscow to freedom with the full-hearted consent of the regime. Those were days when dissident novelists like Solzhenitsyn could only be published in *samizdat*, in hand-typed copies passed secretly from reader to reader. Two well-known Russian critics of the regime, named Sinyavsky and Daniel, had just been arrested for the sin of getting their work published abroad. There had been protests on the streets of Moscow by fellow writers and intellectuals – an event so unusual that Moscow correspondents were making much of the case. And here was Moscow's answer: it had granted a dissident writer, one Valery Tarsis, his request to emigrate to the West. Indeed he had been helped on his way – by Viktor Louis. A plump, puzzled-looking man with almost no English, Tarsis posed for the flash-bulbs while Louis handled our questions. Why was he here? Because he admired England and its liberties. Yet here he was with the blessing of the 'police state' he had been complaining of. So everyone should've been glad. Except that everyone smelt a rat. Especially me. I was wondering how Viktor Louis, whom I had never met before, should know all about my family's tour of the Soviet Union the year before.

That night I trawled through his press cuttings and compiled a dossier which I gave to the editor of the *Evening News* suggesting that their well-informed Moscow correspondent must be working for the KGB and that his present task was to create a diversion to take our minds off the writers on trial in Moscow. I did not have to wait long for a reply. 'You're to telephone this number,' he said, handing it to me on a folded piece of paper. 'Don't let anyone else see it.' I felt I was penetrating John le Carré territory. I dialled the number. 'Yes?' said a voice in neutral. I explained myself and was given an appointment at an address near the Cromwell Road in south-west London. 'Don't ring the bell, go down the slope to the garage. You'll find an entrance. Wait there till someone comes.'

A safe house! Indeed it looked completely anonymous, exactly like its neighbours. The door inside the garage was opened as I arrived by a tall, bony-faced man, who looked every inch Whitehall. The room he led me to contained a wooden hat-stand on which hung his hat and umbrella. He too had just arrived. He didn't introduce himself – presumably MI5 men don't. 'Viktor Louis,' he said abruptly. 'You appear to have done some sleuthing. We've had our eyes on him for some time.' And? What was his game? 'That's for you to find out. Observe him all you can. Then give us another call.' But I had been expecting some helpful information. None was forthcoming. Did they know any?

Viktor Louis seemed relaxed the next day after the press conference he gave on behalf of his charge, Tarsis, who said nothing very much. It was he, Viktor, who had obtained the passport, the exit permit, the plane ticket and now he was to be a guest of his English wife's mother at her home near Dorking. Clearly Viktor did not want him talking to us – not that he could. I suggested that as fellow journalists on sister papers we should get to know each other. Viktor treated me to a rundown on his seven-room apartment in Moscow where all the furnishing was from England. He had installed a Potterton boiler, the only one in Moscow. It was all paid for by his foreign earnings, he explained implausibly. 'Why should I live in the West? I live better than you do here. I am only person in the Soviet Union who can travel wherever and whenever I like. I can afford it. Look, I am giving lunch party for my wife's birthday. Tuesday, the Savoy Grill, one o'clock. Come.' I reported the lunch date to my anonymous mentor, who seemed interested. 'We see this man as a nuisance rather than a danger. But we shall keep an eye on the lunch.' I looked round the restaurant wondering who was there on behalf of MI5. Was he lunching at a neighbouring table? One of the waiters, perhaps? Was the table bugged? Victor's wife Jennifer had brought her mother and her two children. She had been governess to a diplomat's family at the British Embassy in Moscow when she met Viktor. It could have been a normal family party except that now Viktor in his rimless glasses rather reminded me of Beria, the executed KGB chief. Knowing we were being watched but not by whom was an unsettling sensation. Slowly the other tables cleared until ours was the last one left. It must be one of the waiters then. Soon there was only one of those left, a man so marked by his calling that it was difficult to believe he was an impostor. Then he left and we were alone. I casually inspected the central table decoration and even moved it surreptitiously. No wiring. My faith in the efficacy of MI5 took another dip.

During the next few days I learned that Sinyavsky and Daniel had been sentenced at a closed trial to long terms in labour camps. Tarsis denounced the sentences as Stalinist and was in turn deprived of his Soviet citizenship. Before he left for Greece (he was of Greek descent) I asked his opinion of his 'friend' Viktor Louis. 'He is an enigma to all Russia.' Viktor was soon leaving on an extensive tour of the West. I told my editor that it was impossible to prove he was a paid-up agent without some MI5 confirmation. Should we denounce him? 'Write the piece and show it to him. Then tell me his reaction.'

I invited Viktor to my office one evening when everyone else had gone home. I seated him at my desk. He pointed at the top drawer. 'What sort of tape recorder have you got in there?' None, I said and opened it. He looked around the room suspiciously, as if someone might be lurking unseen. 'I know you are working for MI5,' he said. 'I know you work for the KGB,' I replied. He smiled a dismissive smile. We had cleared the air. I showed him the piece I had written about his strange career, including his term in a camp in Stalin's day, accused of espionage. He read it without a flicker. 'This is a dirty trick,' he said calmly. 'Publishing these things could harm me. I might not get another visa. I have done nothing illegal.' Then how could he be harmed? 'Some top people may make inquiries.' I wondered which top people were using him and which were enemies. 'Nothing will happen to me, believe me. They are not going to send me to Siberia again.' He looked defiant. 'All right, so I have been in a camp. What of it? Look at this – my bank statement. With Lloyds in London.' The balance looked a lot healthier than mine.

The editor decided not to print an exposure and Viktor did get more visas. The next year he was back with a pirated copy of the memoirs of Stalin's daughter, Svetlana, which were due to be published with a great publicity blitz in America on the fiftieth anniversary of the Bolshevik

Revolution of November 1917. He offered an advance copy, somewhat amended, to European newspapers and magazines, together with articles denouncing Svetlana's 'betrayal' of her homeland, smearing her character. It was a classic example of doing a 'spoiler', an exercise in 'disinformation' at which he was an expert. We did not meet again but he sent a message through a colleague: 'Tell Peter Lewis that next time he comes to Moscow I will arrange a warm reception for him.' No doubt with some of his friends at the Lubianka. It was years later that his KGB controller revealed in a book that Viktor's instructions used to come to him direct from the chairman of the KGB, Yuri Andropov. But by then he was dead and so was the Soviet Union. I didn't hear from MI5 again and I didn't call them back.

THEATRE CRITICS

I saw the sixties from a seat in the theatre stalls where I spent ten years attending one thousand and one First Nights as a critic, the most unloved and unpopular role at any show. Yet go-getting young writers of my generation yearned to be theatre critics. This was partly due to the fact that the theatre made news. The Royal Court, Stratford-on-Avon and Stratford East's Theatre Workshop were where, in sixties parlance, it was at. The awareness that the play is coming to an end and you are On Next produces a certain flutter of anxiety, not unlike stage fright, until you are used to it. Putting your reactions instantly into words is not as straightforward as it looks. An essential requirement in my time was to know the whereabouts of all the hotels and bars in Theatreland with public telephones (no mobiles then). There one had to turn illegible notes scribbled in the dark into coherent prose in less than an hour, sometimes half an hour. The *Mail* deadline was 10.45 pm. So I never saw the duel scene in *Hamlet*. On bad nights I would stumble to a phone with only a first paragraph written and ad-lib the rest, spelling out every name to the copy-taker. We all knew of legendary transmission errors – Shakespeare's *Two Gentlemen of Aroma*, *Doris Godunov*, Gert's *Faust* or the playwright, Henry Gibson.

Is it fair and reasonable, theatre people often ask, that their weeks of hard work in preparation and rehearsal be damned with faint prose produced in a matter of forty-five minutes? I believe it is. Critics are only behaving like other members of the audience. If you asked *them* as they came out of the theatre what they thought of the show they would not reply, 'Oh, I'll need a day – or a week – to think about that.' Live theatre is instant communication or it is nothing; that is its fascination. Of course intelligent reactions to plays vary wildly which is why critics, who meet in the interval almost every night of their lives, never discuss the show they are watching. Any other show but not this, is the unspoken rule. Contrary to popular belief among thespians, there is no collusion. Theatre criticism was treated as significant in the sixties, due in part to the long rivalry between Kenneth Tynan on the *Observer* and Harold Hobson on the *Sunday Times*. They could not have differed more in temperament or opinion. Tynan, ever conscious of his public image, had discovered Brecht and declared himself a Brechtian Marxist, which did not improve his judgement of plays. He promoted several revolutionary stinkers. His judgement of performances was spot on but it was the elderly Christian mystic, Harold Hobson, who had the better record in spotting innovatory playwrights. He championed Beckett at the time when *Waiting for Godot* was being derided as a joke. And Harold Pinter when *The Birthday Party* was taken off after one week, before his notice appeared. Tynan could not resist making an entrance into the stalls – the white suit, the fashionable lady companion, the greetings to the chosen few. But the crippled Hobson, who could easily have attracted far more attention by his sheer difficulty in getting down the aisle, arrived early in order never to be noticed. He sat in the front row with his crutches laid beside him, eagerly looking for some spiritual depth in the play which the rest of us often could not see. He was sometimes wildly wrong but he was also right when it mattered. He was also the only theatre critic to receive a knighthood since 1914.

Spending five nights a week in the theatre can get confusing. I asked my friend and opposite number, the *Daily Express* critic Herbert Kretzmer, 'Do you sometimes wonder whether what you're experiencing is real life or the theatre?' 'Yes,' he replied. 'You ask yourself, "Who writes this shit?"'

NOEL COWARD

By the time I started reviewing in London Noel Coward's work as a playwright had gone into eclipse, partly because of the contempt with which it had been treated by Tynan as brittle, mannered and concerned with an obsolete social order. In his turn Coward had dismissed the 'new wave' of 'dustbin dramatists' and the 'scratch and mumble' school of acting that were then fashionable. At that moment I was sent as a novice, second-string reviewer to an early offering by the new Hampstead Theatre Club. 'Go and see what these people think they're doing,' I was instructed. 'They're supposed to be experimental and they're doing *Private Lives* of all things. You could well ask why.' The theatre was a modest wooden box round which the November wind howled audibly. Why were they doing *Private Lives*? 'It hasn't been produced for over twenty years. We read it and thought it should be tried again.' I had never seen the play. Having expected an evening of smart, effete twenties banter, I was taken quite aback by the interval. 'Can it be?' I asked myself, marching round outside the windswept theatre again and again. 'Can it be that we have been wrong all this time? That what has been dismissed for years as outdated is a classic English comedy in the tradition of Congreve, Vanbrugh, Wilde?' Dare I say so?

No other papers had bothered to attend so, in a very small way, it fell to me to initiate the Coward revival. The play filled the little theatre with delight for weeks and was re-produced in the West End. Coward came home from exile to cast his eye over it and within a year or two was himself directing his own *Hay Fever* at the National Theatre. This was the production in which Edith Evans, playing Judith Bliss, consistently changed one of her lines to: 'On a very clear day you can see Marlow.' Coward's patience finally gave way: 'Edith, the line is, "On a clear day you can see Marlow." On a *very clear* day you can see Marlowe *and* Beaumont *and* Fletcher.' Usually one heard of Coward's cutting ripostes second-hand but at a theatre gathering not long afterwards I had the good fortune to hear one minted just for me. The secret of Coward's famous style was of course his brevity. But this often brought the conversational flow to a halt on one of his *bon mots*. Desperate for a topic I pointed out a blown-up photograph of Edith Evans on the wall in some Restoration play or other. 'There's Dame Edith in the period when she could remember her lines,' I ventured. The soft staccato voice snapped back instantly: 'There never was such a period!' My favourite was his reply to a nervous actor after a first night: 'Mr Coward, could you see my wig-join?' 'Perfectly, perfectly.'

He was not all *bon mots*. For all his near-royal presence in his beautifully cut brown dinner jacket, in which he would bow graciously from his box to the applauding audience, he never forgot that it was hard work and determination that got him where he was. 'Regular hours are essential – Somerset Maugham taught me that. I get up at seven and am down to work from eight until lunchtime. Then not another word out of me until tomorrow.' He was then in his seventies. '*Hay Fever* took me three days, *Private Lives* rather longer. Five days. I thought of the idea for *Blithe Spirit* on a train going to Wales on a Monday and finished it on the Friday. My trouble is holding myself back.' Beneath the *sprezzatura* there was a self-made man with old-fashioned values. I remembered one of the speeches in his last play, *Shadows of the Evening*, which he delivered himself. 'Courage, humour, kindness…prevent other people from being hell.' Was that his sort of mission statement? 'I should add to those qualities good enunciation. And, before all, talent. Rather important in the mad world of powder and paint, don't you agree?'

TOM STOPPARD

Although it was satisfying to see an old playwright restored to his plinth, the sixties was a thrilling period to watch the blossoming of new playwrights One of the first to burst into view on my watch was Tom Stoppard. His play *Rosencrantz and Guildenstern Are Dead* arrived at the National Theatre in 1967 – nursed there it must be acknowledged by the enthusiasm of Tynan, who had become the theatre's literary manager. It was, as I wrote on the first night, an outsider which came romping home at sixty-six to one. 'We have a stunning new playwright.' Hobson hailed it as the most important event in the English theatre for nine years – referring back to Pinter's *The Birthday Party*. Few plays have won such immediate recognition. Within a year it was being produced everywhere, bound for New York as the National Theatre's first transfer to Broadway, where it won a Tony.

Three weeks after its opening I ran Stoppard to earth with some difficulty at an obscure, unlovely cottage near a crossroads in the Chilterns. He was lying low with his wife, Jose, and their baby son. There was a red public telephone box down the road from which he could call them but they couldn't call him. For a country cottage existence he was very well kempt, with glossy curled black hair, a long, tapered jaw-line and almost Pre-Raphaelite rose-petal lips. He looked faintly reminiscent of Mick Jagger, at that time an idol of his. Success had come to him at the mature age of twenty-nine and he was ready, indeed, impatient for it. I did not ask him what *Rosencrantz and Guildenstern* was about (I thought I knew) so I did not receive the reply he famously gave to another inquirer: 'It's about to make me extremely rich.' We sat on the daisy-papered lawn ('We haven't cut the grass because we like the daisies') where baby Oliver was playing in the sun. We talked about journalism. He had spent his early years on newspapers in Bristol. He had only just relinquished his last bread and butter job, writing a daily serial for the BBC's Arabic Service. 'I'm very well prepared for interviews,' he warned me. 'I'm always interviewing myself.'

This became evident in the readiness of his replies to whatever question. I asked whether he was himself more like Rosencrantz or Guildenstern, who pass their waiting time at Elsinore asking each other questions. 'I don't identify with either. I can always see either point of view and how plausible each of them is. So I spend my time arguing dialectically with myself because I suspect neither is the truth.' His wife broke in: 'Rosencrantz *and* Guildenstern are both very much him.' He was, he admitted, a slow starter. 'I was commissioned to write a novel and given a year to do it. Every few months they would ring up and ask how it was going. I always said fine. I would lie about how far I'd got – twenty thousand words, then forty thousand. One day in desperation I said I had just thrown it in the bin because I didn't like it. But not to worry – I'm working on another one. It's going well.'

Absent-mindedness was another of his characteristics. 'Only Tom would have got underneath a television set, unscrewed each of its legs and then been surprised when it fell on him,' said Jose, the more practical one, who had been a nurse when she met him. 'He once went out to empty the waste bucket and was surprised to find himself at the traffic lights still carrying it.' She had got used to his long periods of mental absence. 'He just paces and smokes for days. People don't realise that that is work.' 'I also read the newspapers a lot,' he interjected. Long before anyone had landed on the moon he was considering the philosophical consequences. 'The day somebody looks back down at the earth worries me. Man will see for the first time that the earth is only that big. All his moral absolutes – right and wrong, not killing people and so forth – will be seen as merely local customs.' It was a line of argument he was going to explore in a later play.

The promised loot had not yet arrived so we ate sandwiches. His royalties would later set him up in a series of Buckinghamshire country houses. He seemed to have always known that was his due. He gave the impression of being simultaneously neurotic and self-confident. 'The day I was supposed to take my driving test I didn't bother to get up. I wasn't ready. I would never be ready. I didn't really want to be ready. I don't like cars.' It was time for Jose to feed the baby.

'The hardest thing I've had to accept is that if I died or disappeared... he would be upset, but his life wouldn't be all that different,' she said, prophetically as it was to turn out. 'Writing is the core of his existence.' Stoppard heard the tail of what she was saying. 'Well,' he responded after a pause, 'I've been married to it for longer.' It was an idyllic day in late spring. Something about the daisies, the gentle slope of the Chilterns, the baby's presence, the promise of wealth and presumably happiness gave it an innocent Eden-like quality that stays in the memory – not at all the sort of Elsinore to which Rosencrantz and Guildenstern are summoned, dark with incomprehensible threats and irrational behaviour. Sooner or later, however, we are all summoned to an Elsinore not of our choosing.

SEÁN O'CASEY

The rediscovery of old neglected writers can be as satisfying as the arrival of a new one. Early in the twentieth century Ireland gave the world three great writers. James Joyce the novelist and W. B. Yeats the poet had gone before I got there. But I just managed to catch the playwright, Seán O'Casey, whose work began to be revived in the sixties. He hadn't seen Dublin in thirty-five years when I found him but he was still writing about its decaying streets and wonderfully articulate human traffic. When the third of his Dublin trilogy, *The Plough and the Stars*, caused riots at the Abbey Theatre in 1926 it was Yeats who castigated the audience: 'You have disgraced yourselves! You are rocking the cradle of a new masterpiece!' But it was also Yeats who rejected two years later O'Casey's bitter anti-war play, *The Silver Tassie*. O'Casey was not a man to stand rejection. He had decamped to London and declared he never would return. Nor had he.

A child of the tenements he had started work – labouring work – at the age of thirteen. His long, thin writer's hands had carried bricks, broken stone, unloaded ships' cargo and pushed a handcart. He learned how to write plays by haunting the Abbey's cheapest seats. Over the fireplace he pinned up a notice: GET ON WITH THE BLOODY PLAY. He was forty-three when the first of them to be accepted by the Abbey was staged in 1923. At the point I found him there was renewed interest in his plays in the London theatre. I wanted to know how he felt about it after many years of neglect. 'Not terribly t'rilled,' he said, sucking an unlit pipe. 'Interested, you could say. I've schooled myself not to be too ent'usiastic about anything.' The Dublin accent was ineradicable. He lay on a bed in an upstairs room on the fringe of Torquay beneath a red blanket. An almost forgotten man, an old man

104

in the attic, he was listening to the sound of the waves he could not see with his trachoma-impaired eyes. He looked like a grounded eagle, his long mouth twisted downwards beneath the beak.

'It's so long since you left Dublin…' I began. The eagle gave a squawk of rusty laughter. 'I nivver left Doblin, nivver! You can't leave that city. Joyce nivver left Doblin. Beckett nivver left Doblin. I carry it about with me like a snail's shell, like an elephant with his howdah. You can't get rid of it. It's a place that remembers old scores. We Irish can be very bitther. That's why all the good writers fled out of it.' To illustrate his point the Archbishop of Dublin had just refused to celebrate Mass for the Dublin theatre festival if any work by Joyce or O'Casey were performed at it. The implication was that their work was unholy. 'An insult to Christ. What a damned impudent t'ing to say!' In response he had banned performances of his works in Ireland. The Irish could be bitter.

He could have done with the royalties. Even as a world-famous playwright he had never made much money – he had always rejected Hollywood's offers to write scripts. 'It's only in the last few years that I began to make a dacent income. I wish some of the money had come earlier so I could have enjoyed it a bit. I never regarded myself as important. Everybody has talent of some kind. A feller with ten talents shouldn't look down on the feller with one. It was the feller with one that took fright and buried it.' He dashed the embroidered cap he wore back from his brow. 'Now I'm talkin' to you like a blasted philosopher. From this out,' he said, quoting himself, 'there's to be no more talkin'. And if anyone does talk, nobody's to listen to anybody!' Was that the Gospel according to St Sean? Another squawk. 'The Gospel according to Sinner Sean!' He lay back on the cushions silently shaking with amusement. He was eighty-two. He knew he hadn't long to live. He turned his misty pink eyes on me. 'Remember I haven't just written plays. I've played with the children. I've played with the children.'

CENSORSHIP ENDS

The struggle against theatre censorship was at its height. Until the Lord Chamberlain's writ was ended in 1968, we had to be made members of a 'club' in order to see 'private' performances of banned plays. This gave the impression that seeing, for example, Arthur Miller's *A View from the Bridge* was a furtive act of moral depravity. We were ushered into the Royal Court by a side door in mid-afternoon to see a 'final dress rehearsal' of Edward Bond's *Early Morning*, as if it were a blue movie. His previous play *Saved*, in which a gang of giggling louts stoned a baby in a pram, had been banned and prosecuted. This time he pushed the boundaries further by portraying Queen Victoria as a lesbian who fancied Florence Nightingale. This felt more like Christmas theatricals at Windsor Castle than a serious play. These disputes kept the London theatre and its critics continually in the news and on television discussion programmes. When the Lord Chamberlain's powers (as Master of the Revels) were abolished by the Theatres Act of 1968 the revels began in earnest. Freedom was celebrated for a time by volleys of four-letter words, stages full of nudity and the representation of sexual acts. Even the National Theatre staged a solemn dance around a golden phallus as a coda to *Oedipus*.

The immediate response to the passing of the Act was the staging of the musical *Hair*. It was not so much a performance as a Happening. Swinging on ropes, hanging from balconies, writhing copulatively, dowsing the audience in confetti or fusillading them with the four-letter word, taboo-busting in a deafening mixture of rock music and psychedelic lighting effects, the cast certainly worked hard to suggest total liberation. The headline-making scene, when they all lie down under a blanket and emerge a few moments later naked in dimmed light, was like the days when the Lord Chamberlain's word was law. Once you have disrobed there is not much more to do than stand and keep still. Exactly what the Chamberlain had always insisted on at the Windmill Theatre.

All this was soon put in the shade by the visit of the 'Living Theatre' of New York. This troupe of hippie anarchists believed in assaulting the audience physically. They came down into the auditorium to scream in your face, go through your pockets, take out your money and tell you to burn it. They lifted my pencil and addressed it as 'Holy Pencil'. They invited me to take off my clothes, as some of them had done already. Their shows were dedicated to bringing about 'the revolution' after which there would be no further need for money, private property, policing, passports, traffic lights, locks and keys – or any form of restraint on innocent human behaviour. The Free Society which they were urging on us was not an erotic experience. When a comely and entirely naked actress elected to park her buttocks firmly on my lap for the interval, she spent it chiding me about the rent she was paying for her flatshare in London – so much more than it would have been in N'York. Did they really expect accommodation to be free? 'It will be when we get rid of the money.' Did they believe that if nothing was locked up, nobody would pinch their stuff? 'Oh no,' she corrected me, 'people would pinch your stuff. But you wouldn't mind! *Because it's not really yours anyway.*' 'Yeah,' agreed a naked male actor nearby. 'Best thing that ever happened to me was when somebody stole all my clothes. My clothes were becoming too important to me.' There was something quintessentially sixties about this conversation. And the situation in which it took place.

KENNETH TYNAN

By then Kenneth Tynan must have feared that he was losing the edge in his drive to liberate us from sexual restraint. His 'erotic revue' *Oh! Calcutta!* proved that he had left it late, too late for the cognoscenti whom he wanted to shock. Before the hotly-anticipated first night in 1970 the battlements of prudishness had already fallen. Flower Power was at its height. It was the only occasion I remember when the audience looked gaudier and gayer (in the old sense) than the performers. Alas, their expectations, like the sketches, fell pretty flat, demonstrating that it is a mistake, in show business as in sex, to promise more than you can perform. The show entertained the coach parties and made him money but did nothing for his reputation for daring, which he attempted to salvage by being the first to say 'fuck' on a television talk show. None of the newspapers which stormed with indignation next day actually printed the word. By the time he followed *Oh! Calcutta!* with a second revue, *Carte Blanche*, which he described as 'a sort of public wet dream', his emphysema was well advanced. He smoked throughout lunch and ate almost nothing. It was impossible for him to give up smoking, he explained. If he couldn't smoke, he couldn't write, without which there was no point to his existence. He had made a fetish of being seen and photographed always with a cigarette held between his third and fourth fingers, as if to distinguish himself from the common addict. He didn't even smoke like other people! When in 1980 the inevitable caught up with him it rated the inevitable headline: 'Four-Letter Word Man Dead.' It seemed, and seems, a dismal epitaph on a writing talent which had been wasted on pursuing celebrity and sexual kinkiness. Tynan wrote that the critic's job was to make way for the good by demolishing the bad. But what he demolished was often by no means bad. 'He made it impossible for me to practise my profession in England,' Terence Rattigan told me bitterly, on his return from tax exile years later. It has since been proved that Rattigan could not well be spared. He had given up his long stay in Bermuda mainly in order to watch Test cricket in person once again. He was residing, impeccably dressed, in chambers in Albany. 'I think it's worth paying the tax for the cricket,' he told me. He planned to write more plays for the Tynan-free theatre – but did not live to do so. But there can be little doubt which of their two names is better remembered, and which made the greater contribution to the English theatre.

ANNA MAGNANI

As a rule critics avoid getting to know actors well personally. It may well mar their stage magic – 'Oh, he's just like that in real life.' Only the most charismatic are proof against close inspection. Anna Magnani had charisma by the bucketful. But when she brought her troupe to London with a Sicilian play, the show looked as if it would never start. Muffled bumps and shouts came from behind the curtain, for twenty minutes. When it did begin all was muddled and inaudible. Magnani, playing a passionate Sicilian mother, flung wine in other actors' faces, seized them by the hair and bared her breasts to the blade of an axe, but even her vitality could not compensate. I did not fail to say so.

Next day I received an invitation to visit her at the theatre – not a compliment that actors often extend to critics. Nervous aides awaited me at the stage door and ushered me to her dressing room door, which was ajar. 'Anna!' called one of them faintly. 'Ees eet Petair Lewis?' came a vibrant voice from behind the door. As I stepped forward her arm shot out and collared me. 'Vieni qui! Come 'ere! You naughdy boy!' I was hauled across the room and flung into the chair beside her dressing table. She flicked token slaps across my cheek to emphasise her words. 'You write bad things about Magnani! 'Orrible things!' Her teeth snapped inches from my nose. Her eyes glistened black as coal. Her hair shrouded her face like a widow's cape as she crouched before me, excitingly.

'Naughdy boy!' She looked as if she might bite but settled for another, playful slap. As a dominatrix she was devastating.

In Anglo-Italian she launched into the cycle of backstage disasters that had dogged their arrival – late planes, lost costumes, scenery that did not fit the London stage. The dress rehearsal had gone on all day.

'And dahrling, I 'ave the fever! But when I 'ear the cries of the public last night I am amazed at England. You are so passionate! Like us! This fury I 'ave on stage – people are afraid of me because sometime I am crazy. Why? I am never secure. Last night I am afraid inside, oh yes, I am afraid of London. So, dahrling, you will write again. Petair Lewis will tell how Magnani has found that the English understand passion?' After that how could I refuse?

THE BIRD

West End first-nighters were not as tame then as their successors are today. You will wait a long time now, perhaps forever, to hear 'the Bird', the custom of booing, hissing or cat-calling plays which fail to please. Why was it known as Giving (or Getting) the Bird? The answer goes back to the eighteenth century. The Bird was a goose. Playgoers hissed like geese when discontented. The ladies did it from behind their fans in order not to look ugly. Kean, Irving, Macready, all of them got the Bird and it was still common in the post-war theatre. 'There's Bird about,' an old actor-johnny said to me in one interval, practically sniffing it in the air. Noel Coward told me he was no stranger to it. 'Dear boy, I got the Bird many times. It's a vastly over-rated tragedy. I used to answer them back from the stage. Still, I shouldn't want to go through the first night of *Sirocco* again. They spat on me at the stage door. I had to send my coat to the cleaners.' John Gielgud got the Bird on tour in a play called *Veterans*, a very funny account of the shooting of a film he had made, *The Charge of the Light Brigade*, in which he sent himself up with gusto. In the course of it he did some swearing at the frustrations and eternal delays of filming. 'I got the Bird, definite Bird. They didn't like to hear me say 'shit!' in my gorgeous voice. In Brighton a man shouted, "Don't say that word again in front of my wife!" I suppose in a way it shows how people care about one – and the knighthood.'

The most raucous Bird I experienced was visited on the popular Peter Ustinov. His *No Sign of the Dove* was by anyone's standard a poor play – as the Flood rose about them, act by act, so did the pretentiousness of his characters' dialogue about life, death and the meaning of it all. The gallery became restive in the interval and increasingly vocal in the second half. By the time Ustinov unwisely took a curtain call they were throwing things. He wrote fewer, and perhaps better, plays after that. The sound of seats snapping upright as their occupiers left was common at the experimental seasons in Sloane Square, accompanied by shouts of 'Rubbish! A disgrace to the Court!' At a Royal Shakespeare Company season of new plays in London one unfortunate actor, who had committed a murder, was required to stagger about repeating the line: 'What shall I do with the knife?' The answer came straight back: 'Stick it in the author!' I miss the Bird. In our present age nobody can boo anyone without fear of prosecution for infringing their rights. Booing is as legitimate as cheering. Hissing is the counterpart to applause. Both are forms of audience participation. I have never heard actors complain of being cheered or applauded. My sympathies are with the paying patrons (paying through the nose these days). They are entitled to complain instead of quietly going to sleep.

JUDI DENCH

The actress with the widest range of any in her time is still manifesting her versatility in her seventies. When I first met her Judi Dench was twenty-six, small, chubbily attractive and as nervous as an electric eel. She was in *The Cherry Orchard* under the awesome director and Chekhov expert, Michel St Denis. She was playing Anya, daughter to Peggy Ashcroft's Madame Ranevskaya with John Gielgud as her moonily self-absorbed Uncle Gaev, who pays imaginary games of billiards while the cherry orchard is lost. As an introduction to acting's Champions League it could not be bettered. Much was expected of her on her promotion from the nursery slopes of the Old Vic to the Royal Shakespeare Company. 'I am absolutely terrified,' she told me. 'I don't think he likes me or my work.' Her elders had been kind but nothing she did seemed to satisfy St Denis, who had visions of the Moscow Art Theatre's first production of the play in Paris a world away. Ashcroft had told her not to let him see her crying. Gielgud said he would be proud to have her performance in one of his own productions. I took her to Rules for lunch, hoping its Edwardian splendours would take her mind off her worries. I had seen some of the morning rehearsal and seen her suffer. She loved Rules's crimson banquettes and the gilding unchanged since the First World War, when my father had dined there before leaving for the Front. 'I say,' she said looking round. 'Do you come here often?'

But there was a slight problem. I had not written an admiring notice of her Juliet, memorably directed by Franco Zeffirelli, at the Old Vic. As the text requires she had played her as, literally, a girl of fourteen but an English schoolgirl, scampering with puppy-like eagerness about the stage. We were not used to that sort of Juliet –

Shakespeare probably having had in mind an Italian girl of more advanced sexuality. Sub-editors in a hurry had headlined my notice ROMEO – WITHOUT A JULIET, which was not only unkind but unfair and not what I said at all. It was almost as bad as the critic who described her debut Ophelia as 'a piece of Danish patisserie'. I was quite surprised she didn't slap me. Instead she teased me, as she typically does, for not seeing the point of her performance. 'Take me out again,' she purred as we walked up to the Aldwych Theatre stage door. 'Fingers crossed,' she added as she braced herself to enter. I was glad that I wasn't reviewing her *Cherry Orchard*.

Nowadays with so many hits under her belt, an Oscar winner and a Dame, it is odd to remember that she had quite a bumpy take-off. It was fraught with obstacles – for example her diminutive height, barely five-foot-two. She can disguise it amazingly. 'You looked six-feet tall on your entrance last night,' I once remarked, quite sincerely. 'Go on! Go on! This is music!' There was also a problem with weight – so easy for her to put on that at our lunches she rarely did more than toy with lettuce leaves and drink mineral water. Yet she loves food. 'Tell me what you had for lunch,' she implored on a day I had driven down to visit her health farm in Hampshire. 'I want to hear every detail. Did you have lobster? Why not? We dream of lobster here. We talk of nothing but the food we long for – much more than sex!' Her looks were never those of a beauty – her features are too strong to be pretty, though they are marvellously adaptable. After her only screen test she was left with no expectation of a film career. 'This American said: "Miss Dench, you have every single thing wrong with your face."' Films came late in life and gave her the opportunity to play dominant women – two queens and James Bond's boss among them

It was in her first summer at Stratford that her talent came blazing out as Titania, a dazzling firework of a Fairy Queen with streaming wild hair and unrestrained libido. You believed she could make short work of an ass. Some time that summer we took a long, memorable walk in the Warwickshire woods. She had only just about got over her long secret passion for John Neville, the Hamlet to whom she had played Ophelia. My own marriage had come apart. There was much to commiserate over with each other. It was then that I realised that somewhere behind the jollity that made her the life and soul of any company there was a Quaker having a Quiet Time. Soon afterwards she took refuge at the Oxford Playhouse in *The Promise*, a Russian three-hander set in the siege of Leningrad. Three youngsters are sharing the hunger and deprivation in a bare apartment. Of her two men companions, one poetic, the other practical, played by Ian McKellen and Ian MacShane, she chooses the wrong one – as they realise at a reunion years later. The extraordinary intensity the trio developed in a searing and true-to-life play made me declare it a natural hit for the West End. So it proved to be. Hal Prince, the Broadway impresario, saw Judi in it and was so impressed that he insisted on miscasting her in his musical production of *Cabaret* as Isherwood's Sally Bowles, brushing aside the problem that she didn't sing or dance. She did wonders with her husky, crackly voice, 'using the gravel' as she put it, but it was hardly convincing. Despite her determination to go to the bad, she looked too nice to manage it – a disappointment, but what could you expect? She rejoined the non-musical theatre gratefully as 'a hoofer going straight'.

In the golden time that was to come she created an unforgettable series of Shakespeare heroines – a magical Hermione, a delicious Viola, an emotional whirlwind of a Cleopatra, a Lady Macbeth who shatters on discovering she could not connive in guiltless murder out of love for her husband. Interestingly, one part she found impossible to play was Regan, King Lear's wicked daughter. Unlike Lady Macbeth, she couldn't find any shred of the character she could sympathise with or understand. The fact that she does so is remarkable considering that she does not choose her parts but leaves that to the advice of a few trusted friends. She doesn't even read the whole script until she arrives for the read-through. It is a tremendous risk to take but she likes risk. 'It makes it more exciting, not knowing what's coming.'

We are getting closer here to her mystery – the Magic Moment that her audience waits for in any performance she gives. At its plainest it is the 'Send in the Clowns' moment when her voice cracks with private anguish in the rather over-sentimental *A Little Night Music*. But it can happen in all kinds of situation – the coming back to life of the tragically traduced Hermione in *A Winter's Tale*, the sudden meltdown of Beatrice after duelling so long with Benedick, the sudden horror of realisation by Lady Macbeth. These are moments when something in her look, her posture, the note in her voice stops the audience from breathing. It is harder to do on camera, to a crew, but she achieved it when John Brown tells his monarch he is leaving her service and the imperious 'Mrs Brown' collapses from being a queen to a lonely woman. It was never any use asking how she does it. She doesn't know, not consciously, and believes that trying to analyse would kill it stone dead. She would not discuss her parts even with Michael Williams, her fellow RSC actor whom she married at the age of thirty-six. She works by instinct, in her case god-given. Such a gift can be difficult to live with for those closest to her.

When they and I both lived in Hampstead – in a pocket handkerchief of a cottage that I once coveted – we would meet at a chic little café-restaurant and bemoan the Labour party's pre-Blair inability to get the Tories out. Michael had a working-class Liverpool background and told me that before going on the stage he had sold insurance. By sheer application he made himself a leading actor and a capable partner of Judi on stage and TV – A Fine Romance brought both of them mass recognition, more than had a lifetime in classical theatre. But when her career took off for the heights his was inevitably overshadowed. One day in a pub at Wasp Green, where she had bought a seventeenth-century house and small Surrey estate, I raised this delicate subject with them both. Had it made their harmonious relationship more difficult to maintain? Our after-lunch coffee had been accompanied by after-dinner mints wrapped in silver paper. While Michael answered my question – by expressing the admiration of a genuinely modest man for acting that was well out of his league – Judi concentrated ferociously on the silver paper wrappings on the table. As she listened she ironed out each of them carefully with the back of a spoon. It was probably harder for her than for him to have the disparity aired.

MUSICAL INTERLUDES

Life fortunately was not all theatre. My love affair with the piano has lasted a lifetime. Music, mostly classical music, has been my indispensable drug. I have always wondered how professional soloists who have to practice many hours a day manage not to kill their repertoire stone dead with repetition. I was given the chance to observe and question their methods. It began when, as a schoolboy, I put my head round the door of the library at Stowe - a magnificent, galleried room – to find Solomon preparing for the recital he was to give there later that day. Without breaking off he nodded to me to enter. The next time he paused he smiled and patted the empty space beside him on the piano seat. Barely able to breathe I sat there inches from the keyboard as his fingers danced like butterflies weaving a shimmer of sound through the variations of the Appassionata slow movement. The leading British virtuoso played it just for me.

Later I found a young Daniel Barenboim sitting in an armchair reading a piano score. 'What are you doing?' 'Practicing.' I must have looked surprised. 'I'm rehearsing tonight's concert,' he explained. 'The best way of hearing how the music should be played is in your head when you're not distracted by what your fingers are trying to do.'

When Arthur Rubinstein was playing in London he always stayed in a Savoy hotel suite overlooking the river and the Festival Hall on the opposite bank. I used to call on him to hear the latest genial despatch from his mountain top. The music for the night's recital was open on the piano when I entered. I had hopes of hearing him rehearse a bit of it. 'I do not practise,' he told me at our first meeting. 'There are certain passages, the big steeplechase jumps that you have to play over before the concert but otherwise…' Instead he sat at a table and showed me the finger exercises he did daily to keep his large hands supple. The little fingers were as long as the forefingers and his stretch was enormous. He did not practice, he said, because in a hotel room he could get only forty per cent concentration. 'But at the concert…' he nodded at the hall opposite, 'the concert is like a bullfight, the hour of truth. I get one hundred per cent concentration. Then come things that I cannot get at home. When I play Beethoven, I am Beethoven. No other music exists. When I finish Beethoven I am ready to become Chopin. This is my talent.' He emphasised his point with Polish chops of the hand. He went on playing (he was eighty-one) in the hope that he could play better. 'If I think I am not getting better I shall stop. Luckily there is no such thing as perfection. Something always stops you short of it.'

Rubinstein had been renowned for his love life and was very expansive on the subject. 'Women excite me as a spectacle. Even if they turn out not to be very intelligent, they give pepper and salt to life. Even when I was deeply in love with one woman I would always look at another.' There was an undoubted sexiness in his playing, which I imagine accounted partly for the rapture of his audiences – as well as the number of women who pined for him. 'I try to give them my heart,' he said. 'The great success I have been favoured with is not so much because I am a very good pianist, it is because I love the people listening to me. It is not a special privilege to play the piano. If you hear the music with love you are just as happy listening as playing. But my life of success with concerts and people and women it is nothing. Nothing in comparison with one concerto of Mozart, one sonata of Schubert or Beethoven.'

He believed that there is some power that enabled him to turn an audience of three thousand people into one. 'There's no explanation for it any more than there is for telepathy, or magnetism or hypnosis. I call it the Power of Creation. We don't understand it any more than the ancient Greeks understood electricity. I love my audience. But before I begin I look for somebody, a young woman, and I play the whole concert for her'. When I last met him he still had several years of concert-giving in him. He did not seem worried about death. 'We are all condemned to death, like criminals. The only difference is we do not know the date. Why worry about it? Live!' But he told me what music he would like to die to: Schubert's String Quintet in C – the slow movement. Me too.

Of the many piano virtuosi I have heard the one who made my receptors jump the most was the blind-from-birth piano genius, George Shearing. He was equally at home with jazz and classical music, which he learned, of course, by ear. 'I don't like being called a jazz musician, still less a blind one,' he told me. 'I am a musician.' I first heard him on a 1949 recording. It was of a piece of his own called 'Consternation' – and that is what it caused me. I had never before heard such bebop. Shearing over-rode the beat, played tricks with the rhythm, ventured chord sequences unknown to Rachmaninov and harmonies beyond even Delius. His dazzlingly fleet fingers could relax into a pianissimo touch to melt the ear. He composed many strikingly original pieces from a jazz standard like 'Lullaby of Birdland' to his settings that made Shakespeare songs and sonnets sound contemporary. He also invented the 'Shearing Sound' – a combination of piano and vibraphone above a rhythm section – which made him a fortune. He was accused of selling out commercially by jazz purists but he disbanded the Shearing Quintet when it bored him and went solo. His arrangements of popular numbers were haunted with echoes of Bach or Debussy and would turn into a fugue without warning. 'I like to honk it up a little,' he said.

On rare returns to his native London, where he started as a teenage pub and club pianist, he would fill the Royal Festival Hall. Each summer he and his American wife Ellie, a singer, took a cottage in the Cotswolds where he loved to listen to the River Windrush. He told me he could tell the differences in sound between rivers, just as he would hear if he passed a lamp-post in the street. There was no cure for his condition, a failure of the optic nerve –'But if one became available now, I would turn it down. If I'd been able to read music, would I have still had my imagination to call on? Thank God for a pair of ears.'

THE AMADEUS

In the music scene of sixties and seventies Britain had more than one Fab Four. The Amadeus Quartet were without question the other one. They were as pre-eminent in their chamber music sphere as the Beatles were in theirs. The three Austrians, Norbert Brainin and Sigmund Nissel, violins, and Peter Schidlof, viola, had famously met as refugees from Hitler in a British internment camp as the war began. They met the cellist Martin Lovett in the audience at a refugee concert and began playing together when barely out of their teens. For twenty-five years they had lived in each others' pockets, toured the world and seen more of each other than they saw of their wives. In their young days they were not known as the Amadeus but by Mozart's other name, 'The Wolf Gang'.

String quartets are as close as families and sometimes as quarrelsome. There are some whose members refuse to travel in the same train compartment, even in the same aeroplane. The Amadeus were renowned for equanimity but I saw a bit of temperament when I called by invitation at Sigmund Nissel's house at the Golders Green end of Hampstead Heath. There was a tanker outside delivering heating oil and the sound of Beethoven, tinny, faint and faraway, coming from the suburban bay window. They filled the front room, sitting facing each other from opposite corners of an orange woolly rug. There was barely room to squeeze in. Nissel motioned to me to sit on the floor. They were well into the Razoumovsky quartet they were practising for a concert that would fill the Queen Elizabeth Hall that night. Nissel, known as Siggy, hosted rehearsals because his house was the most central. At that point the doorbell went. The oil delivery was completed. He got up, still playing, and went to open it to receive the invoice. Not a bar was lost.

A Rogues' Gallery

He sat the stillest of all of them, as befits a second violin, the crux that keeps them all together. Brainin's lock of thick dark hair bounced vigorously up and down with his bow. Schidlof made extrovert sweeps with his viola as his eyebrows signalled surprise, displeasure, sometimes delight at the sound. Lovett smoked his pipe, swaying gently over the rocklike foundation he provided. They talked continually in playing.

'That wasn't very good, sorry.' 'You know what you are doing wrong there?' 'Look, you two are doing nothing. I'm making a tremendous effort.' 'We know. You almost fell off your chair.' When they reached the end of the movement the inquest began: 'Didn't it sound frightful? We're not together.' 'We're ignoring the sforzando three bars after letter C. I think we should do it.'

In a quartet at that level there is no boss. Everyone is equal, equally ready to criticise each other and equally unruffled by the criticism. Ideally. Was this how they'd stayed together, by then for twenty-five years? The Beatles hadn't managed it. One sign of their closeness was the way they would finish each other's sentences.

'We don't get bored. It's not like going to bed with the same woman for twenty-five years.' 'Well it *is*, a bit. You know what to expect…' 'But we are always changing. We don't want to sound like our old records…' 'What keeps us together is that we are playing the best music ever…' 'It takes us a year to discover what there is in a Beethoven quartet.'

But they were still debating this one as passionately as if they had never heard it before

They claimed they could stand back to back in opposite corners of the room and still start together. 'Something in the silence would tell us the moment,' said Siggy. 'Being so close can also be a bit claustrophobic. You see, if anything – God forbid! – happened to one of us, it would be inconceivable to start again with someone else.' Prophetic words. When Peter Schidlof died in 1987 the Amadeus simply ceased as a quartet. Their sound has never quite been replaced. When I hear one of their recordings I see still Brainin's hair tossing, Schidlof's eyebrows semaphoring, Lovett's pipe curling with smoke and Siggy's half-closed eyes wrinkling with half a smile in a suburban front room.

COMPTON MACKENZIE

One veteran writer who refused to adopt the new sexual candour that was suddenly fashionable was Compton Mackenzie. I was lacing up his boots for him at the Savile Club before a dinner in his honour – his eighty-fifth birthday, I think. While I laced he was reflecting on women, of whom there had been a great many in his life. 'I adore women. They've always been more important to me than men. I've always had a somewhat fatal attraction for them. Never known jealousy – but then I've never been refused by a woman.' When going to Edinburgh for the Festival I remember being asked by one of his old flames to give her love to 'Monty' and did. 'Ah, Lenie – such a dainty little thing!' he had said with a fond smile of recollection of a now venerable little old lady. But when he embarked on his autobiography in ten volumes he stipulated that it would not be his 'confessions'. 'I believe a gentleman does not kiss and tell. Even if I wanted to make my private parts public I shouldn't have the nerve.' Such chivalrous reticence had its drawbacks. Ten volumes, over a million words without indiscretions, tended to get boring.

'Monty' enjoyed acting the part of the old Literary Lion holding court from a deep leather chair at the Savile Club with his mane of silver hair, goatee beard and floppy bow tie, nursing a tumbler of whisky and a pipe. 'I'm an entertainer,' he confessed. 'A complete extrovert. People say I'm a case of arrested development. I suppose I am.' When he wasn't at the Savile he was reigning over literary Edinburgh from his bed. It was a velvet-draped tester bed surrounded by books, a bowl of pipes and a decanter of whisky (to ensure it was never in short supply he advertised the stuff). That was where he entertained favoured guests. At two in the morning his visitors might be tiring but he would be in full flow, perhaps giving his imitation of Henry James, who had championed him when he was a young novelist. 'What was the peculiar title of the condiment which we need to import into this humble corner of our vast London, Mrs Dash?' 'Six jars of that Oxford marmalade that you liked, Mr James.' A sigh. 'These hideous encounters with domestic necessity.' Or his mind would turn to Somerset Maugham. 'Willie' had rebuked Monty for his extravagance. 'His ambition was to leave more money than any other author. "I've saved a hundred and eighty-six thousand p-p-pounds, Monty," he would boast. Of course I hadn't saved a farthing. Poor Willie, he never had any pleasure out of life at all. My motto is Stendhal's: he lived; he loved; he wrote.' He certainly lived (and loved) on a lavish scale. Besides turning out one hundred and twelve books he was a secret service agent, the first radio disc jockey, a pioneer Scottish Nationalist, a Jacobite and Gaelic speaker and president of the Siamese Cat Club and Song Writers' Guild. 'I've been bloody lucky. I've eaten my cake and had it. I quite see why people get irritated with me. I enjoy life so much that I shall be livid if I don't live till ninety.' He bowed out a month short of it.

HAROLD PINTER

I was lucky in that my time in a critic's seat coincided with a remarkable flowering of new playwrights. The names of Peter Shaffer, Alan Ayckbourn, Peter Nichols, Tom Stoppard, Simon Gray, Christopher Hampton, Michael Frayn, Joe Orton and Alan Bennett were all established while I was reviewing – a constellation of talent such as had last occurred in England on the Restoration stage or before that in the Jacobean age. In the late sixties there could be no doubt who was the outstanding dramatist of this rich era. The name of Harold Pinter was known to all kinds of people far beyond the theatrical world. The bewilderment his plays had caused at first, beginning with total incomprehension of *The Birthday Party*, had cleared. He had moved the goalposts. At that time most of his plays were first shown on television and became talking points throughout the land the next day. People identified each other's conversational tics as 'Pure Pinter'. The imprecise adjective 'Pinteresque' was invented.

SCENE: *The Aldwych Theatre. On Stage: Michael Hordern, holding telephone:*

HORDERN: Who is this? Who is this? Do you know it's four o'clock in the morning?

                                Pause

VOICE(OVER):   Tell him I want a word with him.
HORDERN: Who is this? Are you a friend of his?

A Rogues' Gallery

Pause

VOICE: He'll know me when he sees me. Tell him I'll be in touch.

HORDERN: (breaking off) Sorry, I don't get this at all. This mystery phone call. Am I alarmed? Surprised?

DIRECTOR: Harold?

PINTER'S VOICE: Not altogether surprised. I think similar phone calls may well have been made in the past.

This was my first glimpse of Pinter, who looked spruce, brisk, spectacles gleaming with purposefulness between his sideburns. He was on a roll of success, following *The Caretaker*. I was a privileged onlooker at early rehearsals of his next stage play, *The Collection*. Four characters were deeply involved in the question whether two of them slept together in a hotel in Leeds during a fashion show. A question not destined to be answered. He and Peter Hall were co-directing the production. He intervened again in a scene between two quarrelsome male characters, coming forward from the shadowy stalls, flicking back his spectacles.

PINTER: This is queer talk. Queer talk. You don't trust him. He doesn't trust you and you are both talking utter balls. Beneath it is this other thing that the talk refers to but you are both talking utter balls!

This was the production at which he gave a famous rehearsal note to Hordern: 'Michael, I wrote three dots and you're giving me two.' Precision was important to him.

It took time, though not very long, for audiences to accept that characters could arrive on stage without any explanation of who they were and where they came from. But were they 'symbolic'? Who were the three men in *The Caretaker*, which he described as 'a play about a tramp and two brothers', people wondered. Was he deliberately suppressing data in order to mystify us? I put this point to him. 'I have a tremendous amount of data; the plays are full of data. But it's contradictory. Unless you know when a character is lying, or mistaken, you can never know the truth. I am not God. I can only proceed from what the characters tell me. I *smell* what they would say or not say. I can't make them say something they wouldn't just because I want to get to the facts. That would be like breaking their arms. It would be cheating'. So was he also mystified – about what happened or did not happen in the Leeds hotel room, for example? 'I am not mystified. I am not *bothered*. There are many permutations of possibilities in sexual events. Thinking of my past, of an affair, say, I've got a good memory but I've forgotten more than I remember. Haven't you? Whether someone put a hand in a certain place or not? The more people try to verify, the less they know'.

He had been in his time a waiter at a London club and a chucker-out at a tough West End dance-hall. 'I've known all sorts of people. Accountants. Footballers. Yes, and a tramp. There are some lines in *The Caretaker* that I heard from a tramp'. Like that memorable boast: 'I've had my dinner off the best of plates?' Pinter grinned. 'No, I made that up'. He insisted that he never carried a notebook. He scorned the often expressed idea that his plays were 'like real life'. 'I don't know what that means. It assumes that there's something called Real Life that you could reproduce exactly on the stage. I like making happen things *outside* normal experience. To shake people up. I enjoy violence – I enjoy using it theatrically. I was going to end *The Caretaker* with the violent death of the tramp. Then I saw it was not necessary'. Like Chekhov, he got rid of the pistol shot.

Pinter could appear very formidable, impatient, judgemental. Then he would take off his glasses and look quite different. The eyes were humorous and oddly gentle. It was a duality that took you by surprise. Which Pinter would he be today? Sometimes he was the stern voice that told me, 'I am trying to write a play. And *I am succeeding* in writing one'. (It was *The Homecoming*.) At others he would gossip happily and amusingly. Of course it was never a good idea to ask him what he meant by a scene or a line. I wrote there was only one line in

The Homecoming which did not seem to flow inevitably from the one before. '*Which line?*' he demanded impatiently when we met next day. I told him. 'Ah,' was all he said.

One person who never asked what his plays meant was his wife, Vivien Merchant, who appeared in most of the best. I wondered if she discussed her characters with their author. 'Why should I? I always know what he means.' It was hard to imagine any other actress being as effective in them. There was a spooky sexiness about her, especially in *The Homecoming*, as the mysterious interloper in a male household.

They had met in rep, in which they had both acted for many years, she more successfully than he. They married at the end of a season in Bournemouth when he was just twenty-six, she a year older. Penurious years followed in theatre digs and basement flats, including one flat where he offered to caretake the building in lieu of rent. When success transformed their lives they moved to Hanover Terrace in Regent's Park. Not just to an apartment but an entire five-storey house on Crown lease with garden and servants' quarters in the Mews behind it. It took a bit of nerve to ring the bell and speak into the entry phone. Whereupon Vivien's husky Lancashire voice would say, 'Oo, coom up, luv.' Long drapes, thick carpets and mirrors everywhere spoke of the change in their fortunes. The bath taps were gilded swans. Those on the wash basin and bidet were their gold cygnets. Pinter's domain was on the top floor, where he wrote in a white cell, which you were not invited to visit. They kept separate telephone numbers.

Lying on the soft white pile of the rug in the drawing room, discussing a forthcoming TV interview with Vivien, who was perched on the sofa, I saw Pinter walk in unexpectedly. He paused as he took in the scene. 'David,' said Vivien, who always called him by the stage name under which they met, 'Peter's come to talk about the programme.' Pinter looked down at me inscrutably. 'I like finding you on the floor entertaining my wife,' he said and paused again. 'At least, I *think* I like it.' As we talked a very slim young man passed to and fro along the iron balcony outside the tall sash windows. He was totally absorbed in a book. 'Hamlet,' said Pinter, indicating the passing figure. It was their son, Danny.

Vivien never called herself Pinter but clung to her stage name, which she made up when starting out at the age of fourteen. When they met in repertory she was by far the more seasoned actor of the two, playing leads to his supporting roles, a dependable, quick study. She was impatient of all intellectual pretension, especially theorising about his work. Her low, gritty voice exuded a challenging sexuality beneath a genteel veneer - never more so than in the famous glass-of-water-demanding, leg-crossing scene in *The Homecoming*. She was his muse. But one could sense that she was not the only apple of his eye. He took a keen interest in his friends' private lives and liked to know the latest developments in adulterous situations. 'I'm keeping a close eye on you,' he said.

Vivien decided one day to open up about the trauma of giving birth to Danny. They were so desperately hard up that they had nowhere suitable to take the baby home to, until a friend came to the rescue. But that was not the worst of it. An obstetrician of the old, totally insensitive school had commanded her to get on a couch for examination in front of his numerous pupils and treated her as a non-sentient prop for his demonstration, like a piece of wood. Her indignation was still fierce; she had never got over the humiliation. There was no question of undergoing it a second time. It had scarred her feelings which must have affected their sex life.

During a fraught and ill-starred Peter Hall production of *Macbeth* at Stratford, she played Lady Macbeth on a steeply raked stage that had been swamped by a symbolically red, shaggy carpet which tripped up the actors. She drove me out to dinner on her nights off. She drove fast, like a man. 'You were right in what you wrote about that bloody carpet.' She was not interested in food, only drink. Rumours about Pinter's long-standing affair with Joan Bakewell had obviously reached her in garbled form. 'Do you know what he sees in this Judith, or whatever her name is? Well, if that's what he wants...'

When the *coup de foudre* arrived later in the person of Antonia Fraser, Vivien refused to suffer in silence. She suffered very publicly in the tabloid newspapers. She continued to work. Then came an anguished telephone call. She had been sacked from *Hamlet* at Bristol Old Vic and wanted to talk. Once more I rang the bell at Hanover Terrace. Its atmosphere had changed as if by black magic. Lights were dim, curtains half-drawn, nothing put away. Alone with the mirrors, like the Lady of Shalott, Vivien looked back at herself with staring, sleep-deprived eyes. Bottles of white wine, nothing else, stood on the kitchen counter. 'It's the first time I've ever fallen down on a job.' She couldn't for once make the lines stick. Danny had just dropped out of Oxford. Pinter had moved into Antonia Fraser's house. 'I never thought he would do a thing like that.' Her confusion was all too reminiscent of Lady Macbeth's final scene. Nightly she walked the house unsleeping, the house of mirrors where there was no one at home on the upper floors. She wore an almost nun-like brown robe and her hair was openly greying. 'Don't stop working, they said to me, and I didn't. It took some courage and vitamin injections. I wouldn't go near the psychiatrists. I said to one doctor, "Have you got a bottle of pills marked Husband?" On our eighteenth anniversary, just before he left, David gave me a card. It said "Eighteen and still my Queen". When we married, I'd never been with any other man. I'm not going shopping now.'

Everything seemed hopelessly dependent on a bond that was broken. I told her I liked her joke about the shoes. She told a newspaper at the time of the split that her husband had no need to take his shoes with him: 'He could always wear hers.' 'He's never stopped blaming me for that remark. He seems to have lost his sense of humour. Maybe they are right for each other. I am uneducated. She writes books. They probably spend happy hours talking about books. But I'll tell you one thing. He'll never write another play.' Apart from *Betrayal* (about an earlier betrayal) he had since written nothing but film scripts and short, angry political polemics for the stage. She filled another tumbler with white wine. 'The will to work has gone. The will to live has gone.' Had she contemplated suicide? I was almost afraid to ask. 'Of course I have. But I'm not the type, you see. Too tidy by nature. I couldn't bear the thought of the mess that someone would have to clear up. And I never could swallow pills.' She gave one of her old boyish grins. Instead of pills she went on swallowing white wine until it brought final oblivion, at the age of fifty-three. It was a terrible, intentional waste. It was no single person's fault. People are like a playwright's characters. You cannot force them to act how you want them to.

She was right about one thing, though. He never wrote another play as good as the ones he wrote for her.

THE SEVENTIES

URI GELLER

In the early 1970s the world was intrigued by a remarkable young psychic from Israel who could bend spoons by merely stroking them. This was a new phenomenon. The Society for Psychical Research, which for a hundred years had investigated ghosts, precognition, telepathy and things that went bump in the night, had never touched a spoon as an experiment. Uri Geller's appearance on Britain's television screens in 1972 was sensational by any standard. Not only did he bend spoons and metal before the viewers' eyes, he had dramatic effects on clocks and watches throughout the land: stopping some dead and restarting others which had been dead for years. What kind of force or influence was he transmitting through our screens?

Geller, in his twenties and darkly good-looking, added to his repertoire mind-reading, card-guessing and making pots of money. He claimed to have been teleported for thirty-five miles. He said he had recorded mystery voices (possibly from space) on tape recordings. He was denounced as a fraud whose tricks could be imitated by any clever conjuror, which made one wonder why clever conjurors had not cleaned up by doing them already. But most of us regarded his ability as supernormal, if not supernatural. I decided to go paranormal-hunting with Mr Geller. So I presented myself at his London hotel room armed with a sturdy teaspoon, an envelope containing a drawing and another containing a playing card. They had been chosen and inserted without my seeing or knowing anything about them.

'Peter,' he said, eager and intense. 'Sit right here in this chair, choose an image and think about it. See it in your mind's eye. Then I will tell you what it is.' I knew better than to make the image a house, a tree or a ball, the three symbols that people most often chose. 'Look into my eyes,' he commanded, squatting opposite me on a stool. 'Look deep into my eyes and imagine your object…' He pulled himself closer until we were practically eyeball to eyeball. His pupils searched mine, which I was trying my best to keep still. In this situation people are apt to trace unwittingly the outline of the shape they are concentrating on and he was skilled at reading the movements of their pupils. I exasperated him. 'You're not really concentrating. Was it a tree?' No, I said, it was the Eiffel Tower. 'Ah well, that accounts for it,' he responded immediately. 'I kept seeing this triangle. I couldn't believe it was a tree. At least I was right about what it wasn't.'

This did not seem to require any great degree of psychic insight. We tried guessing the mystery drawing enclosed in the envelope with no better results. So I produced my spoon, hoping to relieve the tension, which was becoming noticeable. Geller held out the spoon horizontally by the bowl while he stroked the handle delicately with one forefinger. For all his ferocious expression the spoon remained unmoved. 'Metal,' he said suddenly. 'We need some metal.' The room seemed bereft of metal fittings. Anyway, why metal when all that was needed was the Geller effect? We upended one of the armchairs in search of metal but the castors were plastic. There was an aluminium joint deep between the legs. He bent over it. 'There,' he said, straightening up and brandishing the slightly bent spoon. I could not see whether or not he exerted enough force to help it.

He was having a bad psi day. As usual the paranormal was refusing to come when called. I produced the mystery playing card in its sealed envelope. 'Who put the card in?' 'A lady friend.' 'And she didn't show it to you? You have no idea what it is?' 'Of course not.' 'All right.' He held up the envelope between us. We stared at it from opposite sides for long minutes. 'Are you getting anything? What are you getting? Are you getting a number?' 'A large number,' I said. 'So am I.' Something made me say I thought it was Clubs. 'I was getting Clubs,' he said quickly. 'What number? It's the…it's the ten!' From somewhere I had a prompt. 'It's the eight,' I said confidently, though I didn't know why. Geller considered this. 'No,' he said finally, 'It's the ten.' We opened the envelope. It was the eight of Clubs. Geller was examining it as if he had never seen a playing card before. 'Fantastic!' he said, not at all put out. 'I was quite sure. I counted the spots again and again and made it ten...and look! There *are* ten clubs on it. One, two, three, four, five, six, seven, eight – and the two little ones in the corners. Ten!' His confidence was amazing. 'There you are!' Yes, there I was – holding the eight of clubs, I pointed out. But I was not the world-famous clairvoyant. He was. So it goes.

The experience did not make a sceptic of me. I have no doubt that Uri Geller genuinely bent spoons galore in favourable circumstances because in favourable circumstances, I discovered, I could do it too. I found this out in the company of forty-odd parapsychologists from both sides of the Atlantic gathered for a conference at Trinity College, Cambridge. For days we listened to papers of the utmost tedium describing experiments with card-guessing, coin-tossing, dice-throwing, piling up mind-numbing statistics which failed to convince any of us that we had got anywhere near the nature of psi, that mystical grail they were searching for. The elders of the British delegation from the SPR said we were no nearer understanding psi than the society's founders were a hundred years earlier.

On the last afternoon the younger members of the American Parapsychology Association announced they were giving a party that night in a room above the college dining hall and we should all collect spoons from there on our way up. We stood about rather self-consciously holding drinks in one hand and spoons in the other – or forks, because the college's supply of spoons had soon run out. 'All you gotta do is relax!' we were told. 'Act like it's a normal party. If anyone's spoon bends, raise an arm and shout. Once it starts we may get a window.' Ten minutes or so later there was a scream from a woman waving her spoon aloft. Soon there was another call, and another. 'I've got PK!' yelled an exultant American academic.

Suddenly PK (psycho-kinesis, the power of mind to move matter) was busting out all over. With joyful cries people were showing each other their contorted, corkscrewed cutlery. I had almost forgotten I was holding mine when I felt its stem give way, as if it suddenly felt tired. With no help from me the spoon handle had looped the loop, rolling itself into a neat little ring too small for my finger to fit into it. Another spoon I had went the same way so I took the copper bracelet from my wrist and straightened it out flat. As I held it, it wrapped itself twice round my fourth finger so swiftly that I couldn't see it happen. Copper is bendable but to curl it into these two small perfect circles one outside the other was far beyond my skill. Everyone assured each other that they hadn't cheated. There was no need to – and what would have been the point?

Our 'window' lasted about half an hour. We ran out of things to bend. Even knife blades had parted from their handles. By the time the party broke up thirty-something out of at most forty people present had watched their cutlery bend unaided – a success rate unimaginable in a laboratory. What had been going on? Clearly certain helpful conditions had been present. We had group cohesion, from having shared in the conference over three days. We were tuned to the same aim, the pursuit of psi. We had relaxed and treated the occasion like a children's party game, some sitting in circles on the floor shouting 'bend!' Whatever energy these conditions released came from a collective circle of human minds. How this could affect the rigidity of metal or the stasis of matter I could not and cannot explain.

A professor of mathematics at King's College, London, John Taylor, investigated thirty-four youngsters who could freely bend spoons and keys. He speculated that it could be an electro-magnetic force activated by the electricity of the brain, coiled up like an aerial. But the brain's electric charge is not enough to light a small light bulb. Another mystery is why this phenomenon was never reported in previous generations. Besides, what we experienced was not our efforts to make our spoons bend but their collective decision to bend seemingly of their own accord.

If as Einstein told us matter and energy are interchangeable, then one kind of energy (mental) was acting on another kind (matter), which seems plausible, even probable.

I never succeeded in bending spoons on my own. But for years I kept my rolled-up teaspoons and copper rings on my desk as a reminder of what can happen when The Force is with you. Maybe one day we will know how it works and what to call it.

Matthew Manning

One viewer who was especially interested in Geller's feats was a boy just out of school named Matthew Manning. His adolescence had been troubled by violent and spectacular poltergeist activity, both in his home and at school. He found he could bend metal quite as easily as Geller did, choosing keys for his experiments. In one test he bent seven out of eight Yale-type keys by up to thirty-five degrees. He amazed assembled scientists at a conference on psycho-kinesis in Toronto by bending metal rods in glass-encased dials at a distance by simple willpower. I read his then unpublished account of his extraordinary youthful experiences and went to find him at his home in Cambridgeshire. He was then twenty-two, long-haired in seventies fashion with a moustache and wispy fringe of beard that gave him a faint resemblance to the Saviour in some romantic paintings. He smiled placatingly as if to excuse the weirdness of his story. He showed me over his charming Queen Anne home, where his father worked as an architect. The drawing room had been violently disarranged every night when he was younger though his father had surrounded it with string which was never disturbed.

Then we went into a small panelled room downstairs where he used to sleep. The panelling was painted white but it looked grey because of the mass of pencilled signatures that covered it from floor to ceiling. Some were large, sprawling signatures decorated in the Elizabethan style with Xs like crisscrossed ribbons. Others were cramped and tiny. Some were squeezed on to curved surfaces in the ceiling cornice, for instance, where no human hand could find room to write anything. The handwriting was antique in style, often accompanied by dates ranging from 1555 to 1792. More than five hundred names had appeared over a period of six days and nights. The pencils which were left in the room were never observed to move from their place but when members of the family entered they often found a new signature had been added, sometimes only half-finished as if the writer had been interrupted. Pencils grew blunt and, according to Matthew, had to be regularly sharpened. His parents and siblings all agreed that the names appeared without any help from him or themselves.

The first and largest signature was that of Robert Webbe, the merchant who had owned and rebuilt the house in 1730 and died in 1733. Matthew was in correspondence with Robert Webbe through automatic writing. When he emptied his mind and allowed his hand to move without giving it directions, Webbe 'came through' and claimed to be responsible for the signatures. When Matthew's father said: 'Tell Webbe not to write on the walls,' the reply came back: 'I will write as I like. They are my walls. It is my house.'

Webbe also manifested himself physically, by smell. Sudden odours of tobacco smoke, musty books, bad breath would occur on the staircase. Occasionally the front door would open unassisted and loud footsteps would be heard in the hall. They tried putting a tray of sand inside the door. Imprints of a short foot and the points of two sticks were found in the sand.

Over six years their automatic correspondence grew to thousands of words. One of Webbe's communications read: 'You talk to me in mine head. Who are you? Are you the ghost this voyce talks of? I cannot see you but I hear this voyce for many years and I know I go madd. Are you a ghoulle of tomorrow?' The message seemed to come from a past presence haunted by a present one. Webbe was very proud of his house, which he had transformed into that of a Georgian gentleman but he did not live long to enjoy it. Matthew imagined that he was trapped in it by his possessiveness. 'I provided enough psychic energy to allow him to make contact with the present'. Could different eras in time interact – in this case the 1730s with the 1970s? Can consciousness time-travel? Other people have claimed to have experienced time-slips, indeed I have myself. If reality is the product of our consciousness and consciousness does not die with us, then all times could exist simultaneously and be available if only you could

Two fragile couples in fragile harmony: the Oliviers welcome the Millers,
Arthur and Marilyn, to England on 16th July 1956, before the filming
began which was to disturb it for all of them
Courtesy Daily Mail

Bertrand Russell, eighty-eight, sitting on the pavement of Whitehall in protest against Britain's nuclear deterrent, undeterred by likely imprisonment
Courtesy Daily Mail

Symbols of female fifties Britain –
sex and money – Diana Dors (right,
Courtesy Getty Images) shows off
her assets, Lady Docker (below) her
gold-plated Daimler

Comedian and film-maker Jacques Tati in his unforgettable character, M. Hulot

The Maharishi brought
Transcendental Meditation
and 'bliss' to sixties London
Courtesy Daily Mail

Tigress tragedian Anna Magnani,
who portrayed anything but bliss
Courtesy Getty Images

New playwrights…

Harold Pinter (above) gives a note to Vivien Merchant, his wife, before transmission of his latest television play, while Tony Stoppard (left) arrives in 1967 with a debt to Shakespeare

A very teenage Juliet wonders what hit her: Judi Dench with Peggy Mount as
her nurse, Old Vic theatre, 1960
Courtesy Daily Mail

Albert Speer with Hitler looking at dream plans for a future Berlin, while (below) Alec Guinness as Hitler contemplates the model city of Germania, formerly known as Berlin
Courtesy Getty Images

Ralph Richardson gives the Glare appearing at the post-Olivier National Theatre
Courtesy Alastair Muir

Paranormal rivals of the seventies:
Uri Geller (above) and Matthew
Manning (left) exercising
persuasion over a fork

Party Girl: Pat Harmsworth, Lady Rothermere (aka 'Bubbles'),
who wanted them never to stop
Courtesy Dave Bennett

The Boat People trying to escape Communist Vietnam, off the coast of Malaysia
Courtesy Daily Mail

Below, the boat comes ashore to a waiting crowd's hostile reception

Andy Warhol flits like a ghost through London, 1975
Courtesy Daily Mail

America's pessimists: Gore Vidal at his Italian ivory tower, 'The Swallow's Nest', Ravello; Kurt Vonnegut, grimly humorous survivor of the Dresden bombing, February 1945, in underground meat locker, *Slaughterhouse-Five*

A blithe Studs Terkel, radio's gravel voice from the streets of Chicago

A worried John Betjeman: 'How are you, John?' 'Absolutely terrified!'

Laurie Lee (above) at home in The Woolpack, Slad, his birthplace; John Mortimer (le giving a false impression of amused idleness
Courtesy Daily Mail

access them. Modern physics postulates parallel dimensions. Why not parallel times?

Besides automatic writing, Matthew produced automatic drawing in the styles of dead artists. In no more than twenty minutes I watched as he drew a pen and ink sketch of a nineteenth-century French lawyer in gown and floppy legal cap. He signed it with a monogram – the letters H and D. 'Who's that?' he asked. 'I've never seen anything like it before.' To my eyes it was a very convincing Henri Daumier, who caricatured French lawyers in just this manner. He claimed never to have heard of Daumier. He gave me the drawing and I searched Daumier's works, feeling certain that I would find the original there. But I didn't. Matthew had no talent for drawing except when in his trance-like state – this was confirmed by his family and the art teacher at his old school.

Most of his drawings were not good enough to pass muster as being by the artists whose work they resembled. The Daumier did. So did his version of Durer's famous Rhinoceros, which he had done in all its complexity, seemingly without effort. I borrowed it and took it to the British Museum, which owns the original. I showed it to the keeper of prints and drawings, who examined it without questioning its Durer-like quality. I did not tell him its provenance right away. He sent for the original to compare them. Side by side they looked like mirror images, one with the rhinoceros facing left, the other facing right. There were tiny differences. The decorative scrolls and curlicues around the animal's armour were even more complex in Matthew's version. You would have said they were drawings by the same hand – or that of a master forger. The keeper admitted it was a remarkably accurate copy. 'Who did it?' When I told him his attitude changed abruptly. 'You can see right away that it has no real quality.' But this was exactly what people, including himself, did not see. To draw it from memory would have taken a sort of genius. So by what power of imagination had it been produced?

Matthew grew tired of being exhibited as a freak. He spent a few years being sent from laboratory to laboratory, performing kinetic experiments with metal and machinery and appearing on believe-it-or-not programmes on television. He caused chaos across Japan.

According to Japanese press reports, when he appeared on the screen bottles hurled themselves to the ground, taps, fire alarms and car engines switched on, banknotes caught fire, light bulbs exploded and clocks went berserk. Matthew was not proud of these unintended effects. 'I was a performing monkey. All I left behind me was bent metal, broken glass, wiped tapes and disabled electrical equipment. My only qualification was for appearing on talk shows.' He'd left it too late to go to university. He put his strange capabilities to more constructive use by becoming a healer, channelling his supernormal energies into other people's bodies. He soon had a waiting list of patients and a success rate which he modestly estimated as a third. He said success did not depend on whether the patient believed in him or not. He does not know how it works.

DICKENSIAN GHOSTS

Many readers of the foregoing paranormalities will dismiss them as examples of self-delusion, wishful thinking, hallucination or trickery. Or they may think I'm lying. For some reason, I have often noted, disbelievers in the paranormal disbelieve far more fiercely than its believers believe. But there is no gainsaying personal experience of it. Once the nerves of your neck have prickled and your hair has stood up on end - and they really do – you agree with Hamlet's observation to the Horatios of this life that there are more things on heaven and earth than are dreamt of in their philosophy.

I used to be pretty familiar with poltergeists, for example. I have lived with them in three houses and stayed in several others. Our 1860s house in Hampstead, which was being radically restored, seemed to set off a restless spirit or source of energy in its empty frame. Preternaturally loud, crunchingly heavy footsteps made a habit of mounting the bare staircase. On the first occasion my wife and I froze as the footsteps mounted to the first floor kitchen where we were sitting, crossed the landing and stopped dead outside the closed door. I flung it open. The landing, and the rest of the house, was empty but for us. On the top floor of the house where I was decorating in the evenings the footsteps would often follow me. Charlie, my decorator, heard them too. He refused to go up there alone

A Blackheath house, dating from circa 1840, had a habit of swallowing objects of value. Keys and watches and bits of jewellery would regularly go missing and stay missing despite diligent searches. Weeks later they would reappear in obvious places, like mantlepieces and top drawers, which had been regularly searched. More footsteps, light and scampering this time, accompanied by vague childish voices, would pass rapidly along the outer wall of my bedroom, beyond which there was no path but a shrubbery. Indeed they seemed to come from within the wall itself. Outside the room weird metallic smells would suddenly meet my nostrils as I reached the door, growing in intensity then vanishing as suddenly as they came. Trivial though they seem, such experiences leave you feeling that some kind of source is manifesting itself to gain your attention. It happened again at a flat in Marylebone, on the first floor of a standard late-eighteenth-century terrace in London brick dating from the 1770s. Heavy demolition and rebuilding in the basement shook the house for weeks and seemed to trigger off electrical trickery. At night when the house was quiet a kettle would turn itself on unaided; then the electric mixer, television set and CD player followed suit. A standard lamp turned itself on and off at intervals. Once, having left the flat in darkness, my companion returned to find it ablaze with light and noise. Every light (and the electric fire) was on while radio and television boomed away at full volume. Yet the outer door was still locked. There was no break-in.

The most disturbed house of all I came across on a weekend house-hunting expedition on the Suffolk-Essex border. It was an attractive white house set on the edge of a village in a valley with a stream wandering through its large garden. A curious feature of the prospectus was that it was on offer as it stood, complete with all the furniture. The price, 'for quick sale', was a bargain. Four or five of us split up to explore it separately. With two staircases and many rooms we scarcely saw one another. Alone in the main drawing room lined with well-filled bookcases I wondered why I had so strong a feeling that it was a bargain not to take, although it fulfilled my requirements admirably. I climbed the steep garden path to the road where I had parked the car opposite a terrace of old cottages. The occupant of one of them was leaning on his gate. 'Thinking of buying it?' he enquired. I asked if he knew anything about the house. He looked surprised. 'Don't you know what happened there?' He told me a television executive with three young children had lived there apparently happily until a few weeks earlier. 'Then the wife killed herself. With a knife. With the children there.'

I went back saying nothing to anyone except that it was time to go home. In the car nobody spoke – the mood was strangely subdued.

THE SEVENTIES

At last Georgie, my elder daughter, asked me: 'Are you thinking of buying it?' I said I definitely wasn't. 'Oh good. That's all right, then.' Everyone, it transpired, had felt acutely uncomfortable in the house but Georgie, a prey to the paranormal, had felt drawn powerfully along an upstairs corridor into a barely furnished bedroom. A force had pushed her hard in the chest up against the wall and the voice of a distressed woman kept repeating the same indistinct words over and over. She had the impression of blood dribbling down the wall to the floorboards. I sent back the key. The agents, whom I never met, didn't even inquire whether I was interested.

No doubt many people could duplicate or outdo paranormal experiences such as these. England must be full of ancient places which bear traces of the lives lived in them long ago. It is a question of whether you can tune into, access or energise them. Sometimes, however, they seem strong enough to energise you. I had already seen two ghosts, or so I concluded, at Stowe, but they at least seemed to be alive, though living in a previous century. Later on, just off Fleet Street, I came across one that was dead.

Hanging Sword Alley no longer exists. It was obliterated by office development in the 1970s. But for hundreds of years before that it ran, straight and narrow and steeply climbing, between the lower end of Whitefriars Street, where the *Daily Mail* offices stood, and Fleet Street, by way of Salisbury Square. The Alley street sign hung above a flight of steps that led to it beside a pub called the Harrow, much patronised by *Daily Mail* journalists. From the steps it ran between the tall walls of Victorian printing shops or blackened warehouses. Here and there was a recessed entrance, a doorway with a couple of steps. You could imagine the hanging sword which once must have marked one of these premises' predecessors to advertise – what? An armourers? A fencing academy? Or a tavern?

I only walked along the alley at night. It was a short cut from the pub, where Patricia and I sometimes spent the supper break from the night production shift, to Fleet Street, where we worked for newspapers on opposite sides of the street. One night we cut through the alley, though it was dark, empty and felt vaguely disquieting but we were late and it would save time. You could see to the end of it and there was absolutely no sign of life ahead of us as we hurried along. Both of us stopped dead at the same moment and froze. My spine and neck clenched as if seized by a claw. Slowly both of us looked round. In an entrance we had just passed, on a step, someone had left a large bulging sack. Neither of us had noticed it as we passed. It could have been one of those sacks of waste paper commonly seen around printing works. But sticking out of the neck of the sack was a hand. It was a large human hand, spread out and catching the light from a single street-lamp at the crossing of two alleys where we stopped.

I was not keen to investigate but I felt compelled to step back a few paces and draw level with it. It was definitely a hand, not a glove, emerging from the sack at waist height. The skin texture, the veins, knuckles, even pores of the back of a human hand stood out illuminated in extreme clarity. I wanted to touch it but couldn't bring myself to. I can't explain why. After some moments' scrutiny I backed away to where Patricia was standing as if transfixed. 'It's a hand.' I said unnecessarily. But whose? The sack was quite large enough for a body to be stuffed in it. Without another word we hastened nervously on up the alley to the lights of Fleet Street.

The hand belonged to a body, we felt certain. 'Phone the police,' she said. 'I don't know what it is – I'd better go back for another look.' 'Don't,' she said, but I did. I re-entered Hanging Sword Alley, treading on needles. I searched for the doorway. The only entrance I could see looked somehow different. It was in the same place but there was no sack, no hand, nothing and nobody in sight. How can you report a body that is no longer there? Had it ever been there? I might have doubted this but two of us had seen it and felt the same nervous shock at the moment we did so. The unusual clarity with which the hand had impressed itself, coupled with its equally sudden disappearance, made me suspicious. Only a couple of minutes had elapsed before I revisited the spot and there was nowhere along the alley where it could easily have been concealed. The doorway I was looking at was locked, dusty and neglected. It looked as if it hadn't been opened in years. Could we have experienced a time-slip? Could the sack have materialised from another century? But why, and why there?

The Seventies

It was forty years later that I discovered, at least, why there. A friend to whom I was telling the story said sharply: 'Hanging Sword Alley? But that's in Dickens!' And so it is, in *A Tale of Two Cities*, although I had never made the connection. It was where Jerry Cruncher lodged. Besides being the doorman of Tellson's Bank in Fleet Street, Jerry Cruncher pursues a secret off-duty hobby. He is a body-snatcher who goes out 'fishing' at night with a gang, fishing for newly buried corpses. Dickens did not choose Hanging Sword Alley for his abode without good reason. In 1775, when the story is set, the alley was the centre of the 'Resurrectionist' trade. There was a brisk demand for corpses in the City of London for anatomical dissection in the medical schools. A newly exhumed corpse would fetch twenty guineas. Body snatchers would haul them across London if necessary to find the highest bidder.

Not all the corpses had been exhumed. The alleys between Fleet Street and the River Thames were the haunt of eighteenth-century criminals, thieves and cutpurses. Their technique was to accost strangers in Fleet Street, lure them to their lodgings with the promise of drink or women, make them drunk, rob them and in some cases knife them for their value as anatomical specimens. The hanging sword, which may have been a trader's advertisement in Tudor times, took on a far more sinister connotation. The records of the Old Bailey bore out the alley's criminal connections. Dickens could not have picked a better spot for finding bodies in. And nor could I.

LAURENCE OLIVIER

A mystery clings to the name of Laurence Olivier. He was acknowledged to be the greatest actor of his time, a successor to Garrick, Kean and Irving. But he was one of a generation of magnificent classical actors of whom he was not always the best, nor even sometimes the equal. The roll call ranged from John Gielgud, Ralph Richardson, Michael Redgrave, Alec Guinness to Paul Scofield and each of them could touch depths that were outside his range. He was simply the most heroic – and at the ideal time for heroic acting. His film portrayal of Henry V in 1944, expressly made to boost wartime morale, had audiences standing and cheering in the cinemas. Unhappy the land that needs heroes to worship but at that moment we did. And his stage performances emanated a sense of barely contained animal ferocity that was suited to the moment. This established a pre-eminence that he never lost afterwards.

At his peak I was as dazzled by him as anyone in the wartime seasons in which he and Ralph Richardson led the bombed-out Old Vic Company at the New Theatre. In the brilliant sunshine of the doodlebug summer of 1944, on school holidays aged sixteen, I picked my way round the rubble to St Martin's Lane to attend the first matinee of his *Richard III* which had been hailed as miraculous in that morning's papers. I still have the programme which cost sixpence and was no bigger than a folded handkerchief with scarcely room to list the cast. On the dimly lit open stage a wicket gate could be made out, nothing else. A silhouette in a floppy hat unlatched the gate and limped towards us. All you could make out was a nose. It was the lopsided, menacing walk that did it. Then the nose was joined by satanically gleaming eyes. By the time this creature spoke the outside world, the theatre itself, had been wiped from one's consciousness. The voice was light, that of an amused observer of our winter of discontent. The words 'made summer by this sun of York' were held up for our inspection, the final K pricking the air. The audience was transfixed – and we hadn't even seen the hump until he turned to leave. I had never experienced anything like it. It was a 'first' as indelible as the first cigarette, the first air flight, the first sexual thrill. Reared on nothing more challenging than West End domestic comedies and farces, I was blown away by the effect of supercharged acting on the nervous system. It hooked me like a powerful drug and changed my life. My addiction to the theatre was lifelong and later made me a critic.

Ralph Richardson was an equal revelation as Peer Gynt and especially as Falstaff, a performance that was universally hailed as definitive. He was supported by a totally changed Olivier, first as Ibsen's sallow and sinister Button Moulder then as a deliciously doddery Mr Justice Shallow. Shallow's session of drunken reminiscence in his orchard was revealed as one of the funniest crosstalk scenes in Shakespeare – 'And is old Double dead?' – 'Dead.' As the list of his deceased friends grew longer Olivier was no longer sounding the inquiry 'Dead?' It was enough to open and shut his mouth upon it silently with a quiver of the jaw. His variety was astonishing. Immediately after his famous blood-freezing howl as the blinded Oedipus the double bill closed with his gossipy, snuff-box-snapping Mr Puff in Sheridan's *The Critic*. Even in such a trifle he had to make a showman's exit, being suddenly swept up to the flies on wires, still talking as he vanished behind the proscenium arch.

In the midst of such triumphs he and Richardson were summarily dismissed by the Old Vic's chairman, the foolish Lord Esher, on the snobbish grounds that two actors could not possibly run a company which was bidding fair to become the new National Theatre. But it was back at the restored Old Vic fifteen years later in 1963 that Olivier established that long promised, long deferred dream. For another twelve years until the dream was made concrete on a monster scale on the South Bank, he created a National company of mostly young actors like an old-style actor-manager, mentor and father figure to his troupe. The brief golden age he created there is now largely forgotten, except by those ageing and distinguished actors who began or developed their careers there – such as Albert Finney, Michael Gambon, Anthony Hopkins, Derek Jacobi, Geraldine McEwan and Joan Plowright. Maggie Smith, already a West End star, gave up her percentage of the box office for the beggarly-rewarded challenge of the new National. In the early days there was a strong family spirit. Olivier hung out with his actors, lunched in the canteen with them, was generous with advice on the craft of which he was a master – such as: 'In tragedy, go for the laughs.' He believed in acting for acting's sake and when asked what was his policy for the theatre replied, 'To make the audience applaud.' Applause was his life support. There could never be enough of it.

Of his own Shakespearean performances the most quoted was the controversial Othello of 1964. As one of the last white actors to black up for the part he delivered a Moor in full negro character – splayed bare feet, swaying gait, rolling whites of the eyeballs, thickened consonants and deepened vowels. It was a tour de force but for some good judges too near caricature. 'Unspeakably vulgar' was John Osborne's verdict. Sybil Thorndike said he 'lacked the deep agony of the part'. Personally I found it visually fascinating but emotionally empty. It seemed mean-spirited, if not cowardly, to have chosen an inexperienced Frank Finlay to play Iago. Olivier knew how easily Iago can steal the play because he had done so himself in Ralph Richardson's pre-war *Othello*. The imbalance between them as tempter and tempted robbed Othello of some of our sympathy. Finlay, new to Shakespeare, didn't stand a chance and was obliterated. As was intended. Why not cast Albert Finney or Robert Stephens? They could have stood up to him. Of course when filmed his stagey acting looked almost embarrassingly over the top.

'Success won't last – it never does,' Olivier prophesied to Robert Stephens, then his right-hand man. So it proved. There were some disastrous experiments with foreign plays usually promoted by Kenneth Tynan, whom Olivier had appointed the company's dramaturg to get him off the critic's bench. As a result he had to act the company out of several financial crises. Two of his best parts were the brutal husband of Strindberg's hate-marriage in *The Dance of Death* and as the mean, disillusioned actor-husband James Tyrone in Eugene O'Neill's study of his own miserable family in *Long Day's Journey into Night*. But the biggest drawback was Olivier's failing health. All too frequently bouts of serious illness took him away for long periods until the National Theatre Board looked round for a successor, agreed on Peter Hall, founder of the rival Royal Shakespeare Company, and surreptitiously set up the transition while keeping Olivier in the dark. When the news leaked to the press in 1971 Olivier reacted like a wounded tiger. 'I've been given the boot – again!' he protested, referring to the Old Vic's previous dismissal. What made it insufferable to him was to be displaced by Peter Hall, the object of his venomous dislike. Non-acting autocratic directors from university were a type which he distrusted. Besides he had initially offered to make Hall his Number Two. 'Sorry, Larry, I'm going to make it as Number One,' Hall had told him.

Olivier saw the National as an actors' theatre and wanted an actor to succeed him – but he did not have a credible candidate to suggest. Those names he had toyed with, such as Richard Burton, were not available. So he departed from the National in 1974 in a mood of high resentment, shared by 'his' company. When the new building did at last open he refused to set foot in it, except once to welcome the Queen. The whole handover did immense harm to the morale of the old company and to the new Hall regime. When I wrote a book about the National's history I found nobody who was prepared to tell the whole truth about it, including Sir Max Rayne, who as chairman had the last word. They were too frightened of offending Olivier.

For all the fulsome tributes paid him I never met anyone associated with his company who was not, at least, wary of him, or nervous or distrustful. I always felt it was like dealing with an untamed animal; you could never be sure whether it would turn on you. 'Scratch an actor and you'll find an actor,' he was quoted as saying. He was always acting so who was the real Olivier? There was a deep fault in his character which could make him mean-spirited, explosively angry and insanely jealous of anyone's success but his own. 'How was Hopkins?' he would ask his hospital visitors, when his understudy Anthony Hopkins had taken over his part in *The Dance of Death*. 'Not *better* than me?' But years earlier when Hopkins was not doing well in a part he hated,

Macbeth, Denis Quilley was suddenly asked to take over, with the explanation: 'Tony's fucked off!' Quilley suggested he should ring him and ask him to stay until he had had a chance to learn the lines. Olivier went purple with rage, he told me. 'He bellowed, "Don't go near the phone! I never want to see the little bastard in this building ever again!"' Robert Stephens, before his death, gave me the clearest assessment of working as Olivier's associate director – until they fell out. 'He wasn't a man you could say No to – it had to be Yes, Yes, Yes! Though he encouraged his actors he found it very hard to squeeze out a compliment. The minute we began to emerge [he and his then wife, Maggie Smith] as a leading couple he became suspicious. Were we planning a takeover? Larry was jealous of everyone if he felt they might be better than him. The stage was his boxing ring. He wasn't going to lose a fight.'

His rages were legendary and his rudeness gratuitous. Critics he loathed as necessary evils, though he read them – hence his keenness to muzzle Tynan. I was to discover this at our first meeting, at a theatrical reception at Number 10. I had no idea he was there – his lack of height concealed him in a crowd. I was talking to his wife Joan Plowright when, nervously, I recognised his face disguised in thick boardroom spectacles approaching behind her. 'Oh, Larry,' she said sociably, 'do you know Peter Lewis?' – and unfortunately for me added 'the critic.' Unexpectedly coming face to face with someone I had so long admired, I stammered foolishly to the effect that although I had watched him for so many years, I had somehow never yet managed to meet and get to know him. His extraordinarily long, dangerous upper lip gave a twitch that I remembered from his Richard III. With the cutting voice of Richard contemplating a victim he said: 'We can leave it like that *if you like*' – the final K puncturing the air just as it had in 'this sun of York' – and was gone. Alan Brien, the long-time critic of the *Sunday Telegraph*, consoled me with his experience of telling Olivier a story at a party. 'He suddenly interrupted me, saying, "Have you seen my wife anywhere? If you do, tell her I want to go home!"' Alan got his comeback over Othello. He pronounced it as 'the kind of bad acting of which only a great actor is capable'.

The most damaging consequence of his fear of being outshone was his failure to invite any of his great contemporaries to perform at the National Theatre, where the public surely had every right to expect to see them. Where was Richardson, with whom he had shared so many memorable triumphs? He was certainly hoping to be offered a worthwhile part, he told me, but it never came. 'I suppose he didn't buy my acting.' This could hardly be true – had he never been asked? Sir Ralph fractionally lifted a stone which he would have preferred to have left unturned. 'Well, he did once ask me to play some old *dukes*. I said I'd played those old dukes before. I wanted something new.' Old dukes, of course, are never the lead. And Alec Guinness? 'Well, one has to be asked,' he told me poker-faced. He had once been sounded out about a possible *Merchant of Venice* but it came to nothing. Surely, I said, he was a natural choice for Shylock? 'Oh, the part wasn't going to be Shylock. It was Antonio.' I expressed amazement. 'Of course one didn't know who had it in mind to play Shylock.' One did by then. Guinness thought that Olivier did not rate him highly as an actor. He had recently done Malvolio in a starry television production with Ralph Richardson and Joan Plowright. Olivier had seized his arm after watching the run-through and said, 'Fascinating! I never realised before that Malvolio could be played as a bore.'

Michael Redgrave had contributed a legendary Uncle Vanya to Olivier's preparatory season at Chichester which then transferred to the first Old Vic season. But once there Olivier practically drove him from the stage. In the rehearsals for the unhappy *Hamlet* he directed he humiliated him in front of the company by snapping, 'What's wrong with you? You were fine as Macbeth. But as Claudius you are dim.' When Ibsen's *The Master Builder* came into the repertoire and Redgrave found it hard to make Solness's lines stick, Olivier was merciless. He treated it as if the problem was drink. After a less than perfect, nervy first night he berated him in his dressing room as having let down the company and ended viciously by saying he himself would take the part next season and invited Redgrave to come and see it. As a result Redgrave lost his nerve – the very considerable nerve it takes even a first-class actor to face an audience, especially a first-night one. He told me that 'a wall of fear' came down between him and the audience (ironically enough Olivier was to suffer this himself during the run of

Othello). 'For the first time in my life I felt appalled at the thought of having to go on stage. I used to dread the car coming to take me to the theatre.' Yet he had been at the height of his power to move audiences as Uncle Vanya – the best, most heart-stopping I have ever seen – earlier in the same season. 'Now,' he told me, 'I have been made to feel a…d-d-duffer.' Secretly I wondered if the fact that he had scooped the best notices for *Uncle Vanya*, in which Olivier had appeared as Astrov, had triggered Olivier's insulting behaviour. Also he had discovered that Solness was a juicy part. In time their respective performances were compared and several critics preferred Redgrave's.

Olivier's admitted jealousy of John Gielgud went back to 1935, when they alternated in the part of Romeo and Gielgud's was acclaimed by many as the better. It seemed remarkable that our greatest classical actor never appeared at the National Theatre. When he finally did so, as Oedipus in the Seneca play *Oedipus*, it was under the guest director, Peter Brook, at his most iconoclastic. Olivier hated Brook's stylised production and raged at Brook in Gielgud's dressing room, slamming the door so hard that he cracked the mirror on the back of it. Gielgud, who had humbly gone along with Brook's opening weeks of improvisatory exercises and the unclassical staging, full of ritual and chanting chorus work, soon longed to escape. He was embarrassed by the controversial ending when, the tragedy over, a ten-foot golden phallus was drawn on stage for a fertility dance to a jazz rendering of the song, 'Yes! We have no bananas!' In this cavorting Gielgud declined to take part. Nor did he play again at Olivier's National.

Olivier's jealousy of Paul Scofield went back to the brilliant and world-famous *King Lear* Scofield had performed in Peter Brook's production for the RSC. It had made Olivier's own Lear, in some people's opinion, look too much like Father Christmas. When at last he took the National stage it was as *The Captain of Kopenick*, a satire on German subservience to authority. It told the true story of a down-and-out called Wilhelm Voight, who one day put on a Prussian officer's uniform and found that all the doors that had been closed to him were flung open by the grovelling mayor of the town and his minions. Scofield was a wonder of seedy bullied hopelessness transformed by his uniform into the bully himself. 'Scofield is the best Voight I have ever seen,' said the playwright, Carl Zuckmayer. Nevertheless after the repeated curtain calls on the first night Olivier reassured the astonished Scofield: 'Don't worry, Paulie, *we'll get it right*.' Get it right? A mere thirty performances were scheduled, all sold out. Soon afterwards Scofield, who had been appointed associate director and tipped as Olivier's successor, resigned. Guinness voiced the opinion that 'Olivier completely destroyed Redgrave and tried to destroy Scofield'.

The final stroke of jealous ill will came a few years after Peter Hall was established at the National in his place. Olivier had retired to the film studios to play lucrative cameos. Joan Plowright had accepted the role of Martha in Albee's *Who's Afraid of Virginia Woolf?* which was about to open on the South Bank. She had cooked her husband's breakfast and seen him off to the film studios before opening a long envelope addressed to her. It was from his lawyer. It expressed regret at the couple's decision to divorce and offered to help if possible. This was a total shock. When she confronted Olivier with his unheralded decision to divorce her his reply, she told me, was: 'No wife of mine is going to appear at Peter Hall's National Theatre!' As indeed she didn't. The play's opening was deferred at the last minute on the grounds that she had 'lost her voice'. Her husband later wrote her a letter of apology for his behaviour but she naturally nursed a resentment that he assumed her career, as a star actress, should be subjected to his personal grudge.

So it is hard to admire the heights of Olivier's achievements as an actor without it bringing to mind his degree of egotism rare even in the theatre. His memoirs, *Confessions of an Actor*, contain almost not a single acknowledgement of any performances given by his great contemporaries. They themselves admired his technical prowess but few of them actually warmed to his acting. Gielgud, most generous in praising other actors and himself universally loved in the profession, would not be drawn on the Shakespearean rival with whom he was so often compared. 'Great shouts!' he once muttered when I raised the subject of Olivier performances. Scofield said he admired his magnetism and physical presence 'but I was not on the whole moved by him'. Redgrave said nothing but would not go to see him perform.

Guinness, who had once played the Fool to Olivier's Lear (and was thought by some to have outshone him) thought him technically brilliant 'but he always left me rather cold'.

The fact was that Olivier did not 'do' poetry – his Hamlet showed that. But give him a character part, in which he could disguise himself with infinite attention to detail, a Richard III, a Justice Shallow, a Tattle, a Captain Brazen, an Archie Rice, a James Tyrone and he would romp away with it brilliantly. Interviewed on three successive nights on television he characteristically appeared in a completely different guise on each occasion, wrong-footing a baffled Melvyn Bragg. He never stopped seeking acclaim, even though he had received as much of it as any actor could dream of. When I last saw him, frail and aged, the day after he had played John Mortimer's father on television in *A Voyage Round My Father*, I told him how moving he had been in his deathbed scene. He uncoiled like a lizard in the sun and basked in the praise. No one could do enough to satisfy that ego which demanded to be basted and basted yet more.

Ironical thoughts like these occupied me at his memorial service in Westminster Abbey, which was choreographed and directed by Patrick Garland like a royal funeral. The great contemporaries he had undervalued processed up the nave to the altar bearing on velvet cushions the insignia of Laurence Olivier, knight and lord of the theatre. His OM was followed by crowns he had worn as Lear and other kings, and Edmund Kean's sword, which had been passed on to him by Gielgud (who then outlived him by many years) but which he did not pass on in his turn. The procession included even a model of the National Theatre building in which he had refused to set foot. The sword was borne by Frank Finlay, whom he had purposely eclipsed as his Iago in *Othello*. The stars whom he so conspicuously failed to invite to join 'his' National Theatre took part with suitably respectful mien. Paul Scofield and John Gielgud read beautifully. Alec Guinness delivered the encomium on his greatness with total aplomb. The ceremony was a feast of actors playing their required parts – which, I suppose, was only appropriate for someone who never stopped playing his.

THE TWO PETERS

Olivier's successor was the extreme antithesis of the actor-manager. Indeed Peter Hall banished that tradition by creating 'Director's Theatre'. Two Peters, Peter Hall and Peter Brook, dominated a revolution in the sixties, by making the director, not the actors, the star of any production. Both products of Oxbridge, with no professional acting experience, they took a grip on the classical stage when very young indeed. Brook began directing Shakespeare at the Stratford Memorial seasons when he was twenty-two. Having seen his work there Hall, who was five years younger, made a vow he would run the place one day. He was doing so by the age of thirty and created the Royal Shakespeare Company. The first person he invited to be a co-director was Brook. Instead of becoming rivals they became close friends and collaborators. Together they looked to me like gleeful schoolboys who had the theatre scene wrapped up. They had – they had degrees in it.

One night over drinks in the Stratford theatre green room, Brook turned to me and suddenly asked: 'Don't *you* want to be a director?' He said it as if no other job in the world could possibly be worth one's time. Given my lack of qualifications I was nonplussed. 'Me? How could I?' Brook looked at Hall. 'Why not?' he said mildly. 'Think he could do it?' 'Why not?' said a beaming Hall. 'You must be joking,' I told them. In a sense they were but that moment revealed the way they regarded their position. Directors could not be trained – there was no training. Acting ability was irrelevant compared, say, to having had a toy theatre in youth. Apart from a discriminating knowledge of the repertoire the only essential requirement was self-belief – the belief that you could and should realise the classical texts on the stage. Both of them had been convinced of this since boyhood. And look!

A Rogues' Gallery

They had wiped everyone else off the map. People talked of Brook's, not Scofield's *Lear*, of Hall's, not Peggy Ashcroft's *Wars of the Roses*. Hall had made his name at the tiny Arts Theatre through the chance of directing *Waiting for Godot* in its first English production. Brook had taken *King Lear* into that very territory, an existential no-man's-land where Lear and his Fool conversed as if they were Beckett's two tramps, Vladimir and Estragon. They had founded a new style.

As the commandant of the RSC, Hall held court, initially with his wife Leslie Caron, at the company's grand regency villa, Avoncliffe, on the banks of the river, from which he sometimes travelled to work by motorboat. As the son of a rural stationmaster he seemed to exemplify the meritocratic sixties, in which you could become anything if you wanted it enough. With his dapper Elizabethan beard and trim moustache and slim Romeo and Juliet cigar he looked like The Man Who Had All The Luck, profiled in magazine after magazine. He loved wielding power for twenty-five hours in the day and blamed me for calling him 'power-mad' in print, an adjective repeated by many subsequent journalists. I was only reporting what others told me. 'Peter Hall?' Glenda Jackson had remarked irritably. 'I wish he'd stop pretending to be so bloody nice. He's a bloody dictator. OK. You have to have one.' Later he admitted, in reference to the enemies he made in his drive to the top, 'I walked over a lot of people without realising what I was doing.' But he was not as invulnerable as his ever-present smile suggested. One day at Avoncliffe, after Caron was gone and their two children were playing with model cars round our feet, we were comparing notes as divorced fathers trying to function part time. 'It's agony,' he said with quiet finality, 'and it never goes away.' That confession might have surprised some of those who saw him as a Genghis Khan.

His was the biggest classical company in the theatre. It was also the most talked about, thanks above all to Brook who produced one sensation after another. After his *Lear* with Scofield he had restaged *The Marat/Sade*, the murder of Marat in his bath which de Sade had put on with his fellow lunatics in the asylum at Charenton. It was harrowing because it was based on clinical observation of how the mad behave. So was his next 'event' mounted in protest against American conduct of the Vietnam War: *US*, as it was punningly titled, was political theatre designed to infuriate and upset its audiences. It began with a Buddhist monk performing self-immolation. The jerry can was tipped, the match struck and the actor began to contract, seemingly shrinking his fingers, hands, forearms, until like a crumpled spider he toppled over backwards. Blinded prisoners, with large symbolic paper sacks over their heads, descended into the stalls, mewing piteously, searching for the exits. A searchlight was turned on the audience to see which of them got up to help. Some did, absurdly in my opinion, for these were not war victims but actors who were being paid. At the end the cast froze while centre stage a figure in white gloves opened a black box. Out of it emerged a cloud of white butterflies which flickered up the front curtains to the flies. But one butterfly remained in his gloved hand. To this he proceeded to apply a flaming cigarette lighter. We watched it consumed, like a victim of napalm. The burnt butterfly was in fact a paper cut-out. Like much of the show it was brilliant conjuring.

Confusion of the audience's expectations in order to disturb it was the essence of the Brook Effect. His parting gift to the RSC was an eye-opening production of *A Midsummer Night's Dream* set in a dazzling white box rather like a circus ring. Floating above it on trapezes were the immortals, Oberon and company, spinning plates and looking down with amusement on the confusions of the mortal lovers. The clowns, Bottom and his men, came bursting in with saws and planks and circus slapstick routines. Hundreds of productions of the *Dream* have tried to weave rural magic from it. This reversal of expectations without a single green leaf or bower exhilarated and renewed the over-performed play and passed into theatrical legend.

Where could Brook go next? He disappeared to Paris to conduct experiments with a multinational troupe of actors in an old music hall, Les Bouffes de Nord, with a helpful state subsidy. The results were only briefly seen in Britain but he would come back to give lectures in the National Theatre where his touch of genius was much missed. He spoke with a voice as mild as milk. He fixed us with glittering pale blue eyes, one hand caressing invisible spheres in the air. He was not just a director but a guru – he was a devotee of Gurdjieff. 'Precise' was one of his favourite words but his discourses were anything but. Many was the time I took copious interview notes only to look through them vainly afterwards for a coherent explanation of his work. 'We are working towards not a form, not an image, but a set of conditions in which a certain quality of performance can arise' – that was a typical Brookism. For him life was a search and the theatre a holy place in which he conducted it. But in his productions there was always some moment of shock created by his unfailing instinct for theatrical effect that eclipsed all the theory.

Like Brook, Peter Hall loved holding forth. Like him he could hardly be stopped once launched. He loved rehearsals as an opportunity to expound to a captive cast, which he sometimes invited me to watch. For all his boyish geniality nobody dared interrupt or question his expositions on the text, especially on the speaking of Shakespeare into which, he let us understand, he alone had the true insight. When a crisis arose or an actor threw a tantrum Hall would go smoothly into overdrive, reducing the problem to silence. Then he would innocently enquire: 'May we go on with our rehearsal?' His confidence was not always as serene as it seemed. After one last-minute note session full of his reassurances to the cast he confided to me: 'Actually I've spent the whole rehearsal wondering whether to cancel the press night.'

There was streak in him that relished risk. It led him into the mistaken belief that he could also direct big bouncy musicals. Possibly goaded by the success of his former apprentice, Trevor Nunn, he came a cropper with several. But taking over the still unoccupied National building and company in 1974 offered him a surfeit of risk. Unlike Brook's old music hall in Paris, he was saddled with the largest white elephant available, the awkwardly designed and colossally expensive new building on the South Bank planned when concrete brutalism was king. He took arms against a sea of troubles – political, industrial and artistic – defying everyone from the board to the unions. To get it open and to fill its three auditoria to eighty per cent capacity every night is a steep enough challenge for any ego but it was not enough for Hall. He also directed opera at Glyndebourne, Covent Garden and even Bayreuth. He spent weekends making a film. He got divorced and remarried twice and produced several children.

THE SEVENTIES

By the end of his reign the boyish devil-may-care look had long gone. He resembled a massive, heavy-lidded Chinese emperor with plotting, glittering eyes. As his farewell bow he chose to direct all three of Shakespeare's late plays, *Cymbeline*, *The Winter's Tale* and *The Tempest*, simultaneously, using the same company of actors. Beside their problem of learning three parts at once they were also being filmed rehearsing them for a TV *South Bank Show* about him. So whenever he advanced on them with a note there would be a camera, lights and crew peering over his shoulder. The only person who did not mind this was Peter Hall. When his estranged wife Maria Ewing arrived to make her debut at Covent Garden opera house in *Salome*, a production which he had originated in Los Angeles, he added directing that to his workload. With opera in the morning, Shakespeare in triplicate in the afternoon and evening, he administered the National Theatre in his lunch hour. Patient queues of people needing his decisions would crowd his doors and walk beside him along corridors in the hope of getting them.

'You can't do everything. I wish I could stop trying,' he wrote in his diary of those years. Some streak of hubris in him ached to attempt the impossible. Was it greed for power or success? Insatiable ambition? Workaholic addiction? The need to play dictator? His excessive output was responsible for several disappointing productions alongside the notable triumphs such as *Antony and Cleopatra* and *Amadeus*. He made a lot of enemies – Olivier could not bear to hear his name mentioned. But for years he never eased up. After a disappointment he would shake himself like a half-drowned bear and barge on to the next project. At the time of writing he is still hard at it. The urge to direct seems even more compulsive than the urge to act. It offers the seductive sensation of creating artificial worlds and controlling all those who inhabit them. Brook and Hall were exceptionally gifted at this Prospero-like game. But I believe they did harm as well as good to the theatre by imposing the idea of the all-powerful director upon it. Their example was fatally attractive to would-be followers, many of whom lacked their vision.

JOHN GIELGUD

With regal bearing and a long neck as straight as a Greek column supporting a noble polished dome, John Gielgud's mere entry into a room made those in it feel lesser mortals. Then abruptly he would disperse the grandeur with a kindly, often rather naughty remark that seemed to come out of the blue. 'Yes,' he said looking down at the fork of his trousers. 'These days it's all quiet on the Y-Front – don't you find?' On his eightieth birthday he joined me for lunch. 'I hate being eighty. Much rather you didn't mention it. I still think of myself as young. You know, I force myself to take my trousers off without sitting down.' His rather stern patrician features suddenly looked impish.

Devastating candour with no intention to offend was his celebrated hallmark. He spoke as rapidly as he thought, with no time for self-censorship. Reminiscing to a group of actors about his historic career he said: 'Of course the trouble with that *Hamlet* was the Horatio… Was it you, Harry? Well, you've come on a lot since then.' He knew quite well how actors loved to imitate his mannerisms but he could send himself up better than anyone. When Charles Wood wrote a play, *Veterans*, about Gielgud filming an epic (*The Charge of the Light Brigade*) unhappily in the Turkish desert he played himself and had the packed Royal Court hooting like a barn full of demented owls. It took until his comparatively old age to prove that he was a pippin of a comedian. But it was a different story on the pre-London tour. Audiences were shocked. 'One night thirty people walked out. I've never had so many rude letters to say that I had degraded my profession. One woman sent a postal order for 40p because she thought I must be very hard up to appear in such a play.'

He was amazed when Charles Wood, who also wrote the film, came up with the part. 'I was flattered that he had studied me so well.

He made me out to be rather a dear but underneath, guilefully, I get my way by seeming to be innocent and charming. I'm told it's just like me. I tend to get out of a crisis by running away. I am rather a cowardly person, you see'. But, unlike Olivier, not at all jealous. He remarked of a colleague, 'He's got quite a lot of awfully good lines and I think he says them awfully well when he can remember them.' He meant it kindly but he could be just as cutting about himself. It was he who pointed out that he moved on stage as if his knees had been tied together with ribbon. The humility about his work was genuine. 'I think it's a terrible fault that I couldn't possibly play working class.'

He never got over the disgrace of his arrest (by a decoy policeman) for 'cottaging' although it occurred back in 1953 at the height of police persecution of homosexuals. It was immediately disregarded by fellow actors and much of his public. But he would still quite often refer to it as 'my very difficult time' when his career was temporarily eclipsed – as it would certainly not be nowadays. Gielgud was partly of Polish descent, as well as being related to the theatrical Terry dynasty. He spent almost all his last forty years with an Austro-Hungarian refugee, Martin Hensler, who shared his ornate wing of a William & Mary country house at Wootton in Buckinghamshire. Hensler, who cared for the six acres of grounds, turned out to be a domestic tyrant. 'I'd ask you down,' John would say. 'But it would mean – er...*lunch*' – which his unwilling companion would have to provide. It was impossible to visualise Gielgud boiling an egg. He used to list mournfully his many impracticalities: 'I can't drive a car, play cards, tennis or squash. I can't swim or cook. There are very few people who are as unskilled as I am...I can act a bit,' he added as an afterthought. There are very few people who live their entire lives so totally concentrated on one thing – the theatre. His vagueness about the world outside it was perhaps best illustrated in the war. He looked up at the barrage balloons protecting London and said to his companion: 'I do feel so sorry for those boys up there. It must be terribly cold and lonely.'

He regretted strongly that so few of his major performances were on film. Apart from Cassius in *Julius Caesar* there was very little Shakespeare until at the end of his career he did Prospero in the strikingly unorthodox Peter Greenaway film of *The Tempest* entitled *Prospero's Books*. In this underrated experiment Gielgud not only played Prospero as a character but as the author of the tale (in effect Shakespeare), writing it as it goes along. Gielgud was not only prepared for this radical take on one of his greatest theatre parts, he stripped naked for one scene shot in a pool. He never played safe even in his last years. He would take almost any cameo, often in rubbishy films, which would afford him travel to agreeable locations, especially Italy. There was no shortage of such offers after the Oscar he was awarded in *Arthur* as the fastidious valet to a louche Dudley Moore. His inquiry while assisting his employer's bath whether he was expected 'to soap your dick' was just the sort of surprise that delighted the unconventional side of Gielgud. At such moments in life, when he said or did something slightly shocking, his features would melt into a radiant smile. He was not only a superb actor. He was fun to be with.

Ralph Richardson

If I had to choose between seeing a performance by Olivier or one by Ralph Richardson I would have chosen Richardson. This is because of his mastery of mystery, in life as well as in performance. There was never an occasion in his company, on stage or off, when he did not do or say something totally unexpected. I don't believe it was premeditated. He simply didn't care to restrain himself. Unlike Olivier, he never thought his performances were any good. 'I was hopeless as Othello, terrible as Macbeth,' he told me – possibly rightly if accounts of them are any guide. 'No good, no good! I am not enough of a poet to ride those big horses without falling off.' He selected another metaphor. 'Those roles are Grand Op'rah. And grand op'rah I can't sing.' This was demonstrably untrue because his Falstaff by common consent was the best of its time. It had a kind of down at heel grandeur. He himself compared Falstaff's progress to that of 'a gorgeous, ceremonial Indian elephant.' This made the harshness of the rejection scene by the priggish young king, his erstwhile companion in misbehaviour, all the more chilling. Richardson acted this terrible moment with his back to the audience. His back, as the king passed on icily, conveyed unbearable shock. He held the moment, stilling the house, before turning round, features grimacing desperately to hold off tears. I saw him make a similar effect years later in the screen scene of *The School For Scandal*. When the screen falls over, Sir Peter Teazle who is sitting there with his back turned sees that the lady of doubtful virtue behind it is his own wife. The audience laughed at his discomfiture, as Sheridan intends, but something about Richardson's hunched back gradually quelled the laughter which died away to an almost ashamed silence. He made you feel the awfulness of the moment for this doting husband. And he did it purely with his back. I never saw another actor capable of this. But although Peter Hall constantly beseeched him to do it at the National, he would never repeat his Falstaff.

He was equally disparaging about his appearance. Talking of the parts he never played because he hadn't the looks for them he said: 'I don't like my face. I've seen better-looking potatoes.' He thought for a moment. 'I don't *like* the kind of actor I am. But I'm going to change. Change completely.' And change he did. At seventy he joined the avant-garde. With his old friend and acting partner John Gielgud he went into modern drama at the Royal Court in *Home* and later in Pinter's mysterious *No Man's Land* at the National. Both pieces of chamber music held audiences hypnotised. Suddenly the two of them became a staple guest couple. Sunday newspaper supplements printed their lunchtime conversation. Talk-show television couldn't get enough of them. They played up to it enjoyably, like the Morecambe and Wise of artistic show business, although they had the most disparate characters and eccentricities. Gielgud never stopped talking, about the theatre, whereas Richardson's mind was a store of unusual knowledge, especially of the animal world. 'A rat,' he once informed me apropos of nothing, 'has an IQ of twenty-five. Some dogs are a mere ten.'

One evening after dinner, sitting in his study alongside Hampstead Heath, he introduced me to his polecat ferret, Eddie. Eddie occupied a run behind chicken wire along the skirting board and made sudden swishing rushes round the room. Sir Ralph, smoking his huge pipe, took no notice for a while and then went over and took Eddie into his hands and seated him on his knee. In his lightest, tenderest voice he asked, 'What is it, old fellow? Did you want a word with me? A word with Papa?' Eddie seemed relaxed but I could not help staring at a deep red, curved scar on Sir Ralph's upper lip. 'Yes,' he acknowledged. 'He bit me. But it wasn't his fault. You see, I…kissed him.'

It was not only animals that consumed his interest. He loved machinery, collected clocks, loved letting off fireworks and was an intrepid motor cyclist. To all his interests he brought an intense boyish curiosity. His large but choice collection of books lay all round us. 'I like to have four or five on the go, especially beside the bed.' He was invited to advise the The Bodley Head publishing house. I asked him whether he still wrote himself. I had seen an unpublished fragment of autobiography he had written years before, a vivid and typically eccentric description of his weird childhood. His mother had left his father when he was four, taking him and leaving two older brothers behind. They lived very frugally in a pair of converted railway coaches almost on the beach at Shoreham, Sussex. 'We had no front door or back door but we had a vast number of side doors, furnished with brass handles and leather straps to let down the windows.' It was a childhood spent much alone, play-acting on a beach. His chief companion was his black and white mouse. I was greatly disappointed when the writing stopped short at the point when he discovered the magic of acting. Why didn't he go on with his life story? It was so good, so crisply and amusingly written, I urged him in vain. He dismissed the idea abruptly. A possible reason later occurred to me when Gielgud said in passing, 'Poor Ralph. He had such a terrible time for years with his wife's dreadful illness.' He had married an actress when he was twenty-one. Both were at Birmingham Repertory Company and they played together until, after only four years, Kit began to display the symptoms of the sleeping sickness that ravaged Europe in the early twenties. She weakened gradually until she had to be hospitalised for many years. Her death came during the Second World War. Richardson had waited years to marry again, to the actress Meriel Forbes, known as Mu to friends. One could understand it was a story that he did not want either himself or others to tell.

He had a tremendous capacity for strong spirits which sometimes led to the conversation or his behaviour taking a bizarre turn. A sudden stamp and quiver of his entire body would accompany the most ferocious stare I have ever seen, a stare to stop a bus or a rhino at twenty paces. I saw it on the disastrous first night of a play by Joe Orton, *What the Butler Saw*. Set in a lunatic asylum it seemed that every character in the play was barmy and Richardson, as the visiting Lunacy Inspector, was maddest of all of them. The Bird began to stir in the second half. There were shouts of 'rubbish!', 'take it off!' and 'give back the knighthood!' from the gallery. Pandemonium broke out when the curtain rose for the calls. Richardson came on at full glare. It seemed as if some of the audience might rush the stage. A couple of actor friends went round afterwards to sympathise. He greeted them with: 'Has either of you got a little cyanide?'

On a happier occasion, at least to begin with, we were seated at the Savoy on a sofa in the lounge, taking tea. Not that Richardson wanted tea – he had asked for brandy but it was after three o'clock and the licensing hours were then strictly enforced. For his part as a retired general in a new play at the Savoy Theatre next door he had grown a pretty fierce military moustache. Beside me unexpected sounds became audible, sounds of tea being strained through the moustache. I sneaked a glance. Indeed Sir Ralph was sucking his tea from the saucer to the evident surprise of passers-by. He explained lightly: 'Excellent tea they have here at the Savoy but it wants air to it. Tea needs to be drunk from a container of shallow shape.' He refilled the saucer from his cup. 'Vulgar, no doubt, but as we are alone we can indulge our fancies.' He held the emptied saucer up balanced upon three outstretched fingertips. 'Yes! That's the vessel for me!' Then he resumed the filtering. 'If, now, it had been coffee I should have drunk it from a glass.'

Just then a theatre publicist bustled up, uninvited, and insisted on showing him the production photographs. 'Not now, later!' But the man persisted in trying to make him choose some. Storm warnings gathered. Sir Ralph summoned the glare. Thrusting his fists into the sofa he shot to his feet and took off across the floor like a rocket, disappearing down some steps. The offending interloper wondered where he'd gone. After an interval I saw the manager of the Savoy approaching. 'Sir Ralph awaits you in the dining room,' he announced, looking meaningfully at me. As I rose, so did the publicist. 'Not *you*, Mr Fearon!' When I found him, Sir Ralph was still glaring, alone on the balcony of the large restaurant. He motioned me to sit opposite him. 'I don't want to talk to that silly fucker! I want to talk to you.'

His waywardness as an interviewee was often demonstrated on television. He invariably took over the interview, even with someone as sharp-witted as Bernard Levin. Questioned about how he exercised his power over the audience Sir Ralph claimed that it was possible to command the stage even when lying down. He challenged a disbelieving Levin to try it. By gradual steps he talked him off his chair into a prone position on the studio floor. 'There you are, my dear fellow, perfectly in charge' – and he proceeded to walk off the set, leaving Levin to retrieve the situation as best he could.

There was a story, related by Olivier himself, that one night on an Old Vic post-war tour in Paris Richardson disappeared after a performance of *Peer Gynt*, which had not gone well with the French, to walk the streets. Very late at night from his bedroom window above the hotel doorway Olivier saw him return and rushed downstairs to let him in. Richardson brushed past him without a word and then, reaching the first floor landing, seized him, carried him through his bedroom window to the balcony and held him out above a sheer drop to the cobbles below. In vain Olivier pleaded for minutes to be set down. I remembered this, not knowing whether to believe it, when the conversation turned to Olivier. I wondered if they had had a falling out? 'Laurence?' – Olivier was always 'Laurence' to Richardson, never 'Larry' – 'He's my oldest friend.' He paused then said explosively: 'I hate him! Then I meet him again and we're back. I say, "How are you, you silly old fucker? What have you been doing, you old fucker?"' It wasn't easy to interpret this as a sign of unmitigated affection.

The last time I saw Sir Ralph at his splendid Nash house in Chester Terrace overlooking Regent's Park, a biography of him had appeared, a perfectly competent and polite one given that he had refused any part in its preparation. He was not pleased at any sort of breach of his privacy. 'Let us not discuss it,' he warned me as we went upstairs to his study. It looked out over the park just above tree-top height. You could have been on a liner looking out at an ocean tossing with green and purple billows towards the distant shoreline of Baker Street. He pointed out landmarks like a mariner. We drank coffee. As was his wont we drank it from long glasses with handles. He had been filming. Mostly cameos. 'You know those ducks at fairgrounds which you shoot at as they pass across your sights in order to win a prize? Well, that's what filming is like. You wait about all day and then – pow! You've got one shot to hit the duck. On stage you can go back the next night and keep carving away, improving, like shaping a piece of wood.' I got him to talk for once about acting. 'Acting is partly dreaming. To make an audience believe, you have to believe yourself. So you must dream.

A Rogues' Gallery

You partly dream your performance to make it partly true. Nothing is wholly true, even in life. When you say to someone, "I love you very much," it's not wholly true. It's what you've decided at that moment to say.' He went to the window and looked over the ocean. 'People are not what they seem. You are not. I am not. Not just what we seem this afternoon. A person…' he paused for emphasis, 'is a whole pack of cards. *A whole pack of cards.*'

When we went downstairs Jose, Sir Ralph's parrot, was sulking in his cage. He was in disgrace for having bitten Lady Richardson. Sir Ralph stopped to talk to him, not altogether kindly. 'How are you, you old devil? You had better not try that again.' Had he ever bitten Sir Ralph? 'Try that with me,' he informed Jose, 'and I'll wring your bloody neck for you.' On the pavement outside the door stood a gleaming chromium warhorse, Sir Ralph's latest Harley Davidson, on which I had heard he took Jose for rides round the Outer Circle within the park. 'Yes, we ride together every day. As fast as possible. I like to give him the sensation that he's flying.' He was in his eighties. He patted the bike on its saddle, contemplating its beauty. 'Well, goodbye, old fellow.'

Only a week or two later I was shocked to hear he had died. I often used to walk by his house on the park. For months afterwards through a ground floor window a hat-stand could be seen. On it hung a selection of characterful hats and walking sticks – his props for what was his greatest part. Not Sir John Falstaff but Sir Ralph Richardson. He was never the same man twice. He was a whole pack of cards.

P.G. WODEHOUSE

For me there was once no more satisfying way of spending my half a crown pocket money than on a new novel to add to my bedroom bookcase. As my taste matured, P. C. Wren and Rider Haggard, the William books, the Bulldog Drummond and the Biggles sagas moved downwards to be replaced by new novels, sometimes bought mainly for their gay, amusing jackets. I became a bookaholic early on and have been perpetually in need of more shelf space ever since. Easily the largest set was the accumulating oeuvre of P. G. Wodehouse. He was publishing prodigiously long before I began reading him but I kept pace with the Blandings Castle series, the later Jeeves stories and sought out from earlier years the incomparable Psmith. Their orange spines produced by Herbert Jenkins spread intriguing titles along the shelf. *Young Men in Spats, Eggs, Beans and Crumpets, The Code of the Woosters*. I knew I had struck gold but there was ample confirmation in the dust-jacket quotes from the likes of J. B. Priestley, Compton Mackenzie and Hilaire Belloc, who declared Wodehouse to be 'a little lower than Shakespeare but any distance you like above any others'.

After so many years of distant devotion it was with awe as well as eagerness that I climbed aboard the Long Island Railroad one day in the seventies to accept his invitation to lunch. The journey to his lair lay at the oddly named last station of the line, Speonk. Thence one set out through what once had been Indian country but now resembled Surrey for Remsenburg, L. I. An unexpected noticeboard read: The P. G. Wodehouse Bideawee Home. This was not where he lived but was a shelter for stray animals which he had endowed. Basket Neck Lane, my destination, was screened with clipped privet. Ethel Wodehouse – 'Bunny' to his 'Plum' – came fizzing out of the drive of a low white weather-boarded house like a purposeful wasp. Her sharp chin and long nose bore the stamp of authority exercised for many years over six cats, two dogs and an unworldly author. They married within months of meeting in 1914 when she was a showgirl and he a lyric writer for Broadway musicals. Already a twice-widowed single mother, she had brought with her a daughter of eleven, Leonora, whom he adopted as his own and cherished until her untimely death during his internment during the war. When he was liberated and told the news he said: 'I thought she was immortal.'

Ethel Wodehouse waved her guests into her mirrored bar and set about mixing pre-lunch gin with martini and with vigour. 'Plummie,' as she called him, was still in his study. Conversation was in full flow when, like Jeeves, he shimmered into the room unobtrusively. He was well into his eighties but straight, tall and obviously in the pink. He had conceded on becoming eighty that 'the hot blood of the seventies has cooled'. He radiated benevolence through large spectacles and in a voice that chimed brightly in C-major said that he was considering a long-awaited return to London. The reason was *Jeeves: The Musical*, which had been adapted by Guy Bolton and himself, the team that had given New York twenty-odd musicals in pre-war days. 'I should have to go over for that. If only it could be done without travel.'

He turned to me. 'What's England like these days? I suppose there are no such things as butlers now.' This sounded like a well-used gambit. It transpired that he was in process of creating his twenty-somethingth butler. Appleby, 'with a voice like a sound burgundy made audible', had joined the roll of Attwater, Bayliss, Beach, Bulstrode, Coggs, Gascoyne, Slingsby and Vosper (merely to skim the cream). 'The public doesn't seem to mind me going on writing about butlers. It's curious. I suppose there is a certain strength in this nostalgia stuff, do you think?' I assured him the public would not thank him for changing to the then fashionable working-class realism.

Over lunch of traditional roast and veg he listened to Ethel's sister, just back from London, describing a society party where high words had been exchanged and a glass of wine thrown. One participant had been Lord Snowdon, formerly Anthony Armstrong Jones, the photographer. Plum's features lost their benevolence. 'Jones!' he exclaimed, 'What a blighter!' Blighter may *look* mild as a reproof but pronounced as he did it, it was the sleeve across the windpipe. He did not look exactly gruntled either when I asked what he thought of the current BBC television adaptation of Bertie Wooster, who was portrayed by Ian Carmichael as an extremely silly ass with a monocle, accompanied by a weighty, elderly Jeeves (Dennis Price). 'The BBC sent us the tapes,' he was reminded by Bunny. He did not seem anxious to remember watching them. Then he let out a sort of snort. 'They were both so *old*!' he protested. He pointed out that Bertie and Jeeves were both a couple of young rips. Valets were not ponderous like butlers, they were, in their sphere, men about town. 'In my early years I knew dozens of Bertie Woosters. I belonged to clubs where they were practically all Berties. They'd usually got some relative with money or a title. They hung around the club touching each other for quids.'

After lunch he invited me into his study. The typewriter, the trusty old Royal office machine, stood on the desk facing away from the garden window. He plied it still every day. 'I usually manage to wrench about three pages at a go.' There were intervals in the day for walking the dogs, reading and watching a favourite TV soap opera. His life had always been the same, driven by writing book after book. 'My books have never had much to do with life. Even in England I didn't go about much. I got some of the plots out of the newspapers.' But I had never quite understood why it was in America that Bertie, Jeeves, the Drones Club and Blandings were created and created first for American readers, serialised in the *Saturday Evening Post*. 'Yes it's curious. You see that was the only stuff I could write. I couldn't write American stories and the only sort of English characters the American public wanted were dudes and earls.'

Of course we had to talk about the only time that rude reality had impinged on his world of fantasy – his capture and internment by the Germans in 1940 and his notorious subsequent broadcasts from Berlin, about which I had heard disbelievingly at school. No one in Britain heard the broadcasts. By now I had read their scripts which were originally written in camp to amuse his fellow inmates. There was no harm in them whatsoever other than the war situation in which they were broadcast in 1941. It was the wrong moment to make a German internment camp sound almost good fun. Had it been? 'Very like school. When you get a lot of men cooped up together and up against it, it brings out the best in them. They were always doing each other little favours and making fun of the guards. I couldn't make it out worse than it was. Of course, going on the air was a loony thing to do.' He summed up: 'Made an ass of myself' – he used the long A – 'had to pay the penalty.' He had made no sort of deal with the Germans for his release from camp. In fact the release had not been altogether welcome because *Money in the Bank* had been going nicely despite the distractions. Although he had been officially forgiven and stoutly defended by fair-minded people like George Orwell and Evelyn Waugh at the time, the slur on his patriotism had hung on, however often expunged. The penalty was that he had never returned to England, fearing it would start trouble up again. He never gave the slightest indication of feeling hurt but he must have been. It also undoubtedly delayed his long overdue knighthood.

With the pipe drawing and the ice tinkling in Ethel's stinging and copious Dry Martinis we sat in basket chairs overlooking the lawn in the evening. It was a long, well-tended lawn that Angus MacPherson, Lord Emsworth's gardener at Blandings in Shropshire, would have approved of. The yuccas flowered in the distance. Twelve Wodehouse acres fringed us from the hidden shore of Long Island. The birdsong was deafening, the butterflies were huge, the serenity was Salopian. Lord Emsworth could have been lost in the trees. Whether it was Plum's relaxed, warming presence or a lot of strong Martinis, I drifted happily with the feast of reason and the flow of soul. His current book was about Galahad, Lord Emsworth's rackety Edwardian rip of a brother. He had first appeared in the Blandings saga about fifty years earlier. 'Do you know,' mused Plum, 'I'm beginning to feel I *know* Galahad. Like a friend. By the way how long would it take nowadays from Paddington to Shropshire? About four hours? I always make it about four hours.' The likelihood of there still being trains direct to Market Blandings with first class restaurant accommodation seemed minimal but I didn't care to mention it. In the Garden of Eden that he had created for our delight and refreshment that soothing journey would continue to take four hours – until he handed in his dinner pail.

BUBBLES

The nearest to a Wodehouse character whom I encountered in real society was the redoubtable Patricia Harmsworth, wife of Vere Harmsworth and thereby subsequently Viscountess Rothermere. Pat was known among the gossip column set as 'Bubbles', a nickname she hated but brought upon herself by her fondness, amounting to addiction, to champagne. She liked it pink. She used to arrive at parties bringing her own supply, carried for her by a friend or attendant. I watched her sweep past the queue for tables at the Polo Lounge in Beverly Hills calling 'Come along!' to a small Latin-looking follower (friend? servant?) bearing her supply in a wooden box. She was a martyr to Dom Perignon. Parties were the essence of Pat's life and the most important feature of them was who was there. Once she had exhausted the interesting guests she would depart for another, possibly better-attended party. On this occasion she spotted me. 'You're here! Have you seen so-and-so? Or such-and-such?' She reeled off a list of Hollywood names she clearly expected to find awaiting her arrival.

Her presence at any gathering was conspicuous partly by her continually extending circumference and also by the piercingly audible little-girlish voice which seldom fell silent. Her laugh was penetrating and prolonged. Though not perhaps quite in the class of the laugh of Bertie Wooster's dreaded girl friend Honoria Glossop ('like a squadron of cavalry clattering over a tin bridge'), it nevertheless might have shattered a cut-glass chandelier. Smart parties in London betrayed her presence by her swarm of hangers-on, fascinated like myself by her unfailing exuberance. Her cries of recognition were like those of a little girl forever prolonging a fun-loving childhood. She still looked striking and had once been a stunner of the peculiarly fifties, heavily made-up kind. Spotted by a scout from the J. Arthur Rank organisation she had been recruited to the then famous Rank Charm School, a possible route to film stardom. Its members were much photographed in the glossy magazines being escorted to nightclubs, dressed in borrowed jewellery and furs. They were publicity for Rank films. The charm school also taught elocution. It favoured the almost painful bray then considered the hallmark of the upper class and in which most film dialogue was conducted.

So it was that Patricia Matthews, the daughter of a provincial quantity surveyor, became 'Beverly Brooks' on the film cast lists. She had one notable speaking part in *Reach for the Sky* in the somewhat unappealing role of the girlfriend of Douglas Bader who ditches him when he loses his legs in a flying accident. It was a start. Who knows where it might have led had she not just then met the Hon. Vere Harmsworth? Their mutual attraction seems to have been instant. Despite any reservations that might have been entertained by his family, they married in 1957, which spelt the end of her film or any other career. Instead she set herself the target of becoming a leading hostess of London society and the very vocal support of Vere, whose shy reclusiveness was such a contrast to her own ebullient assault on life.

Just as Esmond, the second Lord Rothermere, had been treated as a disappointment by his father, so did he treat his own son and heir. Vere's childhood, spent much in the company of a nanny and servants, must have been lonely and perplexing because it was overshadowed by the record-breaking, long-running and bitter divorce of his parents which dragged its way through the courts over eight years. Vere emerged as a silent, solitary boy who held himself aloof at Eton, did not take a commission during his army service and failed to get into Oxford. Instead he was apprenticed to the family empire in a series of undistinguished positions to learn the newspaper business. From time to time he would be seen around the *Daily Mail* offices where his nickname was 'Mere'. At one office party he reluctantly trailed Pat, who was squealing with enthusiasm at meeting the writers behind the paper's bylines. She was chatting to me when he caught up with her. 'Veah! Veah! This is Peter Lewis – you know, the theatre critic.' 'I know,' said Vere wearily, clearly longing to be somewhere else.

He remained an enigma even when he took charge of the newspapers in 1971 when his father remarried and retired to the South of France. It was assumed there was little love lost between them so that when news came in 1978 that Esmond, now ill with dementia, had little longer to live I was told to prepare his obituary without involving his son. 'On no account approach Vere,' said the senior executives nervously. Nor was I to involve star reporters of the old man's day such as Noel Barber, for whom the South Pole was renamed 'Barber's Pole' after he took a leak there and inadvertently got his member frozen to the side of the receptacle. 'You'll just have to manage on what's in the cuttings library,' they said. It seemed absurd to be inventing tributes to a man whose existence they were trying to minimise. So I found Vere by telephone in New York and explained my task. Would he care to say anything? His response demonstrated once more how ill-founded were the fears executives have of their proprietors' prejudices. He talked warmly of his father for almost an hour and urged me to look up the well-known reporters of those days –'Like that chap, Noel Barber. They were great chums.'

No mention was made among the tributes that Esmond had handed over the *Daily Mail* heading for bankruptcy with a fast-declining circulation. In that crucial situation six years earlier the underestimated Vere had emerged as if from a chrysalis and displayed his newspaperman's genes or instincts. He determined to take the risk of turning the *Daily Mail* into a tabloid squarely aimed at women readers, supported by the sales slogan: 'Every woman needs her Daily Mail.' There were many anxious months before it caught on under the editorship of David English, far outdistancing its middle-market rival the *Daily Express* which turned tabloid in imitation but with far less success. Even so Vere, the architect of the change, kept well behind the scenes.

The mystery of the Rothermeres, as they now were, was the durability of their ill-matched union. Pat's childlike *joie de vivre*, so unlike his brooding silences, may well have liberated him in private. But it became noticeable that Vere was less and less at her side in public as her figure expanded, a figure she did nothing to minimise by choosing eye-catching costumes rich with flounces and frills, embellished with bows and floating panels enough to sail a galleon. All was topped by a luxuriant wig. In 1978 he, but not she, moved to Paris, for complicated tax and inheritance law reasons, it was said, though it might also have been to create space between them. Secretly a legal separation had been drawn up but nobody but the lawyers involved would have known it. So while giving every appearance of being still married they were no longer so in reality.

It so happened that same year I spent much of my time in Paris as a convenient base for foreign reporting. So I shared with Vere the somewhat dingy *Daily Mail* offices in the unfashionable Rue du Sentier. There were two offices, his and mine, so we met frequently on a polite but never confidential basis. We also shared the secretarial services of the charming and efficient Helene Garnier, whose response to requests however outlandish was 'pas de problème'. She was also preoccupied with finding Vere an apartment to share with his oriental mistress, Maiko Lee, whom he had met in a nightclub some time earlier. They duly took up residence on the expensive and exclusive Île Saint-Louis in the middle of the Seine. Pat was also often in France but stayed at their villa on the Cap d'Ail, close to Monte Carlo. From there her voice came ringing down the office telephone asking for 'Veah'. Helene and I took turns at finding reasons for his frequent absence.

Their marriage never really ended partly because of his natural aversion to divorce proceedings but also because there was some deep-seated bond between them that remained intact. One day in Monaco, where I was trying to piece together what was happening to the Onassis fortune now that Christina had succeeded the wily Aristotle, I heard that Pat was at the Cap d'Ail. So I rang her to see what she knew and was promptly invited to dinner. When I arrived at the villa I was surprised to find Vere there too, so soon after we had seen one another in Paris. He was wielding a hose while Pat was – literally – making waves in the swimming pool. The garden overlooked the Mediterranean and along the sea wall outside ran the public coastal path. 'See that path? You can imagine what goes on out there between couples in the evenings. Know what I do?' He waggled the hose meaningfully. 'Put this on them.' It didn't sound as though he meant it as a joke. There was a ruthless side to his character.

The Viscountess did not so much change for dinner as fall into a voluminous white sail of a dress. Her hair, still wet, hung down in curling squiggles. Vere contemplated her across the table and turned to me. 'Doesn't she look like a Renoir?' he inquired. Cautiously I read his expression for irony but he seemed to be quite in earnest. 'Well...' I prevaricated, but he cut me short raising his glass of red wine: 'My Renoir girl!' We drank to that. 'Did you come to my party in Eaton Squeah?' she inquired of me. I said what fun it had been – unusually she had a guest list stuffed with journalists. 'And do you know,' she leaned forward confidentially, 'there was nothing missing! Afterwards...nothing!' Why should there have been, I asked. 'Well! You know what journalists are!' Vere looked amused. 'Did you think they'd take the spoons?' 'Oh no, of course I didn't, Veah.' 'Yes, you did, you thought they'd take the spoons!' It was just one of her frequently tactless remarks. To show I was not offended I assured her that the newspaper paid us enough to buy our own spoons. Vere gave me a sphinx-like look. The talk turned to the gossip of Monte Carlo, of Christina Onassis and her Russian lover and whether the Kremlin had designs on the Onassis fleet with which to dominate the eastern Mediterranean.

When it was time to go I asked to call a taxi to take me back to Monte Carlo. 'No!' said Vere sharply, 'I'll drive you.' 'Oh, Veah, you don't want to drive all that way at this time of night.' 'Yes I do,' said Vere, going to fetch the car. As I got in, Pat stood at the door. 'When will you be back, Veah?' She sounded anxious. He stuck his head out of the driver's window. 'I may never be back!' We drove off. When we reached the town he decided we would go to the casino. But we weren't suitably dressed, I observed. 'Not that casino – the other one.' The other casino was much patronised by American tourists in check shirts and baseball caps. He walked straight past the gambling rooms and made for the central lounge. Tables and sofas were spread about around a raised island bar. Along both sides of it sat unaccompanied women, dressed and made up to kill.

As we talked his eyes returned at intervals to the bar, scrutinising the company. 'See those women? You could have one of them.' No doubt so, I agreed, wondering why he was informing me of this obvious fact. 'That's what this sort of place is for.' 'I know.' 'Well, you must have been to plenty. I know what you reporters get up to abroad on your expenses.' It was not altogether a joke. I pointed out that while one could hire cars, small aeroplanes, even a camel on expenses, ladies of the night were not the sort of item one included. Was it some kind of test? Did he expect me to pick one up and bring her over for inspection? And for what purpose? Was it an exercise in voyeurism? He persisted. 'All you have to do is go over there and select one.' I wasn't in the mood for a painted lady and I did not think my duties extended to procuring one for any purpose. 'I'd rather stay here and talk to you,' I said. So we talked, never once mentioning Paris where he must have realised I knew of the arrangements. I felt that he was in some way disappointed in the evening. Perhaps it was thwarted curiosity – a curiosity he felt he could not indulge for himself. As I say he was a man nobody felt sure they understood.

I liked Pat Rothermere and sympathised with her foolhardy belief that life could remain an everlasting party with her as its star. In 1992 she died unhappily early at the age of sixty-three. Vere mourned her and showed it by writing her a deeply felt love poem which he read at her memorial. Later he married Maiko and they lived in France. But in 1998 on a family visit to London he was struck down by a heart attack. Vere, so inscrutably modest, hid complexities of character which I never fathomed. He said one thing about himself which was unequivocal and perhaps illuminating: 'I am glad I was never an officer. You meet a nicer type of person in the ranks.'

E. F. SCHUMACHER

I must have read many hundreds of books over many years of reviewing and editing. But if I'm asked which one comes to mind as the most influential on my thinking the answer is clear. It was a slim volume by a then unknown author, E. F. Schumacher. Its title: *Small is Beautiful*. Its sub-title: *A Study of Economics as if People Mattered*. I had a deep suspicion of economics ever since it formed part of my Oxford PPE degree course. The set books seemed to be written by men psychologically naïve to the point of juvenility. Their basic assumption was that people are programmed to work only for the maximum profit obtainable and to buy and sell only for the maximum advantage, even if to make only a penny more or spend a penny less. No human being I knew behaved like this. So it seemed unrealistic to base the whole theoretical system on the belief that we are all robots driven by pure greed and nothing more.

Economics as if people mattered was a new concept and its general conclusion was dire. The current thinking that the bigger the enterprise the bigger the profit was driving the human race towards misery and breakdown, and our planet towards exhaustion of resources. It seemed plausible and was brilliantly argued. The pleasure of reading it can be gauged from a brief selection of its aphorisms, each a nugget of wisdom. First and most delightful: 'All predictions are unreliable, particularly those about the future.' 'Man is small and therefore small is beautiful.' 'There is more to life than Gross National Product.' 'There cannot be unlimited, generalised growth. If we use up fossil fuels we threaten civilisation. But if we squander the capital represented by living Nature through pollution we threaten life itself.' 'Our most important task is to get off the present collision course.' The urgency

179

of Schumacher's warning was redoubled by its novelty. For the date he first published it was 1973 – at the height of a boom, which of course soon turned into bust. Almost forty years (and many editions) later the truth of his prophesies has been recognised by general consensus. But it has taken ages and we have still done painfully little to avert the catastrophe he foresaw. Measures to conserve the earth's resources and preserve it from pollution, to keep our environment and the life it supports renewable, are still hopelessly inadequate. They are only too likely to be overtaken by extinction. As he pointed out: 'The single-minded pursuit of wealth – materialism – does not fit this world because our environment is strictly limited. Gandhi told us the earth has enough to satisfy every man's need but not every man's greed. But where is the rich society that says, "Halt! We have enough"?'

Mega-corporations still dominate world trade. But throughout the developed world society is beginning to revolt against the consequences of large-scale, multinational capitalism which rewards the already rich with further riches while the poor remain even further behind. The current nostrum, 'Capitalism with a human face', was exactly what Schumacher was recommending, with concrete suggestions of how to achieve it forty precious years ago. Not many prophets are so speedily vindicated. It restores one's faith in the power of a book, originally issued by a small, fringe publisher, now defunct, to change minds.

When I went to find the great Dr Schumacher, known to his friends as 'Fritz', he was busy planting trees in the grounds of his large house in Surrey. Though sixty-five he looked tall, lithe and vigorous. He was the only economist I know of who had worked as an agricultural labourer. This was because when war broke out he was working in Britain as an academic still not naturalised (he was born in Bonn and educated at Oxford). Promptly interned as an 'enemy alien' he was set to work on a farm for £2 a week. He was soon elected camp leader by his fellow aliens. He immediately had me too under his leadership, fork in hand, helping to plant trees. In line with his beliefs, his large garden was highly productive. It fed a large family and friends. Maynard Keynes, having read one of his papers, got him released from internment and into government service. He worked on preparing the Beveridge Report. After victory he advised the British administration in Germany, then the newly-created National Coal Board. He also worked in Burma. One of the foundations of his thinking he called 'Buddhist economics'. The Buddhist sees consumption mainly as a means to human well-being so the logical aim is to obtain the maximum well-being with the minimum consumption. Hence the rational way to produce is by using local resources for local needs (it also believes that everyone should plant trees). In Surrey he was doing both.

'I go across this hill to Jimmy Anderson's organic farm and put a sack of his wheat in my car. I have a stone grinder which takes fifteen minutes a week to grind it. It takes another twenty minutes or so to do the weekly baking. Think what that leaves out. Hundreds of miles of transportation to mills, bakeries and supermarkets, large fuel costs, much pollution, administration and book-keeping and costly management...' This was undeniable but could it be done by people in general? His recipe was that we should create small-scale production units, fitting the needs of moderate-sized communities, using modest tools and plant. 'Intermediate Technology,' he called it. Now renamed Practical Action it is flourishing today, in impoverished Third World countries of Africa and Asia. There it supplies simple solutions to communities for drought, drainage, drinking water, improving crops, infertile soil and cheap building, all of which can be done by local people themselves. But it works in rich countries like our own. Depressed areas such as Newcastle, Cumbria, Vermont or Montana pioneered mini-plants – brickworks, glassworks, motor-works, paper mills using local recycled waste. Schumacher was no study-bound theorist. He took personal part in setting up such works, firms which manufacture water heaters, measuring instruments, small motors and the like.

Relaxing from our labours over tea he talked about unemployment, which was as much of a problem in the 1970s as in the recessions of the next century. 'People think that in order to have a job someone must provide it. Usually at a very high capital cost. But it is far more normal to be self-employed or to work in small groups on something requiring a modest amount of capital and technology. For example, why shouldn't door and window frames be made by local carpentry shops for local house builders? The first thing to do is to persuade people that they can do things for themselves, as our ancestors used to do.' I would have listened to him forever but, alas, Fritz Schumacher soon afterwards dropped dead. His name and his multitude of followers and organisations like Practical Action continue. His mantra – 'Small is Beautiful' – is still going unheard in the unthinking drive for eternal and unsustainable growth. Ever bigger global corporations threaten the ability of any nation's rulers to control their own economies or even collect their taxes. Large-scale industrialised agriculture rides roughshod over the health and beauty of the countryside. Small farms are not only kinder to the landscape and its wildlife, but smaller farmers lead more rewarding lives. Small sociable shops are being extinguished everywhere by supermarket machines for shopping in, where nobody speaks to anyone, not even at the automated check-outs. Smallish towns with centuries of accumulated character are being submerged in the generalised blight of uniform but messy development that has ruined the urban United States.

Say it every day: 'Small is Beautiful and Big is usually Beastly.' One day soon it has got to sink in.

ALBERT SPEER

After Dr Schumacher a less admirable but equally cultured German preoccupied my attention. Like anyone whose adolescence coincided with the war, I grew up jeering and singing rude songs about Hitler and his gang.

> Hitler – has only got one ball
> Goering's – are very, very small
> Himmler – is somewhat similar
> While Doctor Goebbels
> Has no balls – at all

Which went very satisfactorily to the tune of *Colonel Bogey*. How intriguing it would have been to meet one of these monsters to see if they were actually human. The one surviving member of Hitler's inner circle was Albert Speer, the only one who admitted responsibility and guilt at the Nuremberg trials, the so-called 'civilised Nazi'. When the excuse to go and find him occurred I naturally jumped at it. In 1977 Hitler was back in the headlines. Had he *not* personally given the orders for the Final Solution – as was now claimed by the eccentric, though otherwise well qualified historian, David Irving? And in the final weeks of war did he behave as described in the recently exhumed diaries of Josef Goebbels? After the debacle of the forged 'Hitler Diaries' we were all nervous. Were these genuine? Speer was the man to ask. So I telephoned him at his family home in Heidelberg and after finding him ready, even anxious to talk made an appointment to meet him in Munich.

It was a meeting I looked forward to with extreme curiosity. I wanted to know what was it like to be Hitler's closest companion, his acknowledged favourite over twelve years – the only minister who could disagree, disobey, even defy the Führer and get away with it? And how had so civilised a man fallen under his spell? Sent for as a young architect of twenty-seven he had accepted a Faustian bargain with this Mephistopheles. The bait was the prospect of unlimited scope as the architect that Hitler himself had wanted to be. But it was more than a patron–protégé relationship. Together they spent hours dreaming intoxicating dreams of rebuilding German cities, especially Berlin. It was to be an overpowering Valhalla with triumphal drives as wide as airport runways leading to a dome to dwarf all previous domes. It was to be renamed Germania, 'the world capital'. Its scale would have reduced Berliners to beetles. It remained a fantasy of plans and models, their joint baby. Coming from a patrician family Speer could have spent a busy life as a commercial architect with a portfolio of buildings to his credit. But the outcome of his making the bargain was that virtually no building of his survived him.

Speer's own secret diaries, which he kept on scraps of paper in his twenty years in Spandau jail, had just been published. They revealed him wrestling almost daily with his contradictory feelings about Hitler, whom he by then saw as pure evil. 'How was it possible that he captivated me for so long?' he wrote bemusedly. 'In the last months I suddenly noticed how ugly, how repellent and ill-proportioned his face was.' Yet in earlier years he had 'felt comfortable' in his company. 'I didn't notice his clumsy exaggerations, his ill-chosen ties.' There is a telltale photograph of them together sitting on a park bench at Obersalzburg. They are sitting at opposite ends staring away from each other in obvious tension. The picture calls out for the caption 'A Lovers' Tiff'. There was something here that needed to be explained.

Munich turned out to be freezing and icebound in March – but not within the comforts of the grand Four Seasons Hotel where Speer had a suite. His royalties from his accounts of the Third Reich had made him rich. There were greetings and politenesses in German with him and his wife Margarethe, whom he called Margret, the woman who had waited twenty years for him to return from prison. She withdrew tactfully to let us talk. Speer was tall, suave and still distinguished by his curiously uptilted black bushy eyebrows. For a penitent he seemed very relaxed and sure of himself, even in English in which he was fluent with very little accent. After his release he had thought of resuming as an architect, he said, but had settled for memoir writing for which there was more demand.

He swiftly disposed of the David Irving hypothesis as being hardly worth discussion. 'Of course there are no documents authorising the mass killing of Jews over Hitler's signature. Hitler gave orders verbally. Written ones were very rare. As for Himmler, who carried out the policy, he would never have dared to set up death camps without Hitler's permission. His nature was submissive, very dependent on Hitler's approval, easily depressed if he displeased the Führer. It is not conceivable that it was carried out except on direct verbal orders from Hitler. And he would have known the details. He wanted to know everything down to the smallest detail.' And Speer? How much did he know? He was so used to being asked this question that I had little hope of hearing anything new. He had never admitted knowing any details but once conceded having showed 'tacit acceptance' of what was going on. Many did not accept this equivocation. They said he did not deserve to escape the death penalty. On the other hand his admission of guilt had made him highly unpopular in some quarters in Germany.

So when did he hear about the Holocaust? 'I never really heard about it. What Hitler often repeated to us in private was always some vague general statement such as, "I am going to destroy the Jewish people." He never said anything like, "Now I have given the order to kill them."' So he did not take the threats literally? He gave a just detectable shake of the head. He was never going to be drawn. But he had no doubt of the genuineness of the Goebbels diaries of life in Hitler's shadow, full of details no forger could have known. 'I can hear Goebbels's voice in everything he writes, full of hatred for those he blamed for Germany's defeat, especially Goering whom he calls "the bemedalled idiot". Yet he himself still clung to the belief that if Hitler would only make one more speech everything could still be saved. It is the diary of a man who does not allow himself to see what is happening. It is a very good description of the fantastic, unreal world around Hitler at the end. Goebbels was one of the cleverest and ablest men in the inner circle. I'm surprised that he lost the power to see things as they were. I was the only one who realised, long before this, that the war was lost. I knew that in 1943.'

Speer thought of Goebbels as cool, rational, decisive but two-sided. 'He was a good father, nice to his friends yet he wanted to have all the captured Allied pilots shot. He filmed the hangings of the July plotters and invited us all to watch them being strangled from meat hooks. I refused to go.' Speer showed emotion only in relation to Goebbels's wife Magda, whom he clearly admired, as did Hitler, who thought her the perfect woman. She had married Goebbels in order to remain close to Hitler as 'first lady' of the Reich. She went to him in a rage because of Goebbels's constant affairs with actresses. At her prompting Hitler ordered him to give up his current mistress, the film star Barova, but Magda refused to have him back in the house. In his place she had fallen for his state secretary, Karl Hanke, who bombarded her with besotted love letters. Everything came to an embarrassing crunch at the 1939 Bayreuth Festival, which the Goebbels and Speers were expected to attend in Hitler's box. Speer was an amused spectator of this untypical Nazi scene. 'As luck would have it the opera that night was *Tristan and Isolde*. Frau Goebbels sat there weeping loudly throughout. At the interval Hitler had to stand to acknowledge the audience's applause pretending not to notice the audible sobs coming from behind him. Next day he told the couple to go away and make it up somehow. Hanke, Magda's lover, was sent to join the army in Poland. "With women Goebbels is a cynic," Hitler told me.' I did not have the nerve to ask him whether he thought Magda's daughters, blonde perfect Aryan specimens, were in fact fathered by Goebbels, whose dark, demonic features did not look the least like theirs, or ordered from one of the notorious Aryan breeding farms.

The period that fascinates everyone like a horror film is the final one in the bunker beneath the Berlin chancellery as the city collapsed around it under Russian bombardment. Speer witnessed this on his spectacularly reckless return in a small plane to the almost cut-off capital. The plane was a Fiesler Storch, capable of flying very low and of landing on a virtual handkerchief of roadway in the city centre. He had by then lost his faith in Hitler and had spent the previous months countermanding the Führer's 'Nero' order to destroy everything that was in the Allied path of advance and reduce Germany to ruin. To go back seemed a mad and pointless gesture. What made him do it? For once Speer seemed lost for a ready reply. 'It was mesmerism,' he said at last. 'Goebbels was a good example of being subjugated by Hitler's mesmeric power, rational as he was in other respects. That mesmerism still worked on me to some extent. Why did I fly in when everyone else was getting out? The answer is I wanted to see Hitler again. After our twelve years together I could not just sneak away without saying goodbye.' Hitler already knew that Speer had been traversing the Ruhr and the Rhine ordering that the ready-dynamited railways, roads, bridges and factories should not be blown up. 'But I felt that I had to tell him so personally.'

Did he not wonder whether Hitler would respond by having him shot? He nodded. Only on the previous day Hitler had gone berserk and screamed the bunker down when he learned that the orders to move his largely imaginary troops around Berlin had not been carried out. 'But I found he was too weary, too absent-minded to react. He did not want to know any more. He had decided to kill himself.' He wanted Speer's opinion on whether he should do it there in Berlin or at Obersalzberg to which he might still, just, escape. Speer thought it more fitting to die in Berlin, which was what Hitler wanted to hear. His fear of falling into Russian hands alive was intolerable. Their disjointed conversation was accompanied by the muffled roar of gunfire as the Russians blasted their way through the suburbs. Hitler finally showed emotion. 'Despite our disagreements, I assured him of my unchanging personal loyalty. Believing that everyone had betrayed him, he stood silent with tears in his eyes. But when the moment came to leave he simply held out his limp hand – "So you're leaving? Good. Auf Wiedersehen" – and turned back to his papers.' He was either quite impersonal, or struggling to conceal his emotion.

Speer's next call was on Eva Braun. Usually dismissed as a nonentity who polished her nails and did little else, he thought her a spirited girl and liked her. She welcomed him warmly because she had been certain that he at least would come back to see Hitler. Hitler had ordered her and the girl secretaries to leave for Bavaria but when she refused they had done likewise. Speer admired the calm courage with which she was facing her impending death at Hitler's side. The woman he most wanted to see, Magda Goebbels, had retired to bed, pale with angina. She had already made the arrangements to have her children poisoned. 'I went in to see her. Goebbels was there and stood over us all the time. I knew there was something she wanted to say to me in private but I never found out what it was. He would not allow us a moment together for farewell,' he said with a trace of bitterness still in his voice. 'I liked Magda. She was a charming, cultured erudite woman, full of common sense...and a great friend of mine. I never thought she would become fanatic enough to kill her children and herself. Why? None of the other wives did.' Everyone's imagination of the bunker is haunted by the thought of those six lively, happy children, who used to have tea and games with Hitler even in the bunker, being given cyanide capsules while they slept. 'The world that comes after National Socialism is no longer worth living in. That is why I have taken the children with me – they are too good for the life that will follow.' So Magda wrote in her last letter addressed to her son, Harald. Perhaps that is what she would have told Speer, this Nazi Medea whom neither he nor the world was able to comprehend.

So at nearly four in the morning he left this catacomb of death and walked out through the ruined halls of the grandiose chancellery which he had built for Hitler in 1939. What can he have felt at the sight of it? The hall of dark red marble was blackened, its glass ceiling shattered on the floor like pebbles. Everywhere there were craters and rubble and the detritus of a defeated army. It was the grandest building of his that had been completed. The only building of his to survive was a country cottage he built for his parents. Such was the reward for throwing in his lot with Hitler.

But our session did not end on this sombre note. I asked him about his work as wartime minister for armaments. He cheered up remarkably. Out came his briefcase which he unlocked with almost a flourish. It just so happened that he had the relevant figures with him. Looking at them he was a man transformed. Gone was the smooth impersonality with which he had talked hitherto. 'See, here are the output figures of armaments throughout your bombing offensive. Look – 1943, well up on 1942 and here, 1944 is even better! Weapons production up three hundred per cent, tanks six hundred per cent!' Despite the massive day and night bombing and dam-busting, factories and production plants had been repaired, dispersed, concealed and improvised. It enabled Germany to go on fighting. Here was German efficiency directed by an organiser of genius. It was calculated that without Speer's achievement German resistance would have collapsed two years sooner. 'So Air Marshal Harris was wrong? Area bombing of cities was ineffective?' He almost smiled. 'If he had concentrated on purely industrial targets we could never have survived so long.' So the much vaunted theory of the time that crushing civilian cities would break morale and end the war actually prolonged it. And here, animated and triumphant even thirty years later, was the brilliant architect not of buildings but of war production. Here was the technocrat who had so ably supported Hitler and yet knew, as he achieved his targets, that it was all for a war that was already lost. That was the ultimate enigma of Albert Speer.

ALEC GUINNESS

I felt quite familiar with the claustrophobic interior of the Berlin bunker because it had been partly reconstructed, I assume accurately, at Shepperton studios for a film entitled *Hitler: The Last Ten Days*. I was sitting on a sofa in Hitler's office when someone came in and sat down beside me. With a frisson I took in the over-large grey military jacket with its single gold swastika button and Iron Cross, the pasty face with its limp forelock, the narrow blot of a moustache. There was a second frisson when Hitler began to speak in the suave, cultured tone of an English gentleman. We took tea together from Meissen cups decorated with swastikas.

Hitler is not perhaps one of Alec Guinness's best-remembered parts – the film itself was mauled in the cutting room before it appeared in 1973 – but it was one which he was unusually contented with and proud of, done with great care. He had spent a long time growing and gradually pruning the moustache. 'It's now almost a postage stamp, a fraction too narrow, but that is in order to make my nose look as broad as his. It's terribly embarrassing if I go out in public. I feel I should cover it up.' He had worked hard on the voice. There were no recordings of Hitler speaking in private, only his ranting speeches, which could be used only for one hysterical outburst. 'I am told he spoke in a low voice, none too grammatically and with a bad accent. But I am not doing a "common" voice nor using a German accent. I say "Bear-lin" but not "Bear-leen" which would be more correct.' His face had assumed the droop of defeat beneath the hooded, haunted eyes of the late photographs. The shuffling walk, dragging the left foot, the tremble in one hand and the limp backward flap with the other in a token Nazi salute, he had studied with a survivor from the bunker who was present. This was a cavalry captain, Gerhardt Boldt, who was sent into the bunker with a message then ordered to remain to give Hitler briefings on the military situation. Herr Boldt told me the resemblance Guinness had created was amazing. 'He is the only actor who could be so credible. In fact Hitler was even feebler physically than Guinness makes him. I remember the shock it gave me to find my Führer reduced to such apathy.'

Spending five months reading and watching all available records was not enough. 'It's a question of trying to feel like him. I have become obsessed with Hitler. For God's sake, I hold no brief for his philosophy but I am determined to be fair to him on a human level. The film must not become cheap propaganda. This was a man able to sway eighty million people. You see them at the rallies happy and laughing. He also had a following outside Germany, including in Britain. He was a small man who in some way contrived to be great. Evil as he was, he had charisma – no one can become a dictator without it. Attila the Hun must have had charm. Gangsters often have charm.' He gave me a ghostly smile. 'Film moguls can have charm.' How had he felt trying to get inside such a mind for months at a time? 'Let's face it, evil or wicked people are more interesting to play than good ones.' Although he found the film 'sadly disappointing' afterwards he still counted it as one of the few performances with which he was most satisfied.

He did not usually talk about his work. At our first meeting on a country ramble around Chichester where he was appearing he talked about his other ambition, writing. 'I would love to have been a writer. People like Graham (Greene) living where they please, they have the glamorous life.' He had his writing desk ready prepared at his home near Petersfield. 'I buy reams of expensive fine paper and watch it yellowing and getting dusty.' Everything was ready except the starting spurt on to the blank page. He had made screenplays or stage adaptations of other people's works but his own voice refused to ignite. 'But it did once,' I said. 'What about your short story? About the ship caught in a terrible Mediterranean storm?' It had appeared in one of the little magazines that were published around the end of the war, *New Writing*. It described a horrifying wartime voyage struck by a hurricane in a bucking ship which was outlined in the phosphorescent electronic phenomenon called St Elmo's Fire. What was so powerful was the sense of impending doom building up beforehand and the 'voice' which had woken the writer in his cabin by intoning the warning, 'Tomorrow!' I had never forgotten it. He looked thoughtful. 'That happened to me in the Adriatic when I was in the Navy. I don't remember getting any reaction to its publication.' Well, it had left me in no doubt that he could write.

I wondered whether he had had other premonitions of doom like the one he described there. 'Yes. Of evil.' He told me of his meeting one evening in Hollywood with James Dean, who was showing off his new sports car, a Porsche Spyder. 'Something sinister about that car made me beg him not to get into it. "If you do," I told him, "you will be dead by this time next week." He did – and precisely a week later he was.' Nearly twenty years after that I opened a review copy of his memoir, *Blessings in Disguise*. There were the two stories brilliantly told amid a gallery of subtly and ironically drawn portraits of people he had worked with on stage or screen. Gielgud, Richardson, Tyrone Guthrie and others leapt from the pages in all their amusing quirkiness. He had got past the blank page at last. He also lifted the curtain a little on his disturbed, unstable and illegitimate childhood, the rackety life with a mother who drank and refused to tell him who his father was. One could see why he might have a permanent sense of insecurity and, after the poverty he endured while trying to get started as an actor, an anxiety about money. Surely the films must pay well? 'But on January the 1st the taxman takes it all back!'

The patron who took trouble to get him started in the 1930s was John Gielgud. I once asked Gielgud why Guinness had had such a discouraging start. With typical unexpectedness he replied: 'Poor Alec! His ears were so big and stuck out so much that he used to try to pin them back with chewing gum.' A glance at early photographs confirmed this no doubt mortifying handicap. *Blessings in Disguise* tells you a good deal about his contemporaries' hang-ups but very little about Guinness's. He was obsessively private, referring to himself as 'one', like the Queen. Confession, except to a priestly Roman Catholic, was not Guinness's style. In our suspicious age that led to speculation that he had something to hide – homosexual leanings, perhaps? –

there was no such evidence, other than his liking for the company of handsome young men who worked for him. His lifelong marriage seemed rock-solid, despite his disconcerting habit of disparaging his wife Merula as a cook in front of their guests. Having had to exist on a bun and an apple a day made him eager for rich dining at posh restaurants in later life, after his financial anxiety had been laid to rest by *Star Wars*. How he felt about getting such fame and riches from what is basically a children's story, playing an elderly wizard who hardly tested his talents, can be judged from the remark he made while filming it: 'What I'm supposed to be doing I really can't say.' One boy in America accompanied by a doting mother solicited his autograph as Obi-Wan Kenobi. 'He's been to see the film over seventy times!' said the proud mother. Guinness looked at the boy. 'I'll sign this for you only if you promise me never to see it again!'

Self-denigration came easily to Guinness. At the beginning of his memoir he wrote, typically in the third person, as if he were a stranger: 'The bold statement is never likely to be his: he is well aware he is not in the same class as Olivier, Richardson, Gielgud or the other greats.' Having made this unnecessary genuflection he wrote me a postcard to thank me for my 'kind remarks about the very amateur and no doubt foolish book'. Guinness's postcards typified him. They were frighteningly neat. In a beautifully shaped but miniscule italic hand his lines ran as perfectly straight as did the margins and exactly fitted the performing space available. No doubt his disordered homes, always changing, made him insistent on order and control and gave him a distrust of the 'bold statement'. He pioneered a then quite new style of 'non-acting' on a stage that was replete with what he called 'struttings and bellowings'. 'Oh, I used to shut myself in a room and scream Shakespeare,' he told me, 'but until it's disciplined it isn't acting.' He had no need to bellow – his voice was as sonorous and harmonious as Gielgud's. But his restraint did not mark him out for big heroic roles. He once ran through his failures for me: his Hamlet – 'a disaster'; likewise, his Macbeth (ruined not by him but by miscasting Lady Macbeth and drenching the whole play in relentless light). His Richard III in Stratford, Ontario – 'It wasn't up to much' – and his Malvolio, described by Olivier as a bore: 'I was told there was about a minute at the end that was all right.'

A ROGUES' GALLERY

When he finally got the chance to play Shylock it was in an indifferent production on the wide Chichester stage where he pulled off a characteristic Guinness effect – by getting on stage and staying there for several minutes without anybody noticing. Then came the moment when the crowd of people awaiting the trial were shocked by a sudden rasping sound. It was the Jew, revealed sitting on the floor purposefully whetting his knife. The shocking meaning of 'a pound of flesh', so often thrown away as a figure of speech, suddenly became an urgent and gruesome possibility. Such Guinness moments occur in films too numerous to mention and in so many disguises. But close up his face could turn quite blank, the mask of a mime, which in essence he was. There was a monastic cast to his normal expression. Once we were comparing our experiences of being guests in monasteries – 'The most effective escape I know from the worries of work, money, ambition, security,' he said. 'The only thing I can't stand is the food. The monks insist on trying to cook the sort of food they think you would like instead of their own vegetarian diet. Last time I took my own fruit and vegetables and wouldn't eat. The Trappists grew quite alarmed. They thought I was fasting more severely than they were!' He gave a momentary smile at having upstaged the monks, like a sliver of new moon glimpsed through clouds. Though he could irradiate his face with a seraphic beam, like Herbert Pocket's in *Great Expectations*, and ended it as the character ironically named Smiley, Guinness was no smiler. The mask would quickly empty and he was back inside that locked space he inhabited behind it.

JON SNOW

The coast of Trengganu, one of the most backward Malay states in the far north-east of Malaysia, looked in 1978 like an illustration from a Boy's Own Paper adventure story set in the days of Empire. Houses on stilts stood alongside the river under the palm trees. And precious little else. South Vietnam had fallen to the Communists three years earlier but suddenly there was a mass exodus of the citizens of Saigon bobbing in precarious fishing boats across the South China Sea to land – if they made it – in Trengganu. For once it was in the world spotlight. The refugees were christened the Boat People. As their numbers swelled into the tens of thousands, Malaysia took fright at the possibility of being swamped by immigrants who were ethnically non-Malay, already a third of the population. Everything was being done to prevent them from landing. Police patrol boats intercepted and turned them away or towed them off the shore. Those that got through were met by organised local mobs throwing stones. Those that got ashore were dumped in camps on islands several miles offshore from which journalists were fiercely excluded.

When I arrived the remnants of one of the last boats to beach were sticking pathetically out of the boiling waters on the harbour bar. I was told it had been towed out by a police launch and abandoned to its fate. The locals had watched it break up and its human cargo, including many children, drown. Almost simultaneously there arrived Jon Snow and an ITN cameraman for Channel Four. He was not then the well-groomed news presenter familiar these many years but an eager young reporter with an abundance of tousled hair and very inquisitive, interrogating eyes. He had a naturally commanding air. He wasn't the son of a public school headmaster and bishop for nothing, not to mention having a grandfather who had been a general, KCB, KCMG, etc. But this was combined with a rebel streak that had made him a leader of student protest at Liverpool University from which he had been sent down without a degree. Instead he had served in Voluntary Service Overseas – in those days unqualified young recruits were welcome – in remotest Uganda. Here he had learned about poverty and dictatorial methods at first hand. This had changed him into an opponent of authority, for all his air of having it.

One night we watched the beaching of a refugee boat on the shore near the hotel where the international press were staying. As Snow and his cameraman advanced into the surf, the camera lights brilliantly illuminating the boat and the refugees wading ashore, a hysterical, gesticulating police officer tried to stop the filming. 'You must have pass!' 'I have a pass from the Ministry of Foreign Affairs!' declared Snow loudly (which he hadn't). From his full height he cowed the opposition by announcing imperially: 'We shall proceed to film!' Walking back to the hotel afterwards we were surrounded and ordered to attend the chief at the police station. We said that he could come to see us. So for the next two hours we were kept under guard of two rifle-wielding policemen, sitting on the palm-fringed sea shore. This vigil lost its charm as it grew cooler and we adjourned to the hotel's garden nearby for a nightcap. 'You can come with us,' we told our guards. Our captors kept watch from the shadows. 'I'm going to bed,' I said. Giving them our room numbers 'in case you need us' Snow and I went inside. We discussed the problem of getting near enough the refugees to interview them before they were snatched away behind barbed wire. The obvious tactic was to hire a boat and go out to sea to meet them.

Next day we found a fishing boat and its owner whom we persuaded for five hundred Malay dollars (over £200, a lot of money in Trengganu) to risk setting forth. All day we bounced on the billows of the empty sea. Our skipper, wrapped in a crimson headcloth, was more concerned about being spotted by a police patrol – he put his forearms together to indicate being handcuffed. Then in late afternoon he pointed to the horizon: 'Boat comes now.' As we approached we could see the VT 666 had draped its hull with sheets like washing, bearing messages in English: HELP US! HELP REFUGEES FROM COMMUNIST VIETNAM! WE HAVE RISKED OUR LIVES FOR FREEDOM! DON'T DISAPPOINT US! From a little mast flew a white flag marked SOS. Men and boys hung over the side waving eagerly. Climbing aboard we discovered why the urgent appeals were displayed. They had tried to land further down the coast and been beaten off by police boats. 'What kind of country is this?' demanded a man in an orange helmet. 'Don't they have a government?' He was the skipper, Mr Tuong, who had designed the boat with separate latrines over the side for men and women, built and steered it across a sea notorious for shipwrecks and pirates for four days. It was crammed with desperate people seeking to join the free world. How could we explain to this brave, resourceful man that the free world was not particularly anxious to see them?

The men thrust at us their testimonials bearing witness to the services they had rendered the American forces occupying South Vietnam through ten years of war. They were all skilled or professional men who had paid $2,000 for the voyage. Mr Tuong, a printer, had worked for the US Information Agency. Now his printing business had been confiscated because he refused to print Communist propaganda. A doctor's wife said to me: 'I thought we were all going to drown but I decided I would rather die at sea than live in Vietnam as it is now.' They could not grasp that the American devotion to freedom and democracy in Vietnam did not apply to Vietnamese as refugees in the US. It was accepting a pitifully small quota of one hundred and fifty refugees a week. There were already some forty thousand waiting in the camps. Now here were two hundred more. The hold was carpeted with women and children lying pressed side by side like sardines, sick and frightened but disciplined. The skipper was justifiably proud of his ship. Now, we told him, he had to wreck it by driving it up the beach so it could not be re-floated.

Snow decided that he and his cameraman Claus would remain on board to guide the boat ashore where our hotel stood while I took back the film they had already shot and mobilised a press audience for the landing. It proved spectacular. As night fell the VT 666 charged up the beach belching smoke, splintering its keel. With a loud explosion the engine burnt out. The waiting mob rushed forward unrestrained by the watching police and a pitched battle began with those who were trying to disembark. Snow was in the thick of it, then disappeared in a tide of angry heads. The crowd, unable to get at those on board turned on the watching journalists and began to stone us instead. As we retreated through the hotel garden a Voice of America correspondent beside me was felled by a stone which hit him on the head with a loud ugly clonk. Besieged, the journalists melted away indoors. After the crowd had thinned I sneaked out and back to the boat. The refugees were being carted away in lorries. Jon Snow and his cameraman were pulled off in handcuffs and were driven away to the police cells. I spent the rest of the night trying to get them out.

Thanks to the time difference, London was still at work. I rang ITN and got somebody I knew, Hugh Whitcomb, who set about contacting the Foreign and Commonwealth Office to raise a stink. I filed my piece highlighting Snow's plight. The High Commission in Kuala Lumpur was bereft of all but a night watchman. At length I tracked down the home number of the Trengganu police superintendent. He was not pleased to be woken by my harangue: 'Do you realise what you've done? You've arrested one of the best-known television reporters in Britain! There's going to be a hell of a row – I shall see that there is. The British Foreign Office is already involved...' I broke off to what sounded like an oath and tried to rustle up a taxi to the police station. I arrived only shortly after the superintendent. He had had second thoughts. There was not long to wait before Jon and Claus appeared from the passage leading to the unhygienic cells. Dishevelled, he had lost his Olympian calm. He was cold with fury. 'Who is responsible for this outrage?' The assembled coppers looked blank. If he had his way somebody was going to pay for it. I dissuaded him from our spending any longer in police company, which easily could become custody. Our breakfast at the hotel, I said, was getting cold. His first question as we returned was: 'Have you got our film?' This was retrieved from the bushes where I had hidden it, guessing that my room would be searched. He grabbed the canisters and shot off to the airport. There were no satellite links in those days.

I was smuggled into the barbed wired camp where the refugees were being held. Their reason for escaping was simple: freedom. The

Vietcong had nationalised all small businesses and expected them to work for the state for next to nothing. They hated Communism and dreamed of America, their promised land. Now it seemed that the waiting list for entry could last a lifetime. America's conscience appeared untroubled about the land they had wrecked for nothing, They wanted to forget Vietnam. The Malaysian minister for home affairs, Tan Sri Ghazzali, had been taunting the president publicly: 'Mr Carter, don't leave it all to the UN commission and Brigitte Bardot' (she had espoused the Boat People's cause).

At Trengganu's little airport next day I ran into Tan Sri Ghazzali conducting a public relations exercise for the investigating Willy Brandt Commission, led by Katherine Graham of the *Washington Post*. He was taking them by helicopter to view the island camps distantly from the air. Enjoying the international attention he had dressed for the occasion in black paramilitary uniform, cowboy boots, huge sunglasses and a dazzling white crash helmet. He pranced with self-importance. I dogged his footsteps towards the helicopter, calling out questions which he ignored. At last I shouted: 'Tan Sri! People are drowning. The good name of Malaysia is at stake!' He spun round in fury. 'And why is it at stake? Because of you! *Because of you and your nose-poking!*' The Willy Brandt Commission suddenly looked alert. This was a new side to their smooth-talking host. For once I felt quite proud of my calling as a nose-poker. And it had been enjoyable to share it with so determined a reporter as Jon Snow.

THE SHAH

From steamy Trengganu I flew to freezing Tehran where I had an appointment with the Shah. But by the time I got there in November, 1978, he could no longer keep it. He was barricaded in his palace behind a wall of tanks which Britain had considerately sold him. There may have been less appealing capital cities than Tehran but at that moment of revolutionary turmoil it was hard to think of one – or of a more unappealing ruler. The streets were given over to demonstrations and massacres of demonstrators by his army. The shops were shuttered, the banks bricked up, the bazaar, the schools, university and railway station closed, the airport open only intermittently. The electricity failed more often than it succeeded and if you ventured out after the 9pm curfew, you might either be beaten up by SAVAK, the secret police, or shot. It was a city in the grip of terminal sickness. No one had made anything, sold anything, mended anything or cleared up anything for weeks. I was lucky to find a pair of warm trousers and a sweater hanging from the street railings. This unofficial trader also offered to throw in a long-dead chicken and a sack of old potatoes. This was the state which the Shah's Great Civilisation had reached.

The citizens had had enough of him. The slogan 'Marg Bar Shah' (death to the Shah) was shouted from their cars by day and from the rooftops by night, accompanied by bursts of gun fire. To add to the gaiety it was the month of Moharram, when Shia Muslims (including most Iranians) mourn their martyred Imam Husein. He was killed in an unequal battle with a usurping Caliph in the year 680. Martyrdom is highly regarded by the Shia who processed the streets dressed in black, wielding chains with which some flagellated their own backs until they bled. Many of them claimed they were ready for martyrdom in the struggle to unseat the Shah – and many paid that price. I spent the following days looking down the wrong end of tank gun barrels. Fortunately Mianji, my daily taxi driver, was an ace at tight about-turns at speed. Some days the dead numbered a mere dozen, other days several. They ended up in the huge cemetery on the southern limit of the city, dug into the hard soil, coffin-less and shrouded in white.

I went to see the burials and was harangued by hostile relatives because I was British. Everyone seemed to have a Polaroid to show me of the bloodied corpse of their loved one. 'He was not only my brother but your brother!' shouted an angry youth. A pile of shrouded corpses waiting in the queue for burial was stacked on shelves in a mortuary. There were several mothers searching for their sons. Popular hatred was directed at the Shah, the Americans and the British, whose puppet they regarded him as being, with some justification. Several said they wanted to murder him with their bare hands. The cemetery was the main outlet left for free speech because the deadly members of SAVAK dared not show their faces there.

Tehran is built on a north-south slope. The rich live in the northern suburbs rising toward the snow-capped mountains. The poor – probably four million strong – lived towards the southern end. There was no underground sewage system. Open concrete drains ran downhill on either side of the main road to the cemetery so it was a journey of increasing squalor. Every time it rained the channels disgorged their refuse between blocks of Stalinist flats of increasing nastiness, then came single storey homes, shacks and hovels. The cemetery represented the ultimate in waste disposal.

Naturally the Shah's Niavaran Palace was in the north. But his neighbours, the old aristocracy of Persia, regarded his family, the Pahlavis, as vulgar upstarts. The Shah's father, Reza, began as a sergeant in the Cossack brigade, rose through the ranks and seized power in the 1920s. He was in the habit of going into mosques and firing a burst from his automatic rifle, I was told, to show he was not afraid of Allah. He thought highly of Hitler and planned an alliance with him during the war, which led the British and Russians to invade and pack him off to exile. This left his son, Mohammed Reza, barely out of university, in his place as Shah. In 1953 the present Shah in turn had to be put back on the Peacock Throne by an American-British secret service operation, after he fled to Rome in fear of a coup. This was to ensure that Anglo-Iranian Oil (later BP) remained under Western control. The Shah believed he was under divine protection ever since an assassin fired five bullets from close range. One grazed his head, the others went through his hat. Nevertheless he carried a small pistol in his pocket in case divine protection failed. He would have been stupid not to. My friend, the journalist Margaret Laing, succeeded against difficulties in writing his biography. The first question she was asked when the book was proposed was: 'Are you expecting £10,000 from His Imperial Majesty?' She was not, which baffled the Persian intermediaries. Criticism of any kind was unthinkable. Although he was the only man in the country who need not be afraid of the Shah, she found him distinctly nervous about being interviewed. When she asked about the notorious use of torture he replied: 'We use the same methods as you.'

His people saw him as an Anglo-American lackey and were unimpressed with his grandiose titles – 'Light of the Aryans', 'Chief of the Warriors' and 'Shah of Shahs'. His modernisation programme had given Tehran a top dressing of half-finished tower blocks and seedy cinemas – but no sewage pipes. The money from the second largest oil producing country had gone on weapons, including a huge air fleet, and on palaces and personal investments not only in Iran but Europe and California. He was reckoned the third biggest oil billionaire after the Saudi and Kuwaiti ruling families. I could find no one – politicians, clergy, students, women or ordinary citizens – with a good word to say for him. Without exception they declared he must go. So guided by instructions from the mosques they marched, not in thousands, but a million strong. The thirty-foot-wide avenue bisecting the city from east to west, known then as Shah Reza, ran dead straight mile upon mile. The marchers filled it from edge to edge and end to end. They shouted and beat their brandished fists in unison as if knocking on a door: 'Death to the Shah! Freedom! Islam! Khomeini!' Aged Ayatollahs were carried along on men's backs with beards wagging. Khomeini was present everywhere on placards. The marchers were so young, their leaders so old. But the discipline imposed by the mosque leaders was such that not a shop window was broken.

The western end of the avenue ended under the giant splayed feet of a sawn-off Eiffel Tower in dazzling white concrete, the Shah's monument to himself, known as the Shahyad. It was the most ugly and vulgar slab defacing an urban landscape that I had ever seen. Thousands milled round it making speeches against its dedicatee, defacing it with scrawled caricatures of him and death threats. Of the army there was no sign. The policy of massacre had been put on hold. But it was impossible to get near the Shah. His court spokesman informed journalists: 'The Shah is sad and hurt by the demonstrations. He knows now that some of his ministers have been corrupt but he is sure that the people will continue to carry out his programmes. He is not thinking of leaving.' The British ambassador, Sir Anthony Parsons, in his riot-damaged embassy, seemed actually to believe the Shah would survive the uprising. So apparently did the Americans. Both countries lost any credibility in Iran for failing to realise that their placeman had forfeited all respect in his own country. Any journalist could see that his soldiers were not going to kill their fellow citizens indefinitely. Already there was rumour of defections. But the Shah continued to sit in his palace, just as another Tsar had sat in his, uncertain what to do. This time the Americans and British were not coming to his rescue.

After two months of it, on 16th January 1979, the inevitable was accepted – the Shah fled, officially for 'an extended holiday'. As he stepped out of the palace to his car an elderly subject threw himself at his feet and tried to kiss his shoes. That had once been the way Shahs were greeted by their people. Mohammed Reza, tight-lipped as always, tried to pass without kicking his loyal subject in the face. At the news of his departure from the airport Tehran erupted with joy orchestrated on car horns. It staged its biggest ever traffic jam in celebration. I knew where the Shah was going and, thanks to inexplicable delays in his transit, I managed to arrive at Assuan on the Nile in Upper Egypt in time to await him. The airport was unpretentious, consisting of one lounge, a desk and a baggage trolley or two. But it had done its best – a red carpet was waiting on the tarmac getting dusty. There were some home-made welcome signs stretched on poles across the approach road. The band was waiting. The guard of honour was waiting. The twenty-one guns were waiting to fire a salute. A convoy of black limos was waiting, looking like a funeral procession, which in a sense it was.

Lastly the Shah's friend, President Sadat, was waiting – he happened to be visiting his holiday home near the great Assuan dam. As hour succeeded hour nothing happened except the frequent sweeping of the red carpet which kept getting sandy. Finally at the end of the afternoon the Shah's blue plane dropped on the runway and taxied in blowing a fresh covering of sand over it. Blinking, the Shah stepped out. How small he was, this timid tyrant! Sadat, who was no giant, loomed above him. In a dark blue suit and square sunglasses he looked nervous, pale and worried, like a bankrupt businessman. Inspecting the guard no one had anything to say but the two wives, his third empress Farah Diba being animated in a green beret, and Madame Sadat. The crowd consisting mostly of reporters and some school children watched in silence. On my pocket radio the BBC was broadcasting from Tehran the contrasting cacophony of triumph at his departure. At last he climbed into a black Chevrolet – a thoughtful choice because he owned ten per cent of General Motors in Iran. His hotel, the Oberoi, marooned on Elephant Island in the middle of the Nile, had been cleared summarily of all its guests. No one but the Shah and his small entourage was permitted on the heavily guarded island. The next day he took a Nile Cruise and I followed under sail in a felucca, observing the police boats and frogmen preceding him, searching presumably for mines. For once there was nobody shouting for his death, which may have been restful. When America's ex-president Gerald Ford arrived, on holiday, he joined the Shah and we were allowed on to the island, under guard. Corralled in the gardens I observed the Shah making circular walks on the tended lawns with Ford. Seeing me with my notebook at the ready they both waved. That was the extent of my promised contact with the Shah of Shahs, or, as he had turned out to be, the Shit of Shits. I did not wave back.

He departed for Morocco as guest of the king, but not for long. His Deposed Majesty continued to wander from country to country as the world's most unwanted guest. A former British ambassador, Sir Denis Wright, was secretly despatched to inform him as diplomatically as possible that he would not be welcome in Britain, which had sustained him for so long. President Carter reluctantly allowed him to visit New York for medical treatment for cancer – and thereby procured his own downfall. Students seized the US Embassy in Tehran, demanding the return of the Shah for trial as the price of releasing its staff. The prolonged hostages' affair ensured Carter's defeat at the next election. As for the Shah he proceeded by way of Panama and Mexico back to Egypt and his only friend Sadat. There was nothing left for him to do but die, which he obligingly did the next year, bringing two thousand, five hundred years of Iranian monarchy to an inglorious end.

Meanwhile I made for Paris and his nemesis, the Ayatollah Khomeini, who was even grimmer of expression than the Shah had been. He lived in a bourgeois Paris suburb like a black crow waiting to strike. For two cold wet weeks we hung outside his villa being assured he would give interviews. Occasionally he would walk to the garden gate and address us non-committally in Farsi. Only once were we allowed in to sit shoeless on the floor while he sat in one corner scowling at us. He refused to answer the one question that mattered: when was he going back to Iran? He waited until February. Not even then did he smile at the teeming crowds who received him so hysterically and with so much hope. They little realised what he had in store for them. The Shah's police state had at least been a secular one, where women were not kept in subjection. The black phalanxes of women marchers had put on the chador just for the occasion. You could see their jeans and high-heeled boots underneath. Compulsory wearing of the veil and chador had been abolished decades earlier. Now it was back, together with the suppression of women's rights. So too the suppression of much else taken for granted in the civilised world. Long hair was swept away along with freedom of speech. Even music was banned in public – a refinement that did not occur to George Orwell's Big Brother. Evin Prison, scene of the tortures and executions by SAVAK, again filled with dissidents and the sound of the firing squad. Khomeini announced that democracy was 'the usurpation of Allah's authority to rule'. As he alone was the recipient of Allah's confidences his rule was even more unchallengeable than the Shah's. Iranians who had marched to free themselves from one tyrant found they had exchanged him for another.

THE EIGHTIES
AND BEYOND

WILSON AND HEATH

The eighties was the decade when everything changed in political and social style. Britain had had no domineering leader in the sixties and seventies, only the mock-fights between Mr Wilson and Mr Heath, both of them aggressively middle-class grammar school products compared with their predecessors – Macmillan and Alec Douglas-Home. At the time neither of them seemed remarkable for charisma. They seemed but pale shadows of the giant personalities of the Churchill/Bevin era during and after the war. Yet by comparison their present successors seem but shadows of those shadows. Is this an optical illusion? Does stature grow as politicians recede into the past?

Harold Wilson began his eight years as premier as the epitome of the Briton in a raincoat who smoked his pipe, preferred British grub to any fancy foreign stuff and kept the bottle of HP Sauce on the table. Some wag (I think it was me) wrote snootily: 'Are these the kind of lips we want kissing the hand of our Queen?' How far the image was from the private Mr Wilson I was to discover when he invited me to a party at Number 10 where HP Sauce was nowhere to be seen but quails' eggs were plentiful, along with strong drink. Neither was there any sign of the pipe. Wilson chain-smoked cigars as to the manner born. Holding forth to a large circle with the cigar in one hand and a tumbler of brandy in the other he demonstrated his well-rehearsed changing of the glass. Behind his left elbow stood a waiter with a newly charged tumbler of brandy on a silver tray. As he drained one glass Wilson stretched behind him to deposit it on the tray and take the replacement without turning round or ceasing his discourse. The waiter made a quick exit and reappeared with another full glass of the amber fluid to resume his station at the prime ministerial elbow. I did not know then that his capacity for brandy (or whisky) was a byword among his staff. He used to get through many before and after Prime Minister's Questions but it seldom showed.

The party was being thrown for some theatrical occasion and among the star thespians present there was a sprinkling of theatre critics like myself. Seizing a moment when Wilson was momentarily silent I suggested that the House of Commons might get more lively reporting if it had a few of us theatre critics up in the gallery. 'Theatre critics?' said Wilson. 'What we need is sports writers. What we're playing down on the floor is more like cricket than anything. Take Prime Minister's Questions. You pad up for it. You're well aware of what questions are down on the paper but not the supplementaries. That's when they could send you down a googly. I've got one dodgy question scheduled for next Tuesday about the Duke of Edinburgh. I shan't try to be clever with that sort. Know what I shall do? Drop it dead on the pitch. Dead on the pitch.' But surely there were times when he wanted to play a cover drive? 'If they bowl a long-hop you crack it to the boundary,' said the Yorkshireman. He could do this better than most of his contemporary players. Unlike the opposing captain, Mr Heath, he had a sense of humour.

Smiling shyly in a corner I found Mary Wilson who remarked that this was quite a well-behaved party – so far. 'You should have been here last week when we had the poets.' I was intrigued to learn this from a seasoned observer of male drinking habits. She named one or two guests who had drunk deep and had difficulty in descending the famous staircase which is lined with the portraits of every previous prime minister, beginning at the bottom with Walpole. One of them fell as far as Lloyd George, she told me with quiet amusement. It must have been a welcome change from the trade union barons who always seemed to be at Number 10 in those days and sometimes acted as if they were the real rulers of the country. Indeed Mr Heath when calling an election said it was to decide Who Runs Britain? The answer came back: not you. Wilson was better at managing these militants with beer and sandwiches – and concessions. But it took its toll. He shocked everyone by announcing his resignation in 1974 when his second tenure seemed quite secure. His real reason for going has never been established. He looked a different man, pouch-eyed and weary of it all. But of what all? Could he have been worn down to quitting point by the war of attrition waged by Marcia Williams, his political secretary for so many years, who became also his personal mentor and tormentor? Tales of her tantrums were widespread. She bullied and bawled at him in front of the staff, even before visitors. She became the talk of Fleet Street which was also intrigued by the stories of her affair with a top political correspondent of the *Daily Mail*, Walter Terry, celebrated for his excellent inside information.

The deepest mystery was Wilson's reaction to Marcia's behaviour. He didn't react. He took the stick. He never seemed to object to her imperious demands. Perhaps he thought he was dropping them dead on the pitch. This was never plainer than over the notorious Resignation Honours List of 1974, supposedly written in her hand on lavender-tinted notepaper – 'the Lavender List'. In it were knighted or ennobled an oddly chosen bunch from show business and City business acquaintances of his or hers. The most outrageous name was that of Joe Kagan, the manufacturer of his trademark Gannex raincoat, a Lithuanian refugee who was later to go to prison for fraud. This did not stop him from first becoming Lord Kagan, despite the reluctance of the Queen to bestow the title. I shared her view of his unsuitability from personal experience. He formed the habit of dropping into the office where I was leader-writing to wait for the very attractive columnist Judy Innes, who shared it. 'What are you writing about this time?' he would demand, peering over my typewriter. He would then make unwanted suggestions of what I should be writing about, eating up a lot of urgent time. A more obnoxious character I seldom met. Wilson apparently enjoyed his company and assumed the House of Lords would do too.

With that blot on his reputation Mr Wilson disappeared utterly from view, as did Marcia, by then Lady Falkender. Not so Mr Heath when he was comprehensively dismissed, first at the polls, then by the Tory party who ejected him as its leader in favour of Mrs Thatcher. Instead of taking the expected trip to the Lords he sat on in a Commons seat below the gangway radiating resentment. His was to become the longest-sustained sulk in political history. In his spare time he wrote books about his hobbies of sailing and conducting. He proved no slouch at self-promotion as an author. He clocked up a record of a thousand copies of *Sailing* signed and sold by lunchtime in a Glasgow bookshop. For his next opus, *Music: A Joy for Life*, I was invited to witness his heavy schedule of author signing in Reading, which may have an eponymous enthusiasm for reading. We caught the train at Paddington. In his reserved carriage he was sporting a dazzling sky-blue pullover. British Rail, for such it still was, thoughtfully supplied taped music of a light classical kind for our journey. Knowing of his capacity for taking offence I was careful to avoid politics, so I asked him what influenced him to make the difficult choice, while at Balliol, not to risk a career as a professional musician. It was, he said, on the advice of his professor, Sir Hugh Allen. He told me that if I wanted to get to the top as a conductor I must be prepared to be a shit. 'Like... well, you can guess.' I guessed Sir Malcolm Sargent. 'What he meant was that I should have to be very ruthless.' 'And he doubted your potential ruthlessness?' Mr Heath raised his eyes upwards expressively but did not answer. 'Little did he know what ruthlessness would be required of you in politics?' I persisted. Mr Heath, a master of non-verbal communication, raised his eyes again and shook his shoulders a little. 'You say in your book,' I pursued, 'that "as I did not want any unpleasantness I decided to go into politics!"' The sky-blue pullover heaved with what I took to be silent merriment. At last he spoke. 'You've taken the point.'

He began his part-time musical career conducting a five-piece Royal Artillery dance band, whose signature tune – odd for Heath – was *When You're Smiling the Whole World Smiles With You*. 'I suppose you played for hops and suchlike?' He raised his eyeballs skyward again and even smiled. 'Ted Heath and his Music?' I ventured daringly. He shook again. 'Exactly. I never met my famous namesake but he once wrote to me signing himself: "Yours sincerely, The Other Ted Heath."' By then he was invited quite often to conduct the London Symphony Orchestra, which he had first done when prime minister. He had taken them on tour. For an amateur musician who more usually conducted carol concerts in his native Broadstairs, I said, he had certainly come a long way. Concerts with Menuhin. Friendships with von Karajan and Leonard Bernstein. Why not take it further? His drawing power on the podium was established. A whole new career beckoned as a conductor. The comparative warmth of our conversation was back in refrigeration. 'Of course not. Quite impossible. I am far too busy. I turn down dozens of invitations to conduct.' But surely the political pressure was off? I couldn't have said a more provocative thing. 'What nonsense! I'm up to my eyes in it. I have invitations to speak from all over the world. Princeton. Tokyo. The West Midlands...I haven't retired.'

I realised suddenly that as far as he was concerned political leadership was a far from closed book. He was sitting in the Commons waiting for the inevitable call to return. Once that woman had made enough of a hash of things he would be begged to come back and take the helm again. So it looked like being only a few gigs a year? A curt nod. The conversation, never allegro, still less con brio, looked like slowing to largo, if not to Fine. It seemed a long way to Reading. Well, I suggested, he had looked a lot happier when making music than when being prime minister. 'Prime ministers are not supposed to look as if they were enjoying themselves!' he said, closing the subject once and for all.

He must have enjoyed it less than most.

THATCHER AND CALLAGHAN

Mrs Thatcher's rise to power might not have occurred when, to much astonishment, it did, but for the concerted machinations of a small group of politically and commercially motivated men, none of whom was a politician. One of these was the editor of the *Daily Mail*, David English, the man who had turned the paper into a successful tabloid a few years earlier. On the eve of the Conservative leadership vote of 1975, which Heath was expected to win comfortably, he sent for me. 'You were a nifty caption writer. We're going to do a really hard-selling centre spread on Margaret Thatcher.' We examined all the photographs from the picture library. They were not promising material. When young she looked dowdy and provincial. Older, she became boringly conventional in middle-class hats and pearls with a false smile pasted on for the camera. English spent a long time juggling the best of them, beneath a banner headline: Will She Be The First Woman Party Chief? I chronicled the steps which might take her there from the Grantham grocer's shop. The next evening, when she had won the first round, English passed me in the corridor that surrounded the editorial floor. 'We got her in!' he called with a triumphant arm gesture. It seemed most unlikely that the backbenchers had been influenced by poring over the *Daily Mail*. There was a second round of voting to come – but that was a foregone conclusion. The question was now: could she keep them with her? The Tories are merciless to failure, as Heath had discovered.

I wondered why English seemed so personally partisan – the *Mail* was almost alone in Fleet Street in its enthusiasm for Thatcher, whose stock rapidly declined in her first years as leader. By 1978 it was beginning to recover and he asked me for a piece on 'The Men Behind The Message'.

One of them was her publicity director, Gordon Reece, whom I had known as a TV producer, young, slick and fashionably bouffant-haired. He had appointed the sensational Saatchi Brothers, who were amazing the advertising world with their daring outspokenness. Not the kind of thing English political parties went in for. 'There's nothing wrong with doing something professionally,' Reece told me. Their marketing director, a young Australian named Tim Bell, had been hailed as 'the marketing brain of his generation'. The first fruit of their marketing of the Conservatives was an enormous poster of an endless queue outside a Labour Exchange under the huge headline LABOUR ISN'T WORKING. Newspapers were so surprised at this aggressiveness that they reproduced the poster – thus making it far more effective. Labour spokesmen were outraged. Denis Healey said scornfully, 'Only politicians bankrupt of principle could sell their party like soap powder.' The party's general secretary accused Saatchis of using their own employees to form the 'unemployed' queue (they were in fact volunteer Young Conservatives and their parents). Transport House reacted sniffily: 'We write our own advertisements, with a little help from our friends.' That seemed to be their trouble. 'Our opponents seem to be badly rattled,' said Reece to me with satisfaction. Saatchis came up with a slick, punchy Party Political Broadcast which people actually watched. It had the theme tune, 'Money Makes the World Go Round', and ended with Mrs Thatcher against a background of birdsong telling us that 'a lack of money makes the world slow down'. And an election hadn't even been called yet.

Meanwhile Gordon Reece had persuaded the lady leader to rid herself of the cut-glass accent she had acquired through her elocution lessons. Private polls showed that people found her too shrill and hectoring, too schoolmarmish for comfort. So the National Theatre's voice coach was called in. Other experts were working on her wardrobe, her hairstyle and her make-up. She was being marketed. Not as an Iron Lady, though she was proud of having been given that title (by a Russian magazine), but with an altogether softer, svelter, feminine image. Thanks to Reece, Bell and the Saatchi Brothers, politics in brash American style had come to Britain, rather infra dig by English standards but effective. And then she had an enormous slice of luck.

A Rogues' Gallery

James Callaghan, the wily and ultra-experienced political bird who had held all the major Cabinet posts before becoming prime minister, decided not to call an election that year but wait for 1979. Up till then he looked like a safe pair of hands to handle the mayhem being raised by militant union leaders. Now he opened the door to the notorious 'Winter of Discontent' and made it worse by leaving the country to shiver and come to a near standstill while he sunned himself on Guadaloupe in the West Indies. Sunny Jim returned tanned and refreshed and told the reporters at the airport that he would not declare a State of Emergency because he was not aware there was one, despite the 'mounting chaos' that the newspapers were suggesting. He told them he had been swimming. These ill-judged remarks came out in headline form in the *Sun* and *Daily Mail* as: 'Crisis? What Crisis?' He never really recovered from these words, although he had never actually said them.

As spring and the inevitable general election approached David English beat the *Mail*'s drum ever more insistently for Mrs Thatcher. They seemed to be kindred spirits. Both were self-made with a strong conviction that it was up to you to get where and what you wanted and pay for it. Let the devil take the hindmost. Alone of the Fleet Street editors I knew of, English ran his own small business on the side. His frequent absences on Friday nights were assumed to be because he was collecting the takings from a chain of launderettes. He made no secret of his enthusiasm for sharp practices. He reminisced to me about his days as a reporter in the country where you could spike the competition by removing the diaphragm from the only public telephone, to reserve it for your own use. Waiting one day after lunch in his outer office I watched the room fill up to bursting with journalists all with urgent questions to ask him. Three o'clock, 3.30, even four o'clock passed. At last he put his head round the outer door, took in the crowded scene and announced firmly: 'I'm not seeing any of you until I've spoken to my broker!' And disappeared to his inner sanctum to act on information received, presumably at lunch.

It was time, I felt strongly, that the paper showed a bit of balance where Mrs Thatcher was concerned. We attacked all the others, why not her? I asked him. 'First we'll get her in. Then we'll attack her,' he declared, adding with a meaningful look at me. 'Surely you're one of *us*?' One Of Us! It was the password of the inner circle, a club, if not a conspiracy, dedicated to putting Mrs Thatcher (and her friends) into power. I didn't think I *was* One of Them, I confessed. I had usually been a Labour supporter. 'So was I! I was a candidate! But now...' When the election was at last announced he assigned me to Callaghan's camp and then printed nothing I that I filed. I rang him up from, I think, Cardiff to ask, 'Why aren't you printing any of my stuff?' 'There's nothing political about it. It's just that the Labour campaign is so boring!' But surely he didn't assume that all our more than two million subscribers were Conservative? 'Well, those that aren't can watch television.'

I trudged on with Callaghan, privately admitting that he was a reporter's nightmare. After a leisurely breakfast he liked to spend the mornings pottering around shopping centres making straight for some elderly voter or other with whom he could chat about grandchildren, gardening or bus passes. He left meetings soon after seven – he liked an early night. While he was making himself all but invisible, Mrs Thatcher was putting on the brashest show in town. There was nothing she wouldn't do for the cameras. Show her a sewing factory and she was in there, stitching pockets with the best of them. On her famous visit to Cadbury's she was put into an hygienic white coat and hat while she packed crème eggs and walnut whirls into boxes like a whirlwind. The surrounding television crews, photographers and newsmen, all also wearing white coats and hats by order, looked, in Frank Johnson's memorable phrase in the *Daily Telegraph*, 'like a convention of lunatic surgeons'. This was the first out-and-out television election and the first with a woman contender. It showed. Image was all that counted from now on.

Next came the calf-cuddling. There she was on the farm, holding a calf the wrong way round, with husband Denis muttering in the background, 'If we don't look out we'll have a dead calf on our hands.' Farmer Callaghan looked at the news photographs and murmured to me, 'I could show her how to lift a calf properly with its legs tucked in.' But would he? Big Jim didn't do stunts, other than pat a dog. And he declared more than once that he wouldn't attack her personally.

Indeed he never mentioned her name. You wouldn't know it was a woman he was up against. He feared being called a male chauvinist pig. In despair I wrote: 'He will sign a boy's football but not boot it. He accepts kisses but offers no more than the handshake of a nice old family doctor. He will not stitch pockets for anyone. He toils not neither does he spin anything but comfortable words. What we may be witnessing is the last old campaigner who would like the whole sycophantic, image-massaging, publicity-spinning circus to take a running jump and leave politicians alone.' David English printed that and Jim Callaghan thanked me, although I had also opined that I didn't think he would mind losing, so long as it was done with dignity. So it was. Like Wilson, he seemed to have had enough – of his own party's as well as the unions' provocations.

Soon afterwards David English and I mutually agreed to part company. He knew I was never going to be One of Us. And I could see that we were going to worship, never mind attack his heroine, the Blessed Margaret. He got his knighthood. Our personal differences were well known so I was not altogether surprised when about half the colleagues I invited to my farewell drinks party did not show up. Those that did were surprised to see David English walk in and accept a glass of champagne from me. 'I know you think there's been a loss of quality in the *Daily Mail*,' he said straight out. 'Well, there has. Ten per cent.' I would have put it higher. But I had to admit to myself that there had been an equal loss of quality in its competitors, even the broadsheets. The dumbing-down era had begun and it wasn't going to stop. Not at any rate in my time.

PUBLISHERS' PECULIARITIES

Publishing books used to be considered an 'occupation for gentlemen' – but gentlemen (and ladies) who *lunch*. Literary editors were fair game for the 'selling lunch'. When I became one I was overwhelmed by invitations. I could have been lunched a dozen times a week if I had the capacity. 'Couldn't we discuss your new book over a drink?' I would plead – or even there and then on the telephone? No, it had to be lunch. That was how publishing worked, over lunches that might last until tea time. Between 12.30 and 4.30 there was little point in telephoning. There would be nobody in the office.

The old school of publishing, when names like Jonathan Cape, Allen Lane, Hamish Hamilton or William Heinemann denoted actual people running their firms, were fast receding by then. A few remained – for example John Murray, known as 'Jock' and dressed to suit it in dark green tartan, still presided over the house in Albemarle Street that Byron knew. Indeed the fireplace in his reception room was the very one where his predecessor had burned Byron's too-scandalous autobiography after his death. It was still full of authors, gossip and literary ghosts, but alas is no longer. A curious cylindrical brick building known as the Old Piano Factory in Camden Town housed the maverick firm of Duckworth, and its publisher, Colin Haycraft. He and his star author, Beryl Bainbridge, were neither of them averse to the bottle, often consumed after work at his home nearby. My abiding memory of Beryl Bainbridge at the end of a bibulous lunch, as we were leaving the private dining room after everyone else had gone, was her question: 'Is there anything left in that bottle?' There was – it was nearly half full of claret. Seizing it by the neck, she up-ended it, drained it and passed on with scarcely a pause.

A Rogues' Gallery

London's publishing scene was enlivened after the war by the influx of enterprising refugees. From Austria came George Weidenfeld, so bent on success that for a time it seemed that every exciting non-fiction title was published by Weidenfeld & Nicolson. 'George' was celebrated for his upper-class contacts and lavish publication parties held at his spacious apartments on Chelsea Embankment. It was from one of these that, for the only time I can remember, I was ejected in disgrace. The occasion was the completion of George Melly's autobiographical trilogy, *Owning Up*. This had begun with his louche life as a jazz singer on the road, continued backwards with his louche life as an able seaman in the Navy and finally reached his well-upholstered upbringing in Liverpool. George and I had been at school together at Stowe, where he was celebrated for his lifestyle and his love of traditional jazz and surrealism, both of which the rest of us had then barely heard of. His study was painted black all over. This setting showed off Dadaist exhibits such as an up-ended bicycle whose wheel spokes were threaded with lavatory paper. Jazz was represented by his collection of very scratchy 75-rpm records of old Blues singers, especially Bessie Smith. We used to sit round the gramophone in a reverent circle trying to make out the words she was growling. George would then do his imitations, accompanied by us on guitar, washboard, box-bass, tissue-papered combs or whatever else could be pressed to make sound, if not music.

In subsequent years I would find him singing much the same repertoire in Soho clubs, even Ronnie Scott's, fronting a trad band. His voice sounded much the same (no better) but his presentation had come on wonderfully for he was a born entertainer. He always remained faithful to New Orleans and the South. I once got him to admit that his great unrealisable ambition was to have been born black. But as I entered his party chez Weidenfeld I was met by the braying voice of Sir James Goldsmith holding forth to one of the crowded rooms. 'Melly,' he announced to the assembled guests, 'is a Portuguese Jew! Did any of you know that? Imagine, a Portuguese Jew!' He made this sound like a shameful accusation. I felt bound to come to the defence of my school chum. 'Well, that is hardly the most important thing about him,' I said loudly and sarcastically. There was a sudden drop in the room temperature and an awkward silence. Goldsmith, his mouth open, looked dumbfounded. He was clearly not used to being contradicted. Thinking nothing of this I passed on but soon afterwards, hailing Melly, I was surprised by his reaction. 'You're spoiling my party!' he half hissed. I could not see why. Then our host, the other George, emerged and led me firmly to the door. His large round frog-like face was not by any means beaming with the usual benevolence. 'Mr Lewis,' he said menacingly. 'I think it would be better if you left. Now.' For what reason, I enquired innocently. 'You are upsetting my guests.' It was the red card. And I had no doubt which guest he had in mind. Obviously George did not like his millionaire friends to be upset. However obnoxious they might be.

The Hungarian, Andre Deutsch, had created a more modest publishing house than Weidenfeld. Its reputation was built on its enterprising list of foreign authors, especially American, beginning with Norman Mailer's Pacific War novel, *The Naked and the Dead*. The suggestion that this was going to be banned by the Attorney General, no less, because of its obscene language got its sales off to a good start. Even so, the soldiers' liberal use of the F-word was thought too much for the public (which also used it) to bear. 'Fugging' was substituted throughout, as if that made it somehow inoffensive. With more Mailer novels and the saucily adulterous works of John Updike, Andre was enabled to move to a suitably Georgian address in Great Russell Street by the British Museum. Thither I was invited to a pre-publication lunch of special but secret significance. Short, dapper, charming but Napoleonic, wearing a trademark bow tie, Andre devoted lunch to a discussion of a sensational new American discovery of his, one Peter Benchley, assured of being the next Big Name. There was no holding back when he had something to sell. My role was to snap up the fabulous opportunity he was offering to acquire the newspaper serial rights of a sensational new novel. As he saw me off, loaded with the bulky manuscript, he warned me, 'I expect to hear from you by nine o'clock tomorrow morning and we will talk figures!' True to his word he rang, bright and early. 'Well? Are you ready to bid?' 'Andre, you must be joking,' I said. How was I to maintain interest day after day in a book when the same thing happened in each chapter: someone was eaten by a shark? 'When you've seen it eat one…' After that Andre did not speak to me for some time, while I bore a reputation as the man who turned down *Jaws*.

The third of the foreign trio to galvanise publishing was a large Palestinian raised in Nazareth, of all places. From his penniless arrival in post-war England Naim Attallah had contrived to blossom into an exotic, flamboyant, oriental vision of wealth, no one knew quite how. His mysterious riches were evident in his bejewelled rings, the luxury watches worn on both his wrists, his fine tailoring and accessories, his freshly pomaded shining scalp, his hand-made crocodile leather shoes, his chauffeured limousines. Most publishing offices then tended towards old leather and dust laced with pipe smoke. Naim's décor was velvet and chandeliers and antique furniture. Draped about this setting was his famed seraglio of well-connected, double-barrelled, languidly long-legged, creamy complexioned, posh-voiced young lovelies of breeding, an ever changing chorus or finishing school of attendants without too much to do. There seldom seemed to be fewer than half a dozen Henriettas, Samanthas, Arabellas, Sophias, Georgias, even a Nigella (for it was she) caring and carrying, tending and telephoning, serving or salaaming this Sultan in his court. For his part he was inexhaustible in his sudden demands, wants, inspirations, dismays, anxieties and decisions. Veering swiftly between triumph and disaster his every moment required satisfying, calming or pleasing. Behind his desk mounted on the wall was a symbol of dominance – his tiger skin known as Kaiser.

I had been summoned to the presence to be despatched to Syria, then a little-known and peaceful country for which libraries stocked only one guide book written in the past thirty years. It was my task to remedy this want. If it was a want – for few tourists in those days seemed to have Syria on their map. 'I want it big… I want it beautiful,' he said, conjuring from the air the sort of book to be created by my prose and Robin Constable's photography. 'I have arranged for you to be looked after.' He waved me from his presence like an ambassador bound for a faraway clime. And so effectively did his influence extend in the Middle East that we were received and travelled *en prince*. A chauffeur was at beck and call for the arduous journeys, even into the distant desert to Palmyra, the legendary capital where Queen Zenobia had defied Rome and left ruins far more extensive and impressive than its own emperors had. The publication party was on a scale equal to one of Weidenfeld's, whom Naim, it seemed, regarded as the rival to be challenged.

In times of recession, lavishness was replaced by anxiety and retrenchment in the publishing world, where conglomerates have submerged one historic imprint after another. Naim's fiefdom, Quartet Books, somehow retains its non-conformist identity. He has continued to back his hunches, the outsider and the underdog, especially ventilating the plight of the Palestinians which others prefer to ignore. Along the way he found the funds to rescue *The Oldie* magazine from the losses that threatened to sink it and to sponsor his friend Auberon Waugh's *Literary Review*, to the tune of millions. Without his timely support neither would have survived. Neither can well be spared. While celebrity and safety publishing (in the form of cookery and gardening books) have afflicted too many rival publishing giants, Naim, now in his eighties, has no truck with such a faint-hearted policy. Without his old court he continues to boom with confidence and publish only what he likes.

ORWELL & KOESTLER

Mindful of the approach of 1984, some publishers commissioned me to write a book on George Orwell. It was a difficult assignment because his widow Sonia, though married to him only on his death-bed for the three remaining months of his life, was determined to carry out his request that there be no biography written. Only a few sketchy reminiscences had appeared since he died in 1950. I met Mrs Orwell who agreed that a sketch of about fifteen thousand words to accompany some photographs of Orwell with the baby son he adopted, which had recently come to light, would be acceptable. 'But if you try to write a proper biography I shall stop you!' What about the so-called 'official biography' to be written by an academic, Bernard Crick? 'There is no official biography,' she declared firmly. 'I haven't seen Professor Crick for years.'

Although so long had elapsed, the trail was by no means cold. As I collected reminiscences from friends and acquaintances my word limit soon seemed quite inadequate. It more than doubled with Sonia's tacit acceptance – she read and corrected the proofs as her last editing job (she had already co-edited his works) before her death in 1980. Despite her tigerish reputation as guardian of the flame I never found her unhelpful – nor very helpful since her personal recollections of Orwell as a man seemed oddly distant. For years I had been an ardent admirer, like so many others, of his prose power, his outstanding regard for truth and uncommon sense. For me his style and spirit were summed up in a not-often-quoted sentence: 'If liberty means anything at all, it means the right to tell people what they do not want to hear.' Tall and dominating, his invariably gloomy expression emphasised by the straight pencil line of his moustache, he had clearly been an awkward man to get close to. I met several women who had obviously found him attractive but had turned down his impulsive proposals to marry them. These came in quick succession in 1945 after his wife, Eileen, died prematurely on the operating table just after they had adopted a baby boy. He was then doggedly looking after Richard alone. Their refusals, including Sonia's, at that time were hardly surprising for he was proposing to retire to an inaccessible farmhouse on an inaccessible Scottish island, Jura, where they would be marooned while he got on with writing *Nineteen Eighty-Four* against time – the time his tuberculosis would take to end his life. One of his typical proposals by letter read: 'What I am really asking is whether you would like to be the widow of a literary man?' This was scarcely an alluring prospect – he calculated that before *Animal Farm* he had never earned more than £3 a week from his books and *Animal Farm*, just published in a small edition of four thousand, five hundred copies had not yet brought in any of the riches it was going to do.

His devotion to his small, adopted son was fierce. When I found Richard, then a tractor salesman in the Midlands, his memories of his father were fond but few. But he showed me his birth certificate. The name of his natural father had been burned out by the tip of Orwell's cigarette. There are no photographs of Orwell smiling. The nearest he came to it shows him looking at the boy on his lap indulgently, as at a pet animal. Did he ever laugh? The only person who could remember him doing so was Arthur Koestler, who described it as: 'A sudden bark, a "Hah!" – as if his suspicions had been confirmed.' Koestler and Orwell became firm friends during the war. They were natural allies, united by their disillusioning experiences in the Spanish Civil War which gave them their shared hatred of Communist duplicity. Orwell, having fought and been wounded, had to flee Spain as a fugitive from the Stalinists. Koestler, covering the war as a journalist for the *News Chronicle*, had been captured by Franco's rebel army at Malaga and held prisoner, fully expecting to be shot, until a high-powered campaign of intellectuals in England freed him. Koestler prized Orwell's *Homage to Catalonia* which came out in 1939 and remained largely unsold in the publisher's warehouse until his death. Orwell wrote approvingly of Koestler's *Spanish Testament*, followed in 1940 by his penetration of the Bolshevik mind, *Darkness at Noon*, which made his name internationally renowned. When it came out Koestler was in prison in England as an illegal immigrant. Serving as a latrine digger in the Alien Pioneer Corps earned him British citizenship. Orwell was then a sergeant in the Home Guard. Both look very awkward pictured in battledress. Together they must have been an almost comic sight – the towering Orwell alongside the unusually short Koestler, who tried to overcome his puny height by continually rising on his toes when talking to you and as frequently having to subside.

Their accents were equally contrasted. Orwell tried to disguise his patrician Etonian speech by a classless rasp while Koestler never succeeded in playing down his strong Hungarian/German accent with its Vs in place of Ws. Orwell was Orvell to him. None of this marred their mutual regard and shared gloom . 'Orvell vas a cheerful pessimist and so am I, so I found him stimulating, not depressing, to be vith. His chronic ill-health made him ruthless towards himself. So ze closer you became to him, ze more he felt he could treat you as harshly'. He gave as an example his invitation to Orwell to spend Christmas with him and his future wife Mamaine in Wales. Shortly before his visit Orwell wrote a merciless review of a play that Koestler had just published. When he arrived bearing his baby son, Koestler expected some expression of regret. Orwell said nothing so he burst out, 'That was a bloody awful notice you gave my play!' Orwell replied unrepentantly, 'Well, it's a bloody awful play, isn't it?'

Koestler's self-indulgent hedonism (and tireless pursuit of women) was the direct opposite of Orwell's enthusiasm for his somewhat Puritan lifestyle. Chronically hard-up he enjoyed attempting self-sufficiency by raising vegetables, chickens, even goats. 'He relished bad food. He used to invite me to his regular Soho restaurant, were ze food vas like dog's vomit, and say how remarkably vell one could eat zere in wartime'. On a scorching summer's day Orwell removed his jacket and hung it round the back of his chair. The manager approached and asked him to put it on again. 'Zat vas enough! Orvell valked out and never vent zere again'.

Koestler approved of my mini-biography, indeed pronounced in the *Sunday Times* 'Books of the Year' column that it was far more like the friend he remembered than the large volume by Bernard Crick which appeared in the same year. To me he wrote: 'I liked your book and I think George would have disliked it only moderately.' I took this as a high compliment. One consequence was that he suggested I should write a book of similar length about him. I demurred on the grounds that I did not know enough science. 'I vill teach you ze science!' For some time I made repeated visits to his house on the corner of Montpelier Square. I had been excited by his first exploration of the nature of scientific breakthrough, *The Act of Creation*. No one until then had so tellingly illustrated the similarity of intuitive discoveries between the great pioneer thinkers from Kepler to Einstein. Like artistic advances, they were guided by aesthetic criteria of fitness and elegance. He also compared the eureka moments in both science and the arts to the process of 'seeing' a joke. This sudden combination of one way of seeing things with another – fox-hunting as 'The Unspeakable in pursuit of the Uneatable' – he called 'bisociation'.

He was a bracing thinker to listen to and, just occasionally, dare to argue with. His pessimism sometimes seemed to go too far. I questioned his belief that the evolution of the human brain had 'overshot', leaving our expanded cortex, responsible for rational thinking, undermined by the 'old' animal brain, the cerebellum, which dictated our emotional atavistic reactions, such as 'ze desire to kill people for some cause to which you are unduly devoted'. Surely, I suggested, an evolutionary 'mistake' of that order could not have produced the most successful living species? That triggered Koestler's full crushing power. 'For every species zat survived evolution, vun hundred have become extinct! Now ve have ze power of total annihilation! Ze whole of human history demonstrates zat emotion vill vin against reason! Misplaced devotion to mad ideologies or religious sects is far more dangerous zan our natural aggression.' But he saw some hope in the idea that if other species were out in space they must have also discovered nuclear technology and tamed the desire to use it.

Of course Koestler had many enemies among scientists who saw him as an amateur invading their territory with heretical ideas. What outlawed him even more rigidly was his interest in investigating the paranormal – ESP, telekinesis and coincidence – which I share, but which sends orthodox minds scrambling for the hills. He left most of his fortune to endow a university department of parapsychology at Edinburgh in the conviction that such common phenomena should no longer be ignored by science. He saw paranormal experiences as 'glimpses through the keyhole of eternity'. It was his profound belief that there exists a greater order of reality unknown to us. He expressed it in two images which formed the titles of his autobiographies, *Arrow in the Blue* and *The Invisible Writing*. The 'arrow in the blue' referred to his adolescent experience of lying back on a hillside and staring into a blue sky imagining himself to be an arrow shot with such force as to escape gravity and travel on, never stopping, into infinity. I had precisely that sense of elation, doing the same thing as a child lying on a suburban lawn. For years afterwards I could recall something of the intense excitement it gave me. He interpreted it as a foretaste of escaping from the bounds of space and time. The 'invisible writing' was 'a text written in invisible ink' in which on rare occasions we could decipher hints of an alternative reality.

His own key mystical moments were the result of his imprisonment at Malaga and Seville, not knowing whether his death sentence had yet been pronounced by the Fascists but listening every night to the inmates of neighbouring cells being dragged out to face a firing squad. The emotions he went through in what seemed like a death cell were revealing. In *Dialogue with Death* written immediately afterwards he described the ways his mind tried to deal with the prospect of imminent annihilation. One was to scratch mathematical formulae with a mattress spring on the cell wall, especially Euclid's proof that the class of prime numbers is infinite. This produced in him 'a direct certainty that a higher order of reality exists which alone invests existence with meaning'. He told me that these experiences in his cell had changed him forever. In his book he compared them to Freud's concept of the 'oceanic feeling' – of oneness with something far greater than ourselves. 'I was floating on my back in a river of peace, under bridges of silence. It came from nowhere and flowed nowhere. There was no river and no I. The 'I' had ceased to exist.' Such a feeling comes rarely but I recognise it. It comes unbidden at certain moments such as when contemplating nature, listening to music, reading poetry or on special nights at the theatre when an audience polarises like iron filings in the presence of a magnet. I have known it occur at public acts of worship.

I spent hours in the guest chair in his sitting room, while he would sit in a leather chair with his back to the window opposite the sofa sometimes occupied by his third wife, Cynthia, who was as self-effacing as a personal slave, always awaiting his bidding. Since the age of twenty-two when she began work for him as a secretary in Paris, she had been his lover, mistress, wife and ultimately carer and nurse. Koestler was ill, though he did not say with what (it was a slow-acting form of leukaemia). One day he suddenly interrupted our conversation to tell me that he had decided to kill himself when the illness got bad enough. 'I shall do it here in zis chair. I have ze means,' he said calmly. When sometime later he telephoned me to say that he must reluctantly withdraw from the projected biography and that he and Cynthia were working on a joint book of reminiscence, I feared that the end was near. On 1st March 1983, he carried out his suicide exactly as planned – accompanied by Cynthia. They sat opposite each other as usual to swallow the fatal dose. Although only in her fifties and quite healthy she clearly made her own choice, not influenced by him. 'I cannot live without Arthur...there is nothing else to do,' she wrote as a postscript to his own suicide letter, 'To Whom It May Concern' written nine months earlier. In it he revealed a little of his own feelings at coming to the end of his tumultuous life's journey. He explained he was seeking 'self-deliverance' before becoming incapable of making the necessary arrangements. After paying tribute to Cynthia for bringing him a peace and happiness he had never known before, he added: 'I am leaving with some timid hopes for a depersonalised after-life beyond the confines of space, time and matter and beyond the limits of our comprehension. This "oceanic feeling" has often sustained me at difficult moments and does so now, while I am writing this.' This brave statement is one I would hope to echo in such circumstances. Thus passed from view perhaps the most stimulating mind I have ever encountered.

LITERARY LIONS' DENS

For those who suffer from it the compulsion to write is a mystery. Doing it, everyone agrees, is a misery but not doing it is a worse misery. Writers are 'driven by a demon you can neither resist nor understand', according to George Orwell, whose demon drove him to write himself literally to death. Yet no writer I have met admitted to opening one of his books after it had been published – unless in order to sign it for someone else to read. And the last book never quite comes. Most die with work in progress in the drawer.

The conditions in which to write are vitally important. V. S. Pritchett showed me the pastry board on which, propped across an armchair above his knees, he had written all his short stories and books of brilliant criticism. Anthony Powell took me upstairs to a room in his miniature country house where there stood a low, long nursery-style table, the right height for young children's tea. In order to sit at it he had rigged up a low bench resting, so far as I could tell, on bricks. Uncomfortable as it looked, that was where he had written all million words of *A Dance to the Music of Time*. Once established, writing conditions cannot well be changed, whether it is in bed, like Compton Mackenzie, or on the tops of London buses, where Laurie Lee claimed he wrote best.

The man who claimed to write nothing but best-sellers and be at that time the highest paid novelist in the world was that out-smarter of the competition in any field he entered, Jeffrey Archer. He was not yet either a peer or a jailbird. Like many another visitor I was invited to wonder at the view from his Thames-side penthouse. He could look down from it on the Houses of Parliament of which he was once the youngest member at twenty-nine. The penthouse was also his office (and therefore tax-deductible). As evidence of this a young woman was seated at a computer busily processing his latest batch of output in a far corner. 'Every book of mine goes through seventeen re-writes,' he announced proudly. Seventeen! 'Yes. One must polish and polish.' 'But after that many you must have re-written the original completely!' 'Of course, the later revisions are just points of detail.' He gave me a beam which might have been self-satisfaction – or possibly a tacit acknowledgment that neither of us wholly believed what he was saying. But it sounded good, as did so many of the claims he made about himself.

'Every morning I am brought the typed copy of my previous day's work, which I correct. I have that back typed up the same evening, after that day's stint is finished.' If repeated seventeen times it sounded a very confusing process. But who could argue with his sales figures, which none of the scandals of his personal life seemed to touch? There were indeed doubters who suggested the books might have been written by someone else – his wife? – his agent? – a committee? No ghosts had ever materialised or confessed, though he once joked that his wife Mary 'helped translate his work into English'.

After coffee he took me on a tour of his paintings, a colourful and costly collection by high-priced names such as Warhol. How had he afforded them, especially in the early days? 'I got them all very cheap. Except the Dufy. I never buy at auction, you see. One puts the word round in certain dealers' quarters that one is interested in such and such a painter. Then wait. It won't be long before someone needs to sell but doesn't want the world to know it. That's my opportunity.' He warmly regarded his walls loaded with appreciating investments. In the middle of the highly polished floor stood a single column of bookshelves where calf bindings glittered with gold tooling. Glancing along the titles I saw they were all by him. 'Those are my personal copies. I felt they deserved pampering.' One, I noted with surprise, was a volume of short stories. 'My short stories? My best work! Let me find you a copy.' He selected one in a cheaper binding, wrote on the fly-leaf and handed it to me as I made for the door. 'The thing to remember about me,' he said in parting, 'is that I am essentially a story-teller. A story-teller. *Like Dickens*.' When I looked inside the book, beneath my name he had written the inscription: Happy Reading! Jeffrey Archer. He must have been the happiest, as well as the most revised, author I ever met.

The contrast couldn't have been greater between him and Dirk Bogarde when he came to town with his latest volume of autobiography. He showed me the manuscript, written in a neat hand in nicely bound notebooks. Turning the pages I looked in vain for corrections. It seemed he never needed to make any. The title of the book, suitably enough, was *An Orderly Man*. It described the period when he gave up filming after *Death in Venice* and put his energies into renovating a dilapidated Provencal farmhouse with his friend and partner, whom he always addressed as Forwood. Their suite at the Connaught was as orderly as could be. So it appeared was the idyllic estate in the hot, sweet South of France, about which he had written so mouth-wateringly – for he was a very talented writer. Unfortunately it was not destined to last. Forwood developed cancer and they came back to London for treatment, never to return.

I telephoned my piece about Bogarde and his book. Needless to say the gremlins of transmission got at it so the book title appeared as 'An Ordinary Man', which he emphatically wasn't. I hope he never saw it.

J. B. PRIESTLEY

One of the fixed points in the timetable of countless British families in wartime, including mine, was the Nine o'clock News. On Sunday evenings in 1940 from Dunkirk through to the autumn Blitz the bulletin was followed by a postscript from J. B. Priestley. His was an amazing voice to hear on the uptight BBC of those days – a sonorous Yorkshire rumble without a hint of the strangulated order-giving tones of Authority making public pronouncements. He chatted away informally as if there were just the two of you in a pub. There was none of the usual pep-talk. He seldom mentioned the war, though his best-remembered talk was his tribute to the seaside paddle-steamers that went to aid the Dunkirk evacuation and did not all return. Most were pure escapism; his amused reflections on baby ducklings' behaviour in a pond or a steaming pie produced in a Bradford pie shop after an air raid. They were a safety valve of sanity in dangerous times and in a week or two Priestley's was the most recognisable voice in the country after Churchill's. He was that now forgotten phenomenon, the writer as a public spokesman, in the tradition of Shaw and Wells.

On his *English Journey* through the depressed areas of 1934 he had preceded Orwell's pilgrimage to Wigan Pier and disliked what he saw just as volubly. Post-war came the atom bomb and increasing fear of nuclear proliferation. In 1957 he wrote an article in the *New Statesman* which denounced Britain's taking part in the race. We had just tested 'our' H-bomb to the general satisfaction of the Conservative government and the *Daily Express*. One by one Priestley demolished the arguments put forward for the importance of Britain possessing its own bomb. They were the same as the arguments put forward today – independent deterrent capability, 'top table' bargaining power, though no one could agree on any circumstances in which it should be used. He ended: 'Alone we defied Hitler and alone we can defy this nuclear madness into which his spirit has passed to poison the world...let us declare as an example that we will reject the evil thing forever.' A deluge of letters in support helped Priestley and a group of others to form CND soon afterwards.

He was one of the last novelists to look like a man of letters with his never-absent pipe and tweedy attire (though not the bow tie favoured by Evelyn Waugh and many others) topped with a floppy broad-brimmed hat. He was a prolific all-rounder with not only novels and essays to his credit but thirty-five plays, many of them standard repertory pieces. They soothed audiences into thinking they were naturalistic, then surprised them by playing tricks with time. His sheer output resulted in his disparagement by intellectuals as second-rate. His Yorkshire truculence and self-esteem didn't help – he claimed to have 'not genius but a hell of a lot of talent'. All of which made me eager to meet him. I took the first of many enjoyable walks along the banks of the Avon from Stratford to the village of Alveston. There he resided in Kissing Tree Lane at Kissing Tree House, white and restrained Georgian, when he was in his seventies. They continued until he was all but ninety. The routine was always the same. He was always at work, but relaxed in the afternoons for visitors. Then rather ceremoniously we would proceed to tea to join his wife Jacquetta Hawkes, the archaeologist whose tall, sculptural figure had been familiar as the masthead of the CND Easter marches. Then back to his study. 'I don't know why I'm still working so hard for the taxman. I've written too much for my own good.'

He had a good grumble about it as always. Priestley grumbled for England. 'I don't think the English grumble enough.' With a face that he described as a glowering pudding, with sagging jowls, a drooping under-lip and that voice, he claimed, 'Money could not buy a better grumbling outfit.' And he came from the West Riding, 'where fault-finding and blame are constant and hearty'. He used to grumble at the fees I offered him for book reviews – 'Not as much as I got before the war' – but he was not seriously discontented. A good grumble always made him feel better. Most of the conversation was devoted to grumbling at the state of England where the American-invented Consumer Society was taking root through television and films. 'Man the Consumer is the lowest view of humanity ever taken. This idea that you should want more and more and be paid more and more to get it is contrary to our nature. The English idea of the good life has always been to have enough leisure to enjoy your hobbies. My father was a schoolmaster with £300 a year and on that we lived a frugal but very good life.'

It turned out that he was wrong about the English aversion to living mainly to shop. But he would castigate them as heartily as any other target. 'There are more stupid people in England, many of them in high places, than you'll find in most countries of Europe. The English...' He would warm to his favourite theme with the pipe drawing nicely. 'The English were at their absolute best in the Second World War and have never been so again.' He was a prominent part of that era so why was he taken off the air after only six months? There is a mysterious memo in the BBC archives which says: 'Priestley postscripts ceasing on instructions from Minister.' 'I'll tell you who had them stopped – Churchill! He was behind it.' Why? 'Because he thought I was getting too popular. *Perhaps as popular as him.* Anyway I never understood the fuss about those talks. They were slight things, written in half an hour.'

Despite living in a state of constant grievance about something, beneath the carapace he was an amusing and sensitive companion. Who else in the austerity of 1949 would have written a volume of essays called *Delight*? He presented his readers with over one hundred short pieces about his pleasure in such things as smells, smoking, playing charades or children's games, making stew, dreams and escaping from the treadmill of time. His pre-occupation with time, like Koestler's, was founded on the conviction that there is an alternative reality which we can sometimes sense though not comprehend. On my last visit he was clearly on the last stretch and was thinking of such matters. The preparations to celebrate his imminent ninetieth birthday gave him no pleasure. He clutched not a pipe but a brass handled stick and was silent for long stretches. 'I still regard myself as a writer, you know...although I have no work I'm engaged on at present...' Another silence. Then the half-shut eyes suddenly opened, piercing and blue. He suddenly found his full-powered voice: 'But I may have. At any moment!' He died three days later. He left behind him a hundred titles, many still in print or in performance – he thought more highly of his plays than of his novels. He did not live to see the triumphant revival of *An Inspector Calls* at the National Theatre in the setting of 1945. Its many tours at home and abroad brought it an audience of over half a million people. Quite an audience for a one-time Bradford wool clerk.

ANTHONY BURGESS

Another author who had written too much for his own good was Anthony Burgess, who produced a cataract of novels, non-fiction, film and television scripts and journalism. The reason he gave was that he only began writing full time at the age of forty-two when he was told he had a brain tumour and only a year to live. That year he published three novels to provide an income for his widow. Long after his death sentence expired (if it ever seriously existed) he still wrote and behaved as if he only had a year to live. When we met he always seemed to be in a tearing hurry and a high dudgeon, usually about critics. At a crowded seminar mostly composed of eager students of Eng Lit called to discuss his latest work, he looked increasingly impatient at the questions he was asked until a girl I knew demonstrated a grasp of what he aimed for. 'That's the first intelligent question there's been all evening,' he rasped. You could not say he strove to be liked.

His foremost bête noir was the London literary establishment to which he emphatically did not belong, nor wanted to, but blamed for cold-shouldering him because he was a Mancunian. He came from Lancashire Catholic stock and, though non-practising, looked down on converts like Waugh or Greene as inferior, just as London was inferior to Manchester – although he hadn't lived there since boyhood. He had chosen to live abroad and on visits to London said he always felt an outsider. He looked the part – with tousled hair, rumpled clothes, a perpetual cheroot and eyes permanently creased from its smoke. He probably didn't own a dinner jacket, which was the excuse he made for not attending the Booker Prize dinner, when he learned the winner would be a William Golding novel instead of his own masterly *Earthly Powers*.

A Rogues' Gallery

Despite the acclaim his prodigious output accumulated he talked like a man with a chip on his shoulder. Fame began with his notorious fantasy, *A Clockwork Orange*, in which he correctly foresaw British youngsters living by violence for violence's sake and speaking an argot (*Nasdat*, based on Russian) which only they understood. It became even more notorious as a film, which was banned in some cities for causing rioting and then withdrawn by its director, Stanley Kubrick. Burgess resented the fame the film garnered (he described the Kubrick version as 'The Clockwork Marmelade') to the exclusion of his many other and better works. But he accepted the money it brought in through extra sales.

In Monaco, where he settled with his second wife, Liana, a contessa's daughter, he seemed far more relaxed and optimistic, away from sententious London aesthetes. No writer I knew nursed higher ambitions. His idols and models were firstly James Joyce and secondly Shakespeare, whom he took on as subjects and as rivals. Shakespeare, whose life he novelised excellently in *Nothing Like the Sun* and whose songs he set to music, was, he pointed out, a provincial like himself who never went near Oxford or Cambridge. Joyce he emulated in many books and he made a musical version of *Ulysses* entitled *Blooms of Dublin*, which was broadcast by both BBC and RTE on the centenary of Joyce's birth. His skill and delight in manipulating language could easily summon up Shakespearian or Joycean language but, being Burgess, he had to add Beethovenian to the list. In *Napoleon Symphony* he attempted to create a verbal equivalent to the *Eroica*. Even he admitted that it was arduous to write – reading it certainly becomes so, although there are intriguing passages which echo the music's structure. Burgess admitted that he was attempting the impossible 'and therefore it was a failure just as *Finnegan's Wake* is a failure'. It is hard to imagine any other English novelist attempting failure on such a scale.

In his own eyes he was not primarily a novelist but a composer. He never failed to assure me that this was his true vocation. This or that new work of his was always about to be performed, usually somewhere rather obscure such as on Swiss radio. His output included symphonies, concertos and chamber music but I cannot judge their quality because I never heard any of them nor met anyone who had. 'I'm a musician who also writes,' he would assert. What he undoubtedly was was a writer of greater natural gifts than any other I met. His work is shamefully under-recognised at present.

Another underestimated English writer in exile was Robert Graves. I reached the house he had built long ago in Deya, on a tip of Majorca, after a nerve-wracking drive round unfenced corkscrew bends through the mountains. He took me on his daily tour of the village to receive homage from the young American would-be writers who rented his many properties for the hoped-for magic of being in his ambience. 'They'll get no inspiration from the olive trees,' he commented dryly as we walked back to the house. After lunch with his wife Beryl and their teenage children, who disappeared to smite guitars and drums upstairs, he beckoned me into his study. He opened a desk drawer and handed me a photograph. 'Isn't she beautiful?' She was dark, in her twenties, looked passionate and might well be trouble. 'My muse! Always been in love.' I thought of the passive Beryl. Did she know? Did she accept? I later learned that she did. This was one of a sequence of 'muses', one of whom was to cause a great deal of trouble and unhappiness all round. Graves was in his sixties – the age gap yawned. But this was the price he paid for continuing to write love poetry. It had to be granted that he had written some of the best of it in his time:

> Lovers, when they disentwine.
> You from me and yours from mine,
> Neither can be certain who
> Was that I whose mine was you.
> To the act again they go
> More completely not to know.

Has anyone put it better?

GORE VIDAL

Gore Vidal rated Burgess as 'easily the most interesting English writer of the past half-century'. I did not need to ask him whom he would nominate as the American equivalent. The contrast between the two as social beings could not have been sharper. Gore moved through the literary or political worlds as confidently as a killer whale, exercising his superiority linguistically. In London, where his home was the Connaught Hotel, his suite was filled with a constant stream of callers, literary, socialite, journalistic, all eager for his latest bon mots. 'You're like a visiting ambassador,' I told him, 'but what country do you represent?' 'Sanity,' he replied evenly. 'A small place but some of us are fond of it.' He seemed to have everything desirable – a patrician background in the Washington ruling class, good looks, money and homes in delightful surroundings, whether in Italy or the Hollywood Hills. Though he enjoyed his brilliant reputation he always retained the detachment of the cool, amused observer of a human race which he regarded with cool desperation. He was impregnable because he refused to be personal. People were always speculating about his sexuality. His reply would be, 'I've always done exactly what I liked.' His first sexual experience, he claimed, took place at eleven. Was it heterosexual or homosexual? 'I was too polite to ask.'

In Rome he regarded the turmoil of Italian politics from a balconied apartment overlooking the Piazza Venezia. But his favourite perch was the white villa near Ravello named *La Rondinaia* (The Swallow's Nest) which he shared with his lifelong, non-sexual partner, Howard Austen. Set above the cliffs amid seven acres of lemon and olive trees it commanded views of the ever-changing blues of the Tyrrhenian Sea. There he had no television, entertained little and liked being alone in his white-walled study where he got a great deal of writing done. 'If I lived in New York I'd be on television every five minutes.' In London I took him on walks to see things that might interest him. We lunched frugally at the ancient pub practically on the Connaught's doorstep in Farm Street, where the benches weren't upholstered and the fare was beef sandwiches and beer. He consented to sit in the weighing chair at the St James's wine merchants, Berry Brothers and Rudd, and in a neighbouring passageway was fascinated by a plaque marking the sometime 'Embassy of the Republic of Texas'. But he emerged from Trumpers with a hairbrush for which he was charged a hefty sum, which he afterwards wished he had objected to paying. 'How *pusillanimous* one is!' Always *le mot juste*. He could be ruffled. I once disturbed his serenity by an unthinking remark about British superiority in some respect compared with America. 'What typical British smugness!' We drank wine at *El Vino*, then patronised equally by lawyers and Fleet Street journalists. The critic Philip Hope-Wallace, enshrined in his habitual chair presiding over a daily champagne circle, grew increasingly restive as his audience's attention kept wandering to Gore. 'I don't really want to talk to him,' he said but sauntered over and soon was dominating the circle.

'You could easily have been an English or European writer.' 'No! I live in Europe because it's the best place to observe America. The United States has always been my subject. It's the country that most interests me – but not to live in.' His fellow countrymen got nothing but reproof from his pen. Though rattled by him they wanted more. To him both Democrats and Republicans were equally noxious wings of the same Property Party, concerned to protect the 4.4 per cent of the population that he said owned the United States. 'People don't like to be owned.' But he was never really satisfied with being the national Cassandra crying doom from the wilderness. Though he despised politicians, including the Kennedy family to whom he was distantly connected through Jackie, he ran twice for Congress. Just after his second defeat, in California, we met at the Plaza Hotel, New York, and consumed corned beef hash in the Oak Room. He was bitter at the disappointment of not getting the Senate seat. 'I'm a frustrated man of action,' he mused morosely. 'I hope I am more than just a prose writer. I feel...' – he sought for the word – 'under-used.' But surely he commanded more attention as a commentator, essayist, television wiseacre, than he could hope for by making speeches in the Senate? He assented. He did not want to join 'the opportunistic lawyers bought by the big corporations'. He had higher ambitions. He wanted to be president. 'The presidency is the only thing I ever really wanted and didn't get.'

KURT VONNEGUT

The other fascinating American writer of the time, for my money, was Kurt Vonnegut. He was as disillusioned and gloomy about America's future as Vidal in print. In person he invariably seemed in the best of spirits. His long lugubrious face looked as if it had been wizened since birth but he was far too tall to be a gnome. Beneath his tousled jungle of hair, rioting eyebrows and eyes glittering with scepticism hung this long, tobacco-singed moustache sagging with despair at both ends. Yet his most memorable characteristic was the laugh that lighted up all about him. Like a car trying to start on a cold morning, it would cough up wheezily to a climax, then burst into loud back-firing life – a series of explosive, squawking explosions – pow! pow! pow!

While listening, you could not help remembering at times that the man laughing so infectiously had seen the aftermath of the Dresden fire-bombing of February 1945 in awesome detail and then spent twenty-three years trying to figure out an effective way of conveying it in writing. To begin with he couldn't remember it. 'There was a complete blank when the bombing took place.' He revisited Dresden, where he and fellow prisoners-of-war had afterwards been assigned to 'corpse mining'. Eventually he succeeded in dealing with it in a startling mixture of truth and science fiction. *Slaughterhouse Five* (the address of the underground meat locker where he and other prisoners survived) had huge sales and impact and made him famous and rich. His reaction was a trio of shoulder-shrugging words that ran through the text as a comment on every death recorded – 'So it goes.' 'What else can you say,' he demanded, 'of the biggest massacre in European history?' The three words became a mantra for the betrayed Vietnam War generation. They also betrayed the German origin of his immigrant family. They are the counterpoint to the casual German greeting, 'Wie geht's?' The ethics and effectiveness of the obliteration by firestorm of Dresden and of Hamburg and other cities, by 'carpet' or area bombing, have been debated ever since. He knew the answer. 'It didn't bring the end of the war a single day nearer. The only person who benefited from it was me. I must have earned about five dollars for every man, woman and child who was killed there, through my book.'

His house in the East Sixties in New York seemed to be full of young people, many of them his own grandchildren with whom he seemed to be on such easy terms that he might have been their age. His writing style seemed artless like direct, informal conversation with the reader. If Gore Vidal represented the high culture of America at that time, Vonnegut represented the counter-culture. To the young and iconoclastic, who still seemed plentiful, he was definitely 'cool'. He illustrated his books with comic doodles and cartoons usually of himself, like a schoolboy doodling on boring textbooks. Being classified as a science fiction writer irked him. As a trained scientist he reckoned he was writing science fact – projected into a future which he thought technology was bound to spoil. Not that anyone else saw this. 'Americans need to feel there's a frontier,' he told me. 'They need to feel they're going some place, like Mars. Opportunity is supposed to be limitless in America. But we aren't going anywhere. It's a myth, like believing in Santa Claus. We've been lied to. What's unbearable about that I don't see. Life is absorbing enough the way it is.'

Meanwhile television was spoiling children's gift of imagination – 'the imagining is done for them' – and computers were robbing them of human sociability and relations with other people. 'Technology is starving people's souls. As for my trade, writing, it's over with. Technology entertains people better. Mine is the last generation to be totally formed by books.' He remained a joker to the last. He threatened to sue Pall Mall cigarettes, which he smoked continually, for failing to kill him as promised on the packet. The last book he published was entitled *A Man Without a Country*. He had finally lost faith in the America which he had known and loved as a mid-Westerner from Indianapolis. Like a fellow mid-Westerner, Mark Twain, he preferred the succinct aphorism to lengthy analysis. 'When Twain came East he was treated as a barbarian.' He died after a fall, aged eighty-four, in 2007 – just too soon to see the prophesies in his last book come true. He had forecast that almost everyone would lose their money in a vast financial scandal and that America would be bankrupt, most of it becoming owned by the Japanese and Koreans. He was only slightly out. It was to be the Chinese.

'I don't care whether I'm remembered or not when I'm dead,' he said to me. He was a realist. Writing, to him, was 'a job'. I was told that his last words to an audience were: 'I'm out of here.' I am not, by a long chalk, the only one to remember and cherish him. We had some laughs. So it goes.

STUDS TERKEL

The gritty voice of Chicago was that of the radio commentator, Studs Terkel, and that raw and windy city was Studs Terkel's muse. His daily radio talk show on WMFT was listened to far and wide. For five days a week for forty-five years he broadcast relaxed but deep-probing interviews and his guests were as various as Big Bill Broonzy and Bertrand Russell. I was invited to be one of them because Studs, formidably well read, idolised George Orwell and I had just published my modest biography of him. He was also becoming known for his books of street interviews with the disregarded blue-collar, working-class America – somewhat like Henry Mayhew's interviews in Victorian times with *London Labour and the London Poor*. His collections like *Division Street, America*, *Work* and *Hard Times* had opened a lot of eyes. Studs' trademarks were his cigar, red muffler, microphone and gruff friendliness of manner which got people to talk to him unreservedly.

I should have been on the look-out for his disarming technique but I arrived at the studio to find him already in full flow in his braces. He waved me to a seat diagonally around the table so that we seemed to be sharing the microphone rather than confronting each other across it as is normal. It was flattering to see that his copy of my book had been page-marked throughout, with many passages underlined. Thorough research was unusual for an author-interview on radio, where you usually felt that the presenter had glanced at the title and blurb and possibly the first chapter. Such interviews usually lasted only for three to five minutes before being swept away by the next record. Studs talked to me for forty-five gruelling minutes, mostly about Orwell. But this was the early spring of 1982 and the British Navy was sailing for the Falkland Islands on a danger-fraught mission to retrieve them from Argentine occupation.

Without warning Studs removed his cigar and shot me the question: 'Well, Peter, whaddya make of this Falklands business? What's England doing sending a task force all that way to a bunch of islands nobody's heard of?' Unexpectedly called upon to justify the war policy of Margaret Thatcher, whose views on most subjects I regarded with sincere loathing, I tried to justify defending our remnant of Empire. The islanders, though far away and not at all numerous or rich, were British, after all, and wanted to stay that way. Studs eyed me coolly. 'Know how we see it? Like two bald men fighting over a comb!' This was a cutting swipe and it floored me, then made me angry. How dare our supposed partners tell us what not to do with our own territory? I think I said – but there is no record to consult – that we couldn't let a bunch of Fascist generals, who had made their opponents disappear from the streets of Buenos Aires in their thousands, deprive British subjects of their freedom. I hope I said, 'I thought you valued liberty in the United States. What's that statue doing in New York harbour?' Studs looked delighted. He liked a good argument on his programme and this one continued for some while.

Afterwards he put on his muffler and invited me to lunch at a club where Chicagoans greeted him warmly. As he introduced me to his friends one or two of them looked at me strangely or with a hard stare. 'Say, are you the Limey who tried to give Studs a hard time on the air this morning?' I hastened to say it was he who gave me one. Studs must then have been turning seventy. He went on publishing interviews until his death at ninety-six. He was an old-fashioned New Deal American who had suffered in the Depression. He was outspoken, unsentimental, egalitarian – and when he fell silent America seemed to have no more of his sympathetic kind to replace him.

ANDY WARHOL

If there was one American more infatuated with the tape recorder than Studs Terkel it was Andy Warhol, who told me: 'I didn't get married till 1964 when I got my first tape recorder. My wife. We have been married ever since.' He started taping everything without exception about the same time as Richard Nixon. But why? 'Everybody I meet is so fabulous,' he breathed in a voice so soft it might have been cotton wool made audible. The fabulous creatures who occupied his private zoo at that time were the likes of Bianca Jagger, Liza Minelli, Lee Radziwill and Caroline Kennedy. But did he not get tired of hearing his own voice, which took up much of his cassette library? 'Oh, I don't play them back. I just store them. In a box.' In that case, I asked, feeling more and more like Alice in his Wonderland, why record them? He lifted the small machine in his hand. 'It's like working. A machine that's working to make sure that all this energy doesn't disappear.'

Acolytes from the Warhol entourage were on hand to keep changing the tapes or batteries as required. They presumably preserved them like papyri of Ancient Egypt in some great underground archive. I spent a day accompanying him through restaurants, department store windows, along carpeted corridors and down lift-shafts. Wherever we went recorders were turning, flashbulbs were popping, reels of film were being exposed and every last syllable of his high, babyish voice and shake of his floppy mop of dazzling white hair was being saved for posterity, down to the last pimple – his pimples were worrying him that day. And everywhere we went someone took out a watch and muttered, 'Oh dear! Oh dear! He'll be late!' More and more he reminded me of the White Rabbit.

THE EIGHTIES AND BEYOND

He had just come, he said over lunch, from an exhibition in Italy of his one hundred and fifty paintings of black transvestites. Did he know that many transvestites? 'No, only nine or ten.' Most of the paintings were the same as each other. Why do the same painting over and over again, I asked, feeling by now thoroughly like Alice. 'I like to do the same things all over again. All artists do the same picture over again, all their lives.' 'You mean that Rembrandt's or Monet's canvases are really the same picture?' He nodded. 'To me they are.' In that case why go to see another? 'I don't.' His latest portfolio was a hundred or more prints of Mick Jagger, done not from life but from Polaroid photographs he had taken. 'I try to make them as much like the Polaroids as possible – but they aren't as good.'

I recalled that when he started he used to paint identical cans of Campbell's tomato soup. He smiled in fond reminiscence. 'Yes. That was because I had a tin of Campbell's soup every day. Always the tomato. I couldn't afford expensive lunches in those days.' What was he doing for a living? 'I was doing the windows of the stores on Fifth Avenue.' 'You were a window dresser?' 'We called ourselves Staplegun Queens. It was a very happy time.' And was he surprised when his soup can pictures sold? 'Yes, I was.' More and more of them? For more and more money? 'Very surprised.' 'Why did people buy them?' 'I really don't know,' said the cotton wool voice. 'I'm really surprised they did.' His position was impregnable.

He talked about his next film, to be called *Bad*. In the 1960s he made several films of nothing happening to a man asleep, for instance, or of the Empire State Building just standing there. 'Now I believe in more dialogue.' His great unfulfilled ambition was to have his own TV show. He would set up the camera somewhere in New York and just leave it to run. 'The show would be called *Nothing Special*. You can get fifty or more TV stations in New York. This would be a more restful kind of entertainment. Nothing special. If anybody came by that would be special. If not you could watch the weather. Do you know that in Paris there's a channel just showing the clock? When I'm there it's the only thing I watch.' Why not watch a real clock? 'A clock on television is more fascinating than a real clock...' The baby voice was fading like the smile on the Cheshire cat because he was again being

249

hurried away. Once more the White Rabbit was late. The snowball of hair, which he had told me was washed everyday in Clairol, was bobbing in the middle of his flock of acolytes. It was, of course, a wig. A wig, I could imagine him saying, was more interesting to wear than real hair.

Not long after his visit to Swinging London he was shot, but not killed, by one of his madder female acolytes. His fame has lasted a great deal longer than the fifteen minutes he promised everybody. Why this should be so is an intriguing question. Warhol discovered the principle which was going to underpin the art market for years ahead: Anything can be Art – if you declare that it is, and maintain that you are an Artist. There was no need to create or invent any longer – potential Art lay all about you in the form of soup cans, Coke bottles, Brillo Pad boxes, whatever. It also subsisted in sheets of Polaroid snapshots, once they had been silk-screened and tinkered with and given a daub or two of lurid paint. Brand images were the key: they could be Marilyn or Mao, Elvis or Elizabeth (the Second or Taylor, no matter) and especially Andy, the brand himself. Images for a world obsessed by brands, repeated over and over by mass production. He called his studio The Factory, implying that Art was now a commodity manufactured by technology. Indeed one of his posters put it frankly: Art Is What You Can Get Away With. All he had to do was sign and staple-gun it to the walls of galleries and wait for the dollars. They arrived by the bucketful. It was a system that has been gratefully copied ever since by the likes of Damien Hirst, aided by grateful art dealers.

In a way getting shot when he did was a good career move, worth tons of publicity. And he was running short of subject matter. He hadn't thought of sharks, oddly enough.

JESSICA MITFORD

'Abroad is bloody and foreigners are fiends.' It may have been that sort of sentiment offered by her father that drove Jessica, the fifth of the six Mitford sisters, to make a bee-line for abroad and stay there. From an early age she saved up her 'running away money' and used all £50 of it to bolt to Spain at the age of nineteen and join the Republican side in the Civil War. Two years later she left for the United States to continue the revolutionary struggle with a husband who had been in the International Brigade. They joined the Communist Party – a natural step for a born rebel against her Hitler-loving family – her father and mother, Lord and Lady Redesdale, and sisters Unity and Diana. In California, where she had settled in Oakland, near San Francisco, her upper-class county voice stood out like Crown Derby china. She was Comrade Posh until 1958 when she left the Party for civil rights campaigning alongside her new husband, a lawyer named Bob Treuhaft. Jessica was a rebel never without a cause.

The object of her ridicule and righteous indignation when I first met her was the pompous and predatory American funeral industry. She had cosied up to them, subscribed to their trade journal, *Casket and Sunshine* (note the upbeat title), interviewed them charmingly and allowed them to hang themselves with their smarmy, money-grubbing self-esteem. When her book, *The American Way of Death*, came out there was extreme embarrassment in the embalming rooms. Evelyn Waugh had been bad enough. She detailed the wiles by which funeral directors (she infuriated them by calling them undertakers) screwed their mourning customers for thousands of unnecessary dollars. The National Funeral Directors Association had her denounced in Congress as an 'anti-American Communist'. Forest Lawn, the Ascot of Los

Angeles cemeteries, wrote to every clergyman in LA calling the book 'a Communist plot'. She longed for them to sue, as they had promised. But she never got her day in court. 'There was,' she told me lightly, 'the occasional telephoned death threat at night.'

The counter-attack boosted her book to the head of the best-seller list. She became a national name for her witty responses on network talk shows. She testified at Federal Trade Commission hearings into the practices of the NFDA. Their spokesman tried to justify their practice of recommending expensive caskets for Loved Ones but he was no match for a Mitford. Mitfords love to tease – and Americans don't understand teasing. 'What if a grieving widow selected a yellow casket for a husband who had died of jaundice?' she was asked. Should she not be gently persuaded to change the colour?

Mitford:	Not at all. Yellow would be my choice for jaundice. For scarlet fever I would choose red. It's best to have everything matching.
NFDA:	Suppose a husband chooses a casket too narrow for his heavily built wife?
Mitford:	He'd probably been urging her to diet for years and was getting even at last.

Did the book manage to reform over-pricing? Casket makers complained that it dented their sales. 'But the scene is still pretty exorbitant. The ultra-cheap alternative coffin which a manufacturer promised me to name the Jessica Mitford never materialised. But there has been a large increase in cremations, from five to forty per cent, which are, of course, much cheaper.'

Some years later we met in London on the eve of the launch of her companion campaigning book, *The American Way of Birth*. After the morticians she was laying into the obstetricians, 'who are, if anything, worse. The cost of giving birth in America would appal any English mother-to-be'. She listed fees which obstetricians charged for scarcely putting in an appearance and the price of a twelve-hour hospital stay ($1,200) to disposable slippers ($15). If you wanted to spend serious money there was the luxury birth-suite with four-poster and dinner *à deux* afterwards. There were teaching cassettes to be played to the foetus during the no doubt tedious hours it spent awaiting delivery. Her scorn especially highlighted the strap-on 'empathy belly' for husbands who wished to demonstrate that they were both in this thing together. It was guaranteed to produce backache and press uncomfortably on the bladder. 'For many men it opens up a whole new world of feeling,' ran the promotional literature.

Jessica beamed at this. But she was deadly serious about the appalling infant mortality figures – America she assured me was twenty-fourth in the world table – and scandalised by the wretched provision made for the thirty-seven million mothers who had no health insurance. One in four births was by Caesarean which gave doctors less inconvenience and added $1,000 to their fees. 'They are right up there with company presidents, you know.'

She herself had her child in a Washington hospital charity ward where nurses were very reluctant to answer patients' bells and bring bed-pans. In typical Mitford fashion she organised industrial action. All nine women on the ward wet their beds on cue, deluging the nurses with wet sheets. 'After that one only had to touch a bell and a nurse came running.' The Americanism 'feisty' might have been coined for her. Long before Presidents Clinton and Obama she was campaigning for a revolution in health care against the American Medical Association's opposition to what it called 'Socialised Medicine' – 'that deadly S-word'.

She was a born investigative journalist. *Time* magazine called her 'the queen of the muckrakers' and a muckraker in her seventies is an impressive sight, even though she was always on the verge of letting her amusement break through. 'And what a mercy,' she said with satisfaction. 'It's got nothing to do with the Mitford industry' – of which she was impatient, although she had contributed to it with *Hons and Rebels*. She had never fitted in with the family. 'When I was fourteen I asked my mother whether she realised she was an enemy of the working class.' Lady Redesdale had replied indignantly, 'No I am not. I think some of them are perfectly *sweet*.' Jessica must have felt she had a lot to atone for.

BERNARD LEVIN

The doughtiest fighter in British journalism in my time was Bernard Levin. He had the zest of a schoolboy and looked like one, with round spectacles gleaming and a coil of unruly hair springing aggressively above his forehead. He immediately built a formidable reputation in Fleet Street as a fire-cracker critic – of Parliament, television and the theatre. He wrote a daily column which made mincemeat of the current follies of the world, with special attention to his bête noires – political fixers like Harold Wilson, lawyers, judges, and lazy, complacent institutions such as the banks, gas boards, airlines and trade unions.

TW3 made him a national figure. Every week he mounted a stool and set about challenging an invited group from the studio audience – public relations men, lawyers, Tory ladies, CND protesters – in the most forthright terms. They seldom gave him much opposition because they were too winded by the force of his attack. 'There is only one word to describe British catering,' he typically began to one victim, the hotelier Charles (later Lord) Forte representing the food industry. 'And that is disgusting. Unless I were to add tasteless, uneatable, boring and revolting...' Forte stared back dumbly like a stranded fish. Nobody had been so rude, person to person, in television interviews before. Bernard, a sincere hater of the meretricious, pompous or pretentious, always had his arguments marshalled with deadly efficiency.

One night the husband of an actress to whom he had given an adverse review came up and swung a fist that knocked them both out of vision. After a brief period of chaos he resumed his perch and said to his opponents for the evening, who happened to be anti-nuclear demonstrators, 'Now may we get back to non-violence?' They applauded.

At this period he and I shared an office and formed a friendship that would last forty years until his death. He was the spikiest but least boring man to sit opposite. He rattled off his daily column with scarcely a pause, then looked across the top of his typewriter and would demand, 'Haven't you finished yet? Do you realize that you are the only man I know on whose wrinkled forehead one could play noughts and crosses?' Provocation and disparagement were his normal line of discourse though he did not disparage his own abilities. More than once I heard him rip the copy out of his typewriter saying to himself *sotto voce*: 'Clever old me, clever old me!' Secretaries slaved for him willingly. He always thanked them at the end of the day.

When he handed over the *Daily Mail* theatre critic's seat to me, who had deputised for him for some time, he threw a party to mark my first First Night in his stead. This was hardly helpful. I had to write the review at one end of the editor's office while he opened champagne for the guests at the other end. I had barely got going when he peered over my shoulder at the first paragraph. 'He's made a joke,' he announced to the company. I seldom wrote a notice under more trying conditions. He also presented me with three volumes of Bernard Shaw's collected theatre criticism with the inscription: 'For Peter, with the assurance that he will find in them many a phrase that he can steal and the hope that when he comes across the hundreds that I have already stolen he will keep quiet about it.'

As he quit the office each evening he would give me a condescending smile: 'Off to the theatre again, are we? No doubt some masterpiece by William Douglas Home awaits you. I wish you joy of it. *I* am going to the opera.' As he usually was. Like many otherwise rational people he was addicted to opera. In Bernard's case it was a ritual of almost mystical significance. It involved the booking of the chosen companion – blonde English Roses preferred – the sending of flowers for her to wear, the donning of evening clothes including a flamboyant opera cloak, the chauffeured limousine, the supper table at the Savoy or a Michelin-starred restaurant, the whole ritual of a bygone belle époque.

But music was the primary pleasure in his life and the music of Richard Wagner blinded him, as it does so many, to the preposterous goings-on in the Ring cycle as well as the disgusting character of Hitler's favourite composer. One evening at his flat he seated me at the optimum point between the latest loudspeakers, handed me the full score of *Die Walkure* and, before switching on the recording, presented me with a slender ivory baton in a box. 'In case you feel the urge,' he murmured. The vision of Bernard all alone, conducting the oceanic volume of Wagnerian sound haunted me afterwards. But, as he ruefully acknowledged, he was unable to play any musical instrument except the baton.

The shared outing I remember most fondly was our fishing expedition to the wilds of Connemara. Neither of us knew one end of a rod from the other but this did not deter him. Two days before departure he approached to impart a solemn confidence: 'I have decided *not* to take a dinner jacket.' Given the remoteness of our country hotel this was welcome news. It rained a good deal, the fishing was unproductive and he panicked when he found an eel squirming on the end of his line. 'Get rid of it!' he cried throwing the rod at me. In other ways the visit was a success as it was designed to cure us both of our addictions. I was to give up smoking and he was to give up reading newspapers. We were both in our separate ways twenty-a-day men. As an incentive I was allowed one cigar after dinner and he was allowed to have one article read out to him. Only *The Field* was available. The article I read was entitled 'Walking a salmon up to the gaff'. He heard it out patiently.

'Why did I become a writer? Because I had a very great deal to say and not a scrap of any other talent. I spent my adult life fighting with words, which I have tried to use to stem the tide of evil.' Though this made him the best-known journalist of his time, his carapace of confidence concealed an inner shyness and frequently depression. When someone in the office exclaimed in his hearing, 'Wouldn't it be wonderful to be as sure of yourself as Bernard?' he turned on him with real venom: 'You stupid, blue-shirted, bloody Scotsman! Do you think I would behave as I do if I were not eaten up with self-doubt?'

A search for unsatisfied spirituality led him to give up his columns and go away for eighteen months 'to think' – not the kind of retreat to which journalists are much given. He wrote of his 'gnawing awareness that an alternate reality lies elsewhere, sensed just beyond the light cast by the campfire, heard in the slow movement of a Mozart quartet, seen in the eyes of a Rembrandt self-portrait, felt in the stab of discovery when reading Shakespeare'. The nearest thing to faith came to him through great art. His last companion, Liz Anderson, was a Roman Catholic but he told her she would never make him one – he would prefer the Church of England. He asked for a C of E funeral.

Before that he was subjected to the severest imaginable test of faith, philosophy or endurance. Symptoms of memory loss began several years before they disabled him. His conversational powers seemed unimpaired when he was first diagnosed with Alzheimer's. Which of us, after reaching seventy, did not forget names? Were the doctors possibly wrong? 'I'm afraid not. I have pills to slow it down but the outlook – well, it's too bleak to think about.' I still would not believe it until the night when he found it impossible to remember the name of Oscar Wilde.

His ability to enjoy writing, reading, the theatre, even the opera came to an end. The magic of music still worked for him, although after a concert he would wrestle fiercely, but without clarity, to express what he felt about the Bach or Schubert we had been listening to. Gradually silence descended between him and the world. There was a publishing party to launch his book on the sixties in paperback. The room was full of the people he had dominated as a talker for so long. But I found him sitting in a corner alone, ignored by every one of the 'friends' busy jabbering away to each other.

It was tragic to see the most articulate person I had ever known, a walking dictionary of quotations, who said he knew by heart three thousand lines of Shakespeare, no longer able to frame a sentence. His last public appearance was at a party given by the BBC for the fortieth anniversary of *That Was The Week That Was*. The studio was filled with writers and performers watching film-clips of him at his lethal best. He stood up to acknowledge the tributes and applause with an embarrassed half-smile. He murmured 'thank you' to all those who came up to shake his hand while I stood beside him fielding their well-meaning enquiries. I wondered, did he recognize his earlier self on the screens? Did he even remember the show? Can memory persist although the faculty to express it is wiped out?

Sometimes visiting him in hospital I thought I evoked a hint of recognition – for example, by quoting one of Belloc's *Cautionary Tales* which he used to recite in their entirety. Rarely and abruptly, as if a cloud had dissolved between us, he would speak in his old voice: 'It's very, very lonely' or, with real passion, 'The bastards! The bastards!' I did not need to ask who the bastards were. Inevitably there were tantrums of frustration, like those of a thwarted infant. In hopes that he could still recognise them I put on tapes of Mozart, Schubert and Beethoven. Sometimes he closed his eyes – possibly in sleep. Sometimes after a few bars he would get up and shuffle away. But on my last attempt he remained seemingly alert through a movement of a quartet. 'Isn't that beautiful?' I said without thinking when it ended. For once he looked me full in the eyes and said with every appearance of meaning it, 'Yes! It *is*!' We clasped hands. For a few moments he seemed to have come back from wherever it was. There was still a Bernard to come back.

At his funeral a few weeks later I felt his presence watching us intently. Even dementia, I believe, cannot shatter what Orwell called the crystal spirit.

JOHN BETJEMAN

Despite the explosive laugh that shook his whole body so often, John Betjeman off-guard wore an expression of dejection, like a schoolboy who had been disappointed of a promised treat. The long, loose upper lip would sag over the prominent teeth and the eyes gazed out apprehensively beneath the noble Roman dome of a forehead. 'How are you, John?' 'Absolutely terrified!' He meant it. He looked it. One did not need to ask what it was of which he was terrified. Death – and worse, hell – ran through his poems like a *darkmotif*. It was also a major part of his television persona as the venerable old party who aroused affectionate sympathy when he spoke up for unfashionable buildings and places. Was he beloved because he was so fearful?

Presented with a half-bottle of champagne that he liked you to bring him at mid-morning, the lips firmed, the eyes sparkled again. He wore his emotions very visibly. 'What shall we talk about? Not the ghastly Herr Doktor?' Even then Doctor Professor Nikolaus Pevsner was cataloguing, or re-cataloguing, or re-re-cataloguing the Buildings of England, like a diligent auctioneer, listing their size, style and specifications: 'Late Georgian frontage of five bays...' There was, to say the least, an absence of human feeling in such work. To Betjeman, for whom buildings were living expressions of their epoch and architect, he was the Enemy.

I first heard him talk about architecture as a schoolboy. Cut off from the outer world at Stowe deep in Buckinghamshire a group of us formed a club and invited him among others to come and talk to us. He came. At the end of his talk a clever boy asked a question which led to the complete unraveling of one of his arguments. Betjeman thought for a moment. 'You're absolutely right! Corks! I'm sunk!' – followed by the Betjeman horse-laugh. His stock couldn't have risen faster. We were quite unused to our elders and betters admitting mistakes in so carefree a manner. Conversation afterwards turned for some reason to Frank Pakenham, later Lord Longford. 'Lovely man. Always has his shoelaces undone. Isn't that *darling* of him?' Later I learned that Betjeman too had trouble tying his shoelaces. From that time on many of us became Betjemaniacs.

At Wadham College, Oxford, the warden, Maurice Bowra, and Betjeman were old friends and he was often to be seen around the front quad. 'The trouble is,' said Bowra, 'John keeps wanting to take me to look at Keble.' That puce palace of Victorian Gothic was still regarded as the outer darkness architecturally and I used to wince when bicycling past it. Betjeman was just beginning his campaign to restore William Butterfield and his fellow Victorian architects to respect in the teeth of the modernists who opposed 'any kind of ornament because it collects dust', as he put it. He succeeded ultimately. Although I could not share his enthusiasm for Keble College or old Liverpool Street station, through whose contorted stairways and passages I had lugged an army kitbag all too often, I had to applaud his defence of St Pancras, which was to be totally vindicated. Thanks mainly to him preservation became a popular cause.

Television expanded obligingly at the precise moment he needed it to become our guide and mentor to his favourite churches, stations or suburbs. These reached a high point in the gentle mockery of *Metroland*, his valediction to the Baker Street line to Amersham and beyond. Having lived much of my childhood along it, I knew that when you lifted the brass door handles of the old wooden compartments you saw engraved beneath them the slogan: *Live in Metroland*. It had been put there to give a touch of imaginary glamour to a set of modest wooden stations that grew sleepier and leafier the farther the commuter travelled from Town. Betjeman imagined his dream:

> And all day long in beastly London Wall
> The thought of Ruislip kept him warm inside

It was always tempting to review his books or theatrical evenings in a pastiche of his jog-trot verse. But he rose far above that at his best. He could be subtle and complex in meter and rhyme scheme and a master of the sudden dips from the banal into the fearful. He did not become the best-selling poet since Tennyson on the strength of agreeable light verse, mild snobbery ('Phone for the fish-knives, Norman') and jokey sentiments about tennis and riding girls.

Towards the end of his life he had the idea that I should write a short unofficial biography of his life and work. He seemed less than thrilled at the prospect of the massive two-tome (subsequently three-tome) *Life* by Bevis Hillier, commissioned by his publisher Jock Murray of Albermarle Street. We had preliminary discussions but Parkinson's was already taking hold. I wondered how much he was up to remembering. There was above all the problem of coming clean at last on his private life. For years his virtual separation from his wife Penelope, the redoubtable horsewoman, and the companionship of Lady Elizabeth Cavendish, who lived a few doors away in Chelsea, had been kept a secret from the public. Out of regard for him, his Mid-Wife Crisis was not even hinted at in the newspapers of that time. Would this be a problem? Would Lady Penelope talk? His face sagged apprehensively. 'You see, I simply don't know *where she is.*' This attempt at evasion was swiftly ended by his secretary: 'Oh, we know where she is. We had a postcard. Somewhere in Wales.' The goodwill of the two women whom he loved for their very differences was never put to the test. Jock Murray got wind of the project and firmly squashed it. There was to be no competition with the official tombstone, which was only completed twenty years after his death. So I never discovered whether the anguish of balancing his affections between the two was the cause of his very real fear of damnation. His sense of sin and belief in hell, supposedly induced in infancy by a Calvinist nursemaid, was unusually severe for the times he lived in. 'I believe my religion is largely one of fear,' he once admitted. His cherished Church of England at least tolerated his doubts but he thought The Management, as he called it, might reject him as unworthy 'for what I have done to Penelope'.

Our last meeting was a sad one for me because our joint project was over. 'How are you?' 'More and more terrified!' When I was leaving he gave me the slim volume of *Uncollected Poems* that had just tardily been published. His hand was now shaking so much that his signature wobbled into incoherence. Betjeman is a long word. The book contains his poem to Archie, his celebrated teddy bear, which Jock Murray had excluded from previous collections, probably for fear of critics sniffing at it as sentimental. It is nothing of the kind. It is one of the toughest of his poems. In it we are told the true significance of Archie, who sits dolefully above his bed:

> He has no mouth but seems to say
> They'll burn you on the Judgement Day

After recalling the many experiences they had shared, Archie speaks again:

> In double-doom notes, like a knell,
> 'You're half a century nearer Hell'

Archie was not exactly a bear of comfort. He was there to keep the score.

I used to worry whether the poet's death would be as terrifying as he supposed. It was with relief that I heard he had died quite peacefully. Holding Archie.

LAURIE LEE

Laurie Lee liked teasing. His spectacles gleamed with mischief in the low lights of the Chelsea Arts Club. 'Go on, then, Peter, take the plunge. Sell the Jaguar. Chuck in the expense account. Take yourself off to the country and be a real writer.' This was the song the sirens always sang. Now it was coming from the husky Gloucestershire voice whose Rs rustled like a wire brush drawn across a snare-drum. It was all very well for him to play the tempter – *Cider with Rosie* had just sold its millionth paperback. 'But I haven't got a Jaguar,' I objected lamely. 'Only a figure of speech,' he retorted. You could never be sure when he was winding you up.

There he stood, acknowledged as a master of landscape painting, the village boy who had walked across Spain carrying a fiddle at the age of nineteen, but who seemed more at home in the smoky chatter of London's Bohemia. Tourists went looking for him in Slad, Gloucestershire, but Chelsea, SW3, was where he liked to be lionised by rich and titled ladies. The country cottage was for weekends. Every book he'd written, he'd written in London, he told me, on the top decks of buses or in his seat beneath the mirror of the bar of his pub, the Queen's Elm. 'I like noise around me when I write. Buses give you motion and privacy. No one can get you on the telephone.' That, of course, is unfortunately no longer true. He also preferred metropolitan food, wine and company. As we set about a well-lubricated lunch with Kingsley Amis, Amis told a story which went on, perhaps, a little too long. Laurie looked at him with the mischievous gleam. 'Eat up your oysters, Kingsley,' he said kindly. 'Before they get cold.'

The valleys and deep-buried villages around Stroud – Slad, Sheepscombe, Miserden, Bisley – were very familiar to me because for years I spent holidays in a cottage at Far Oakridge belonging to my friend Norman Shrapnel, the veteran Parliamentary sketch-writer and novel-reviewer for the *Guardian*. I once suggested that it would be pleasant if the two of them should meet. Laurie's face registered anything but eagerness. 'Shrapnel?' he said, flinty-eyed. 'Gave me a shocking review once,' – no writer ever forgets – 'over-writing, I think, was the word he used.' Thinking of Norman's spare, dry, deflationary style I could well believe it. Laurie was always on the verge of over-writing, of over-doing the charm, but J. B. Priestley got it right when he commented: 'He often trembles on the very edge of affectation but always dances out of danger, coining phrase after phrase to delight us.'

Outside his clubs, which included the Garrick, and his pubs Laurie was far from sociable. I knew no one who had been invited to his flat in Elm Park Gardens where there was a locked study to which even his wife and daughter were not admitted. Evasiveness was second nature to him. His publisher, Andre Deutsch, said testily one day: 'If you see Laurie ask him from me what has happened to his book on his Civil War experiences. I've been waiting for it for years. Is he really writing it?' When I duly mentioned the last installment of his autobiographical trilogy it brought forth a masterly display of evasive tactics. The book was virtually written. In fact, he was even then carrying the pencilled manuscript with him for safety. The trouble was the typing. 'You see no one else can type it and there's this problem with my machine. The Ts and the Ls stick so you have to lift them back off the roller by hand. That slows things up a lot.' Yes, he had been sent new typewriters but they were electronic and the slightest brush of your cuff sent them mad. 'The text comes out looking like Serbo-Croat.' Also he found summoning up that time of forty or more years ago was very arduous. 'I'm having to dredge very deep. Still,' he added, brightening, 'you can tell Andre that if I can lick the problem of my bloody typewriter I may even have another book in me.'

When *A Moment of War* at last appeared six years later, it was a shock to those who had waited so long for it. It sang of death rather than the joy of being alive which he usually conveyed. In the harsh winter of 1937-8 he had walked over the Pyrenees, been promptly arrested as a suspected spy and spent much of his few weeks in wartime Spain in prison cells. There had been a brief period at or near the front where the Republicans were losing before he was invalided home. The book was dedicated 'To the Defeated' and it reeked of hopelessness and bitterness in vividly depicted cold and squalor. Praise for the prose was accompanied by disbelief. The British battalion commander of the International Brigade declared that the actions he described were largely fantasy. By then he was too blind to read notices of his book, which was widely praised on publication. Doubts about its veracity were not made public until after his death.

Like all his books, this one belonged in the territory between realism and poetic vision. He began as a poet but he discovered that he was better at expressing poetic sensations in prose, illuminated by his lightning flashes of precise imagery. His talk sparkled with images. He would reminisce about the Cotswolds: 'Beech leaves in spring like fresh washed salads. We lived as on a raft in this great green sea.' In rural Spain he had witnessed the tail end of an historic way of life. 'Nothing moved faster than the horse. I might have been the first Englishman they had set eyes on since the Peninsular War.' He managed to make contact with strictly supervised Spanish girls, including one who nudged him into a dark corner, surreptitiously opened her blouse and brought forth a peach. 'She gave me a gift of voluptuousness – a breast-warmed peach.' I discovered I was not the only listener to have been beguiled by the story of the breast-warmed peach.

Was there an actual Rosie? He sounded ambiguous on the subject, never revealing her identity. He once suggested to me that she was a composite of half a dozen girls whose names he reeled off. But you don't climb under a hay wagon with a composite girl. He admitted the celebrated title was a bit fanciful. 'There was very little cider and not too much Rosie.' But he did recall coming with her out of 'a dark, hot summer wood' where he had held her hand. 'Coming into the sunlight was very like coming out of the Odeon on a Saturday afternoon.' Hay-cart or wood, it doesn't really matter exactly what happened in the Slad that exists only on the page. The overcrowded kitchen was real, where no one would listen when he tried to tell them what had happened to him at school. 'So I went and sat in a tree writing. It was the only thing that I could do.'

A Rogues' Gallery

Looking at him in old age you could still make out that grumpy child who knew how to make the others indulge him in order to provoke his golden words. He remained in many ways a helpless boy who (like Betjeman) couldn't tie his shoelaces, nor drive a car nor answer the telephone. When *Rosie* was first published he was deluged with letters from readers claiming to have had similar experiences. 'Many of them implied that they could have written it themselves if they'd only got out the pen.' It went on to sell six million copies. Buoyed up with money he did what seems to me still an extraordinary thing. After thirty years away he went back to Slad and bought a house. 'I shouldn't have gone back,' he admitted once. 'When you leave the village you leave forever. Unless you come back ruined you're never forgiven for leaving in the first place. I was treated coolly. There was always this book. I had made money from writing about them. Some said it was a pack of lies, a pack of lies, though most of the stories in it were common currency in the village. The taboo I broke was to put them in print. That took a long time to live down. Mind you, people never recognise themselves. They'd say, "Old George now, you got him to a T." But they didn't know they were in it. Village life is secretive, close-fisted, close-mouthed. We were like a tribe. There were marks on us that said Slad. I was blowing the cover on a secret.'

Time healed the rift and he became a local hero. He deplored the changes in the village. But the view from his stone cottage just below the Woolpack, the sweep of the valley, did not change. 'Every hollow in that landscape, every branch of every tree, every curve of every field, every twist of every hedgerow is the mythology of my life.' When his sight failed he had it still, hoarded inside and written down. 'Our job is to recollect and preserve,' he told me seriously. 'We have only a short time. There aren't going to be any second helpings. To lose any of it is to waste it.' He had always made time to stop and stare at this life. So he was able to tell us, who haven't, what we'd missed.

JOHN MORTIMER

John Mortimer had two styles of doing anything. With languor – or with extreme languor. He liked to pass himself off as a barrister who occasionally wrote something. His considerable height was topped by a sensually cherubic mouth from which issued a high, almost girlish voice. It was the laziest voice I can recall. He gave the impression that he could scarcely find the energy to lift his glass of champagne. The drawl and the bored expression must have lulled many a hostile witness in court into being unprepared for the sudden knife-thrust of a crucial question. He liked to defend murderers and when reporting duties occasionally took me to the Bailey we would share the lunch hour in a wine bar whose proprietor's name helped inspire the name of his best-known character – Rumpole. 'What brings you here today, John?' 'Oh, I'm doin' a little murder. What have you got?'

His first and, to my mind, perfect short play for radio was *The Dock Brief*. In it Michael Hordern brought to uncanny life one of the clapped-out, down-at-heel counsel who used to haunt the criminal courts of my youth on the off-chance of being given a 'dock brief' to defend some unfortunate accused who had no legal representation. Mortimer cast a cynical eye on most of the practitioners at the Bar and it showed in his pointed satire on this case in which a confessed murderer is acquitted through the incompetence of his counsel. Though it made ideal radio (which won the *Prix Italia*) it was transferred to the theatre and then film, losing a little of its sharpness in each translation. Mortimer had early experience with the wartime Crown Film Unit. He was soon turning out film scripts as well as plays and television. It was true that one of his major credits, the adaptation of *Brideshead Revisited*, was largely discarded by the director when shooting – not necessarily to the film's advantage. His own stage plays were usually flawed but his adaptations of Feydeau farces for the National Theatre were masterly. His languor was a disguise for intense industry. He would get up at five a.m. and write at furious speed before the courts claimed his attention. He also turned out lucrative articles at the request of the newspapers on any topic with a bearing on the law. By this means he maintained a large family, the product of two marriages to women named Penny, which must have caused, or perhaps saved, confusion. They were by no means his only relationships.

He was never going to be content within the confines of court. He commiserated with one jury for having sat through 'one of the most boring cases I have ever known'. 'The English law,' observed the judge, 'does not exist purely for the entertainment of Mr Mortimer.' In private he deplored the antique jargon and costume of the courts, the hose and buckled shoes and wigs and inward-looking minds. 'Most of our judges have spent their lives since they were undergraduates living on staircases in quadrangles and dressing up in gowns to mix only with other lawyers. They have never been exposed to real life.' But he endured the fustian panoply in order to fight infringements of liberty, especially censorship of any kind. We used to argue about extreme cases. He maintained that child pornography, which he detested, should nevertheless not be banned.

He was also a keen pursuer of women, who always responded warmly. He propositioned my then lady friend when I was absent for only a few minutes. Despite his large helpings of success in life he entitled his autobiography *Clinging to the Wreckage*. There was enough wreckage to justify this, particularly in the stormy relationship with his first wife, Penelope Mortimer, whose novels reflected it. His predilections came out in the end when a hostile biographer planned to reveal that one of his affairs years before had produced a 'love child', now a mature man in his forties, as an addition to his other offspring. Mortimer spiked his guns by revealing the secret himself before the book could be published. But his extreme libertarianism had its limits, as I was surprised to discover at the first night of a rather revolting American play. It was set largely in the bath houses of New York, where it had been a *succes fou* with gay audiences. Seeing me there in the capacity of critic he accosted me after the curtain fell. 'What are you going to say about this?' He was visibly agitated. 'It's a disgrace to the stage.' I found myself arguing, with him of all people, that such plays had a right to be heard, however disagreeable to us personally. 'Oh, well,' was his snorted parting shot, 'roll on AIDS.' Admirers of his defence of such cases as Schoolkids *OZ* might have found this shocking.

He did most of his writing at the beautifully situated white house that his father had built in the 1930s near Turville in the Chilterns. Living alongside the Chilterns myself I got to know it. It was still very much his father's house. He sat at his father's desk and slept in his father's bed. Even the walking sticks in the hallstand were his father's sticks. Both his father and the house became familiar to the public when he wrote *A Voyage Round My Father*. Clifford Mortimer, a distinguished barrister, was totally blind but refused to acknowledge or even speak of it as he pursued his career in the divorce courts. His arbitrary and contrary character attracted major actors like a honeypot. Beautifully done on its first outing by Mark Dignam, the role went to the West End in the hands successively of Alec Guinness, Michael Redgrave and finally, in the television version, Laurence Olivier.

So completely did John identify with his father that he allowed the filming to take place at home, in the very house where he represented himself growing up with this puzzling parent. He attended the shooting, which included the scene of his father's death in the very room and bed where it had taken place. It must have required considerable detachment to watch this moving scene re-enacted as drama. Beneath his genial affability he maintained such detachment. His father found the idea of ending life which he so much enjoyed, infuriating: 'I'm always angry when I'm dying.' He played his father's role to the end.

EPILOGUE:
VOYAGE ROUND MY FATHER

Looking back over this album of snapshots of some seventy-five extremely varied human beings, I am struck above all by the strength and uniqueness of their characters. Some had character on a nearly superhuman scale, like Churchill, Bertrand Russell or Arthur Miller. Others, like Ralph Richardson, Spike Milligan or John Betjeman were freakishly outstanding. There are also those who personified folly and fraud. But where, I wonder, could I find a band of such originals today? None of their celebrity was manufactured – it was earned.

It occurs to me that people who flourished in the period of this book, 1950 to 2000, had one common influence which occurred before the book opens. They had lived through world wars, the First, the Second or both, and their aftermaths. That experience leaves a sediment behind, a ballast to the character that seems often lacking in those who never knew it. This is a theme which I want to explore in this final section through the medium of a character especially close to me. My father.

Although it ended ten years before I was born, my childhood was permeated by the Great War, as everyone called it then – they could not believe there would ever be a greater. Even in short trousers we were paraded at the local war memorial to stand to attention for the two minutes silence in Remembrance of something we did not remember. Whatever they were doing at eleven o'clock on 11th November, everyone stopped doing it and men took their hats off (most of them still wore hats) in honour of the Fallen. During the silence it was hard to know what exactly to think about. I had never known any of the Fallen, for obvious reasons. Nevertheless the dying melancholy of the Last Post has affected me ever since.

Afterwards the poppies were discarded but the war never went away. A photograph of my father in service dress, looking faintly amused in soft focus, stood on my mother's desk. I was to have my photograph taken in similar uniform with the same soft focus at the same studio, Hay Wrightson on Bond Street, thirty years later. In other houses one saw similar photographs, some of them bordered in black. My piano teacher displayed her dead brother's portrait together with his Military Cross with its mauve and white ribbon. Men on crutches swung along with one trouser-leg pinned up at the knee, exciting no notice. My headmaster's legless wartime batman arrived daily at my prep school in a motorised wheelchair. He was called simply 'Bell' and sat all day in a glorified cupboard cheerfully cleaning and mending our shoes and football boots. He seemed to accept his stumps so we did also. We never asked him how he came to lose his missing legs.

We played war games (before the invention of Monopoly) called Attaque, whose pieces were battalions or battleships – the enemy always German. We soaked up the exploits of Biggles, the flying ace, over the Western Front. The war poems that we learned were not the disillusioned Siegfried Sassoon and Wilfred Owen but Rupert Brooke's *If I Should Die Think Only This of Me* and Laurence Binyon's *For the Fallen*. We knew there were corners of foreign fields where young men did not grow old as we that were left did. Dying for your country, your highest patriotic duty, was an opportunity which we had missed.

From the wireless we knew the insistent optimism and good cheer of the songs of the trenches. You packed up your troubles in your old kit-bag and *smiled*, boys, while you'd a Lucifer to light your fag and your loyal sweethearts kept the home fires burning. When Brother Bertie went away to Do His Bit he didn't say goodbye, he said good-byee! ('Wipe the tear, Baby dear, from your eye.') He was tickled to death to go, as if he was nipping off for a rollicking time. Or was it, just possibly, irony?

Nobody, not a single elder or teacher, told us what the war had been about or why we were right to fight it. My father never talked about the war. Sometimes I heard from my mother that some pieces of shrapnel had at last worked their way out of his leg. I knew that he had been wounded, quite badly, but that I was not to ask about it, as though it was a slightly embarrassing secret. He never wore his medals, which never left their case. Other men wore theirs at Armistice Day ceremonies but he didn't attend a single one. On his bookshelf stood his only war book, German at that, *All Quiet on the Western Front*. In an obscure drawer he had hidden his service revolver, a heavy Colt .45, just like the one that would be issued to me in my turn. I did not know then that your chances of hitting anyone with it were minimal because of the kick which sent your hand flying.

He had been wounded in 1917 at the onset of the battle of Passchendaele. Why would he never talk about it? Why did so many men of his age keep the same silence? Was it too upsetting to describe? For us or for them? Or was it because it could not be described or conveyed to anyone who had not shared it? At last he grudgingly volunteered a little of it to me when emphysema was ending his life – partly the legacy of having been gassed.

'We had no gas masks when it started. They told us to pee on our handkerchiefs and hold them over our noses.' Later, going through his papers, I came across the two black notebooks he had kept as diaries after going to France, still faintly legible. From them and from what he told me in his last days I was able to piece some of his story together. He volunteered, aged nineteen, for the Honourable Artillery Company, the Army's oldest regiment, at its headquarters at Finsbury Pavement in the City of London, where he had begun work at fourteen in an accountant's office.

'The HAC was my university – they were all Varsity men.' Stationed at the Tower of London he supervised the exercise in the moat of prisoners who were waiting to be shot for spying. 'Boys used to stand on Tower Bridge Road and spit at them.' Bored of waiting to be supplied with guns, an HAC battalion was drafted to France in 1915 to join the infantry, all of them volunteers anxious not to 'miss the show'. They sailed up the Seine to Rouen. From there they reached the beleaguered Ypres salient. After months of static trench skirmishing, shelling and mortaring, he was sent to cadet school in 1916 and gazetted as a second lieutenant to the Wiltshire regiment, which had lost most of its officers at the Somme. His colonel told him not to expect promotion – that was strictly for regulars. But the losses to come were so heavy that within a year he found himself commanding a company, or its remnant, at the age of twenty-two.

The day-to-day discomforts of the line in seemingly constant rain are broken in his diary by such terse entries as: 'Shelled with gas again. Several men bad. I got a slight touch… Bagged 11 Huns. Total now

21… Shaw killed – my other best pal gone.' Occasionally he escaped to a billet in a French farmhouse well behind the line, with good meals, a horse to ride and the farmer's daughters to entertain him. There were home leaves: 'Arrive Victoria 1pm. Very happy.' Then, ten days later, 'Depart Victoria 9am.' It was a war you caught a train to, like going to the office. The families and girlfriends who shared their leaves had no idea what awaited them at the other end of the line.

From his last leave in July 1917 he went straight into the opening battle of Passchendaele, the supposedly decisive push. His company was ordered to take three miles of ground as far as Inverness Copse. As they began to advance a German machine gun post opened up at them in No Man's Land. My father, a good shot, dropped on one knee and took out the gunner but did not stop for a sniper, who was standing in a shell-hole and firing at them. 'I've always worried about that decision. There's no telling whether I would have got him or whether he got many of my men.'

They advanced half a mile beyond the objective. There were no other troops to be seen and none of the messengers sent back to report to headquarters returned. He decided to report the situation himself. By the time he had run out of the range of German snipers he had bullet holes in both legs of his trousers. On arrival he was told that the neighbouring regiment to their right had not showed up. There was an undefended gap of three-quarters of a mile. After three days and nights of solid rain they were ordered back from their lonely salient. Over mud, churned up by the biggest artillery barrage of the war many feet deep in places, he led forty-four men in single file for three miles, trying to miss the worst of the shell holes. 'When we finally got to our line I turned and looked back. There were only twenty-five men left behind me. The rest had disappeared without my knowing. They must have gone into the mud… I haven't thought about that for over forty years…' His voice trailed off into choked silence.

A few days later he was asleep in a dug-out with two others when a shell exploded above the sheet of corrugated iron that was acting as a roof. He was hit in the head and leg. 'All I remember is being carried back by stretcher with the most violent headache. At the casualty clearing station someone looked down at me and said, "You're in luck.

You've got a Blighty One."' During the coming weeks almost all the Wiltshires officers were wiped out.

This experience was a barrier between us that could never be surmounted. All the memoirs, poems, film footage of that nightmare cannot supply the horror and disgust of the real thing. My father had put it out of his mind for forty years because, I imagine, it was unbearable to contemplate. Or had he? 'When men are dying,' he suddenly said to me once, out of the blue, 'they scream for their mothers.' A whole generation had gone missing. They were either killed, maimed like Bell the Boots, or had closed off the damaged part of themselves in a locked compartment somewhere inside them.

It affected his character. He put duty and responsibility for others above all other priorities. I would get letters of reproof from him for having made a joke about some minor happening as a school prefect or a junior officer, which seemed to him a frivolous disrespect for duty. It made for heavy-handed disapproval which I resented. But I had not been responsible for the survival of others in the hell-holes of the First World War.

In the Second he kept a distance – apart from fire-watching. He declined to fraternise with the regular officers of the Irish Guards who were billeted on us - adjutants and their batmen who kept the house astir. Not even my mother could loosen the knot that war had tied in his soul. He was quick to dismiss men who did not meet his stern standards of character. 'A poor fish'; 'A lightweight'; 'A shyster' – those were his terms for the sort of men you could not rely on. I wondered if he thought I was one. Would I have stood up to the tests he underwent?

Much later in life I thought I could see the reason for his silence. 'The Great War For Civilisation', as it was called on the medals which he never wore, had achieved nothing for humanity. Its appalling sacrifices had been for no high ideal, beyond the loyalty between those who were its victims. His diaries say nothing about victory. They peter out in September 1917 when he embarked for England and military hospitals. There are no reflections on war, the meaning of war, the pity of war. What was there to say, then? Now, as the last veterans of the Great War have died out, people are finding ever more to say. There are nine hundred books about it, yearly increasing in number. The Great War. The Great Waste. Will we never be free of it?

Although I did not in the end have to fight it, I think the Second World War changed me just as the First, with far greater reason, changed my father. In September, 1939, I was keenly anticipating a summer holiday at Frinton-on-Sea – until we got there. The hotel was like a transit camp. Everyone seemed to be in the process of leaving. The dining room was empty, the beach deserted. The next day, 1st September, the cars parked along the cliff-edge played their radios in unison tuned to the News. Their owners sat inside them monitoring Hitler's invasion of Poland. Everyone looked grave; obviously war was soon going to include us. On the sands below where I went undeterred with my spade, building sandcastles had become a thing of the past. We were marshalled by military-looking fathers to fill sandbags. Boys paired off, one to swing the spade, the other to hold open the limp bag. The sacking smelt of tar and tying knots at the corners was not easy. But we were excited to be a humble part of the defence of our island. Sandbags like these were soon piled up around countless official buildings, sagging and leaking sand on to pavements. I wondered if some of the leaky ones I later saw were mine.

That evening my father announced that we were returning home next morning, without even having dipped a foot in the sea. The road to London was jammed in many places. In a country hotel dining room where we stopped, two elderly men in uniform with red tabs and Sam Browne belts sat with their wives and soon began booming to each other across the room about the services they were about to offer to the War Office. 'What sort of show did you have last time?' They reminisced about it like a party they had enjoyed long ago. 'You were in the War – you could have told them so,' I said to my father after we left. 'Brass hats!' he snorted. 'Why would I want to talk to *them*?'

On Sunday morning, 3rd September, we gathered round the curved walnut spokes of our wireless loudspeaker to hear the pinched tones of Mr Chamberlain, the prime minister. Forcing his words through a strainer of disbelief, he spoke of 'Pooland' and our demand for an undertaking to withdraw. 'Ay hev to tell you now thet no sech undertaking hes been received…' From Herr Hitler, whose signature on a piece of paper he had trusted. Then the siren went. This was what we had been warned to expect – total and instant obliteration by the bomber that always got through. Voices were raised in the garden. Passers-by were running up the drive seeking shelter. Soon the house seemed to be bursting with strangers, apologising for intruding but… we had no shelter to offer them. Together we listened for the drone of the engines. None came. The All Clear broke the silence – an anticlimax. I had expected worse things from Herr Hitler.

Air Raid Precautions and the Blackout filled life that September. Our old-fashioned house had a large number of windows unreachable from indoors. Intricate wooden screens with strings and pulleys to lower them from the floor above had to be made by hand and installed by my father with myself following him like a dog carrying a hammer, screws and tacks. Stirrup pumps appeared with red buckets; fire drill was carried out. It was better, much better than normal life.

Then came evacuation. My prep school was evacuating any pupils who wanted to go to Somerset. Like my friends I begged to go. Chard turned out to be a dour, grey little town. Its ancient grammar school, where we were billeted but not welcomed, regarded us like a gang of street urchins from the London slums rather than respectable suburban boys with pink cheeks and clean knees. They avoided contact with us. We were consigned to the oldest Tudor wing, built of stone with windows that admitted fearful draughts. The abysmal food, or what was left of it, was served to us when everyone else had finished.

A fierce winter set in. Our dormitory, whose windows were permanently open, suggested a game of Dare after lights out. You had to climb out of a mullioned window at one end and walk along the narrow sill with almost nothing to hold on to until you reached the open window at the other end. My intestines can still feel the crawling sensation at the sight of the frost-covered schoolyard glistening twenty feet below. The icy window frame burned your clutching fingers and the narrow stone sill felt slippery beneath your bare feet. Being a Dare you had to do it or be shamed by those that did. I have suffered from vertigo ever since.

On Sundays there was nothing to do after church but write letters home. There was nothing to say until, amazingly, we were bombed before almost anyone else had been. For no apparent reason a German landmine landed in a nearby field breaking several windows. Our headmaster, a veteran of the Dardanelles, was discouraged. By the summer term we were back home at our suburban school – just in time for the Battle of Britain. We were experts on the aircraft involved, theirs as well as our own. Most of us had fingers permanently sticky from the balsa wood cement used in making models of Spitfires, Hurricanes, even the hated Messerschmitt. Living within a few miles of the big RAF station of Northolt we often watched fighter planes climbing into the sky. The only sign of battle was the occasional putter-putter of machine guns in the clouds while we ate picnic sandwiches in the woods below. One Messerschmitt which crashed intact nearby was put on show outside the council offices as tangible evidence of our victorious struggle. It never occurred to us for a moment in 1940 that Britain could possibly lose.

What seems remarkable about the Blitz that followed in the autumn was how unquestioningly we accepted the discomfort of shelters, usually dank holes in the ground by day, while at night we slept on the floor under stairs at home. We soon abandoned the practice and went back to bed, rising only for the Alerts. When the early sirens wailed I liked to go outdoors with my father on the excuse of checking the roof for incendiaries. The sweeping searchlights occasionally picked out a glint of metal in the heavens. Every boy could tell theirs from ours by the engine note. Their bombers gave out repetitive jabbing purrs, like a vacuum cleaner being pushed in short strokes along a carpet. The important thing was to find out where the nearest bombs had fallen in order to be there early to collect pieces of shrapnel. We traded in jagged bits of shiny metal, always claimed to be genuine German bomb casing, not shell fragments.

From September to the following May the raids became routine. People would look up at the night sky and say, 'Jerry's late tonight.' It was 'Jerry', never the Boche or the Hun of my father's war. Jerry sounded friendlier, like someone you might even have a drink with after it was over. Our gardener, Thorn, summed up the attitude of stoical acceptance when we asked whether his home had been damaged in the previous night's raid. 'Nothing to speak of,' he said. 'Jerry shook us a ceiling down.'

How minor our tribulations were was brought home to me forcefully when someone I knew and loved was bombed and horribly injured. Dorothy, who had looked after me like a second mother from the age of six months, had left us only a few years before. She had married and was living in Wimbledon when there was a direct hit on a row of houses, including hers. After uncountable hours buried in the wreckage she was dug out with her legs smashed and her flesh saturated with particles of debris from the blast. We spent months visiting her in hospital, staring awestruck at her hands and cheeks mottled blue and her head shaved to cleanse it from the debris. She described hearing the rescue squad at work at last, after being trapped alone for so long. 'I called out, "I'm in the kitchen," only of course there wasn't any kitchen.' Six others in the house died, including her husband. Some of her neighbours were never found. Her painful, partial and courageous recovery made a profound impression on me. Until then I had assumed that war was exciting. I now saw how ugly it was. You could not count on your luck to keep you unscathed.

The government issued posters calling for patriotic efforts of various kinds. We were exhorted to dig for victory, lend money to defend the right to be free and to avoid careless talk which cost lives. The one that affected me most was to 'Make Do and Mend', the exact opposite of the motto of our current consumer society where it is practically your duty never to mend anything. Some people showed their patriotic thrift by re-using envelopes covered in deleted addresses and labels which scarcely left room for the stamp. Even the stamps turned a pale anaemic hue because of the shortage of dye. A consequence is that to this day I resist throwing away wrapping paper, especially the strong brown sort. As we did then I fold it and carefully put it away feeling that it will be needed again one day, if I can only remember where it is. The same applies to string, which lies about coiled up in the corners of drawers because it is re-useable. I shan't re-use it but throwing it away would feel almost immoral.

My departure for public school used up the clothing coupon allowance of my entire family for a year ahead. The very next term the school uniform was abandoned for the duration. The rest of my schooldays were passed in sports jackets mended with more and more leather patches and in baggy corduroy trousers which sighed as you walked along. Stowe's overgrown grounds provided the setting for the warlike exercises of the school Junior Training Corps (formerly Officer Training Corps but this was now thought an undemocratic assumption). Most of us distinctly lacked keenness, knowing that all too soon we would have to soldier in earnest. The keen ones tended to attract surreptitious mockery. 'How are the nettles your side of the hedge?' called one hearty NCO. 'Growing in luscious profusion, Corporal,' came the lugubrious reply.

During the Doodlebug summer of 1944, Londoners soon became familiar with the sight of Flying Bombs wavering over the rooftops spitting flame from their tails and emitting a buzz like an angry hornet. We began to pay little attention – until the moment when the noise and flame suddenly stopped and the object began its silent fifteen-second dive to earth. These were ugly moments of shameful prayer – 'Please, God, don't let it fall near me!' – accompanied with the guilty feeling that you were praying for it to fall on someone else. The reality of war was the noticeboard on which was pinned the long roll of Old Stoics decorated, killed or missing on active service (two of them won the VC which won us half-holidays). The names began to appear of boys we had known as seniors or prefects. Within two or three years of leaving they were dead. The headmaster read out the lengthening list each Remembrance Day with visible grief as we reflected it was to be our turn soon. As it turned out we were wrong. The dropping of the two atom bombs relieved us from the prospect of fighting the Japanese to the last man. I cannot pretend that I regretted the coming of a nuclear weapon at the time – it seemed like an extension of the German V2 rockets which had bid fair to devastate London. We were too relieved to care how the war ended, so long as it did.

Music, which reaches a part of the psyche which cannot be contacted by other means, played a large part in almost everyone's war and provides some of my most poignant memories of it. Not only popular music, the songs of Vera Lynn, but the heroic blasts of Beethoven, who became a favourite symbol of resistance (to, not by the Germans). When the radio announced that the German war was over it followed it with Beethoven – the Fifth Symphony, first movement, with its opening motif which for us spelled V-for-Victory. I spent much of my summer holidays at the Henry Wood Proms at the Albert Hall with my eyes fixed on the horn section – I was learning the French horn, which is like trying to tame a wild animal. Nearly everyone in the audience smoked and a hazy cloud hung over the promenade. There were notable premieres. Shostakovich's Leningrad

Symphony, written in the besieged city, was smuggled to Britain in a diplomatic bag. Occasionally a composer would mount the rostrum in army battledress to conduct his new work. Dame Myra Hess, masterful as a warship, cruised across the platform to perform Beethoven's Fourth Piano Concerto to boost morale, as she had with her lunchtime concerts in the bomb-damaged National Gallery, price one shilling.

Then in 1944 the Proms were cancelled for the first time because of the Doodlebugs – which was why I picked my way one brilliant summer Sunday afternoon to the Cambridge Theatre to hear a live performance of *The Enigma Variations*. Something about the tension in the air, the expectation of more rockets, the rubble in the streets and by then the sheer weariness of war united the audience as the nobility of the music seemed to lift us off the ground. The *Nimrod* seemed to sum up five years of endurance, survival, sadness and loss together with a belief in persistence that seemed especially British. It was like another National Anthem. The audience merged into a single emotional whole such as only music seems able to evoke. People wiped their eyes and blew their noses as they got up afterwards to leave. When I hear talk of national unity in the war I recall that afternoon. Churchill had spoken, indeed roared for us. But so did Edward Elgar.

My father had come out of the first war without a job to go to – until the British Empire Exhibition at Wembley, where he ran the large amusement park, gave him the idea of inventing one. There was no one professionally organising exhibitions so he called himself an Exhibition Organiser, hired a small office and filled the gap. Planning was his forte. Before we set off for a seaside holiday he would issue us each with instructions on what to take and do before leaving, as if it was an attack on the Western Front. 'You have no respect for detail,' he would complain of my disorganisation. The exhibition business soon surrendered to him and we grew used to seeing pre-war newspaper photographs of my dad in striped trousers and spats carrying a top hat a few paces behind royalty, even the King himself. He needed them there to open the show. When the Royal Tournament came round our seats behind the royal box enabled me to study the two princesses, Elizabeth and Margaret Rose, dutifully carrying gloves like their mother. But I preferred the hectic eve of the Motor Show when the new models were unveiled for exhibitors only. I vividly remember sliding into the driving seat of an Armstrong Siddeley Sapphire, a heaven of leather and walnut woodwork. Such designs have never been surpassed.

The war put an end to public gatherings and therefore to commercial exhibitions and knocked my father's success out of his hand. He found a new berth in newspaper management. He had no formal education beyond the age of fourteen so his ambitions for me were correspondingly high. After Oxford I was to serve apprenticeships in accountancy and stock-broking so that I would be perfectly qualified to become Something in the City, which he regarded with reverence as a place where My Word Is My Bond. Unfortunately there was nothing I less wanted to become. This conflict of aim inevitably got between us. I became a disappointment, lacking serious purpose – and a proper respect for detail.

In his world men were rated by their reputation for running companies or businesses. Like them he wore Savile Row suits, Jermyn Street shirts and ties and a Homburg hat and carried an expertly rolled umbrella (he taught me how to roll one). Like every man of his generation he smoked continuously – Du Maurier cigarettes, which lay about the house in brilliant red boxes of two hundred. When I was thirteen he offered me one, with a glass of sherry. His 'tipple' was a stiff gin and mixed Vermouth which he called a snifter. His generation shared a peculiar set of circumlocutions which even then sounded obsolete. You did not say you needed a pee – you must 'pump ship'. Somebody who was drunk was not pissed, he was 'three sheets to the wind'. 'Playing silly-buggers' meant not observing the rules. Any social solecism was 'bad form'. Swearing was restricted to 'damn' and 'bloody' and even these were bad form in mixed company. It was the form to call acquaintances by their surnames. Christian names implied an unusually close degree of friendship, unlike today. It was certainly not the form for us to exchange a hug or, worse, a kiss, in public when greeting or parting, even though we were father and son. We shook hands as neutrally as possible.

He and his circle lunched at their clubs (the East India in his case) or at approved restaurants such as the Savoy or Simpson's in the Strand. At Simpson's the upstairs dining room was a kind of club patronised by business leaders who stopped by each other's tables on the way in or out to exchange banter. My father always occupied the same table and was served by the same waiter in a long white apron. Arthur looked like an Aubrey Beardsley drawing. The waiters knew the wants and foibles of their regulars through and through and spoiled them expertly. Arthur never waited for him to order, he simply placed the smoked salmon before him with a plate of brown bread and butter and the greeting, 'I've cut your crusts orf.' Then he would steer him firmly through the menu. 'What's the beef like?' 'Yer don't want that. Yer want the lamb, it's just 'ow you like it. What'll you have with it, roast or boiled? Leave it ter me, I'll see it's all right for yer, leave it ter me.' Everyone was served with the same overcooked vegetables, the cabbage soaked and tasteless and compressed into a circular cake which was cut into triangular wedges. To follow there were boarding school puddings and custard. Simpson's was renowned for its roast joints wheeled to the table and carved to the client's liking followed by a discreet tip. My father's half-crown was passed beneath his hand and palmed by the carver so that no vulgar gift of coin was ever visible. For Arthur a ten-shilling note was left on the plate beneath the bill. The old waiters bent over their charges like nursemaids examining children of uncertain health and temper. Deference was paid but of the familiarity that obtains between officer and batman. My father never looked as if he expected it. He was fond of Arthur. The ritual ended with Arthur brushing him down. 'Yer'll be in termorrer? Take care of yerself, now.'

Later, when I took him out to lunch to return his hospitality, he conceded that he could not be my guest at Simpson's. I led him to a smart enough restaurant. He looked round distrustfully at several well-known Fleet Street columnists and Vicky, the celebrated cartoonist, at neighbouring tables. He studied the menu through his spectacles and then asked for something that wasn't on it. 'Do you mean to say you don't have fritto misto?' The Italian head waiter was apologetic. 'Mi dispiace, Signore. Today the necessary fresh ingredients were not all available, mi dispiace.' Instead he recommended the veal, which turned out to be excellent. My father regarded it frostily. Veal was a viand that was simply not served at Simpson's. 'Try it, it's very good.' 'What is it?' 'Veal, of course. What else could it be?' He poked it suspiciously with a fork. 'Could be goat,' he said.

Years later I reminded him of this embarrassing display but, of course, he remembered it quite differently. 'I did no such thing, my dear boy, whatever put such an idea into your head?' There was never any point in arguing with him. I both loved and feared him but we were not destined to be comrades. Every man has a quarrel with his father, wrote some famous son. I wish I could remember who it was. He spoke for me.

The gas or the cigarettes, or both, did for him in the end. When he was dying he seemed to regard death as an old acquaintance he knew he would meet again. I asked him how he would like to be commemorated for his unique achievements in his field, including the conception and building of Earls Court. His reply delivered with unusual force shocked me. 'It doesn't matter a damn, old boy. None of it matters a damn any more.' In due course I wrote his obituary for *The Times* and the address for his funeral, crowded with men in suits whom I did not know. All the time I was conscious of his vehement verdict: 'None of it matters a damn!' Now I realise why he said it. With very few exceptions, whatever you have done ceases to matter once you stop doing it. When so many of the names in your address book have been crossed out there are few left to remember. Except in the family circle, where I miss my father as much as always.

When he could no longer manage it he asked me to shave him. I still wince at how clumsily I did it. It is hard to shave a chin not one's own, especially with an old-fashioned single-sided blade. 'You're very patient,' he said, though we both knew how untrue that was. When I was forced to leave overnight he wanted to be sure I would be back next morning to shave him again. I promised to be but, hating any kind of fuss, he departed in the small hours of that night without even waking anyone. When I next saw him he was lying on a wooden trestle table in an outbuilding. The backs of undertakers' premises are less genteel than their frontages. They hadn't yet started work so I contemplated his chin as nicked and raw as I had left it. It was too late to make amends for that as for so many other disappointments I must have caused him. Like it or not, that is the image I have to remember.

If there had been no world wars I wonder how different we would both have been. Common danger, common interest, common responsibility and care for something greater than oneself – these are powerful influences on behaviour. The flavour of England without those wars would certainly be different. Now that the last personal memories of its wartime self are all but extinct, I seldom recognise my country. I would like it back, which is why I have compiled this album.

INDEX

INDEX

A Rogues' Gallery

Silverman, Sidney 46
Simpson, Alan 38–9
Sinatra, Frank 31
Smith, Bessie 220
Smith, Maggie 148, 150
Snow, Jon 195–6
Snowdon (Anthony Armstrong
    Jones) 26, 170–1
Solzhenitsyn, Alexander 93
Sondheim, Stephen
    A Little Night Music 116
Soviet Union (USSR) 11, 19,
    49, 92
    Committee for State
    Security (KGB) 92–3, 95–6
    development of hydrogen
    bomb (1953) 50
    Kremlin 177
    Leningrad 92, 116
    Lubianka 96
    Moscow 93–4
Spain
    Civil War (1936–9) 46, 228,
    251, 265
    Majorca 239
    Malaga 228
    Seville 228
Speer, Albert 183–6, 189
Sputnik 50
Stalin, Josef 95
    family of 95–6
*Star Wars Episode IV: A New
    Hope* 193
St Denis, Michel 114
Steel, David 49
Sillitoe, Alan

*Saturday Night and Sunday
    Morning* 13
Stoppard, Tom 125
    *Rosencratz and
    Guildenstern Are Dead*
    101–3
Storey, David 16
    Home 16
    This Sporting Life 15–16
Strasberg, Paula 6
Strindberg, August
    Dance of Death, The 148–9
Suez Crisis (1956) 19–21, 54
Sweden
    Stockholm 27
Syria 222

Tarsis, Valery 93
Tati, Jacques 75–8
    Jour de Fête 75
    *Les Vacances de Monsieur
    Hulot* 75
    Mon Oncle 75, 77
    Playtime 75, 77–8
Taylor, A.J.P. 50
Taylor, John 136
Terkel, Studs 246, 248
Terry, Walter 211
Thatcher, Denis 217
Thatcher, Margaret 211–12,
    214–17, 247
Thomson, Roy 29–30
Tippett, Michael 51
Truman, Harry S. 50
Turing, Alan
    suicide of 35

INDEX